ACROSS AND DOWN

OTHER BOOKS BY EUGENE T. MALESKA

Sun and Shadow

Three Voices
(*with Arthur Bramhall and Herman Ward*)

The Story of Education
(*with Carroll Atkinson*)

Simon and Schuster's
Crossword Book of Quotations Series

Simon and Schuster
Crossword Puzzle Book Series
(*with Margaret Farrar*)

The Junior Crossword Puzzle Book Series
(*with Margaret Farrar*)

The Simon and Schuster Book of
Cryptic Crossword Puzzles Series

A Pleasure in Words

D
ACROSS
AND
W
N

THE CROSSWORD PUZZLE WORLD
BY
Eugene T. Maleska

WITH AN INTRODUCTORY CHAPTER BY
MARGARET FARRAR

A FIRESIDE BOOK
PUBLISHED BY
SIMON & SCHUSTER, INC.
NEW YORK

Introduction Copyright© 1984 by Margaret Farrar
Copyright © 1984 by Eugene T. Maleska
All rights reserved including the right of reproduction
in whole or in part in any form
A Fireside Book
Published by Simon & Schuster, Inc.
Simon & Schuster Building, Rockefeller Center
1230 Avenue of the Americas
New York, New York 10020
FIRESIDE and colophon are registered trademarks of Simon & Schuster, Inc.
Designed by Helen Barrow
Manufactured in the United States of America

1 2 3 4 5 6 7 8 9 10

ISBN: 0-671-50472-X

*This book is dedicated to
all crossword puzzle fans*

CONTENTS

FOREWORD

WHEN THE IDEA *for this book was broached, someone suggested a catchy title — The Last Word in Crosswords. Delightful! But as Euripides once said: "In this world second thoughts, it seems, are best." Let someone more assiduous, more ambitious and more pompous write that book. Mine would be merely a modest attempt to present facts and viewpoints about recent and current trends in the Kingdom of Puzzledom — a land that I have traversed as a solver, constructor and editor for the past five decades.*

This book is not even intended to be the next-to-last word. For example, except for the introductory chapter by the great Margaret Farrar, very few attempts are made to relate the history of crossword puzzles or their kin. Nor am I perspicacious enough to predict the future of the black and white squares, except to say that I dread the incursions of computers and wonder if they will ever adequately replace homo sapiens.

Humans are what this book is all about. First, it addresses itself to the millions of fans whose reactions and suggestions (and even silence!) have continually affected the course of the pastime, and without whom crosswords would not exist. Second, the book deals with some of the ingenious constructors, ever striving for new and exciting ways to entertain and inform the solvers. Finally, it speaks of the editors whose behind-the-scenes task is so important in the long run.

But, from another point of view, the puzzles themselves are the heart of this book. Their evolution since their invention by Arthur Wynne is traced with special emphasis on the advances that have taken place since the 1930s. Aside from traditional American crosswords, such offshoots as Cryptics, Puns and Anagrams and diagramless puzzles are discussed in detail, along with directions for solving each type. The finale gives examples of some of the best puzzles that represent various themes and devices which constructors have conjured up since the 1940s.

In essence then, Across and Down *tries to live up to the promise in its title — no more, no less. The reader is invited to learn the inside story of the Crossword Puzzle World from several different angles.*

I am extremely grateful to Margaret Farrar for consenting to embellish this book with an account of her role from the inception of crossword puzzles until her retirement from The New York Times in 1969. As most readers know, the Queen of Puzzledom is still actively involved as an editor of various Simon and Schuster puzzle books, and every fan and constructor joins me in wishing that she continue ad infinitum.

My appreciation also goes to my A-1 spouse (alias 1-A) who has played such an important part not only in the creation of the book but in fifty wonderful years in my life. Finally, thanks are due to Peter Cancro for typing the manuscript and to Robert and Lois Hughes for proofing it.

Pax, amor et felicitas
E.T.M.

INTRODUCTION
In the Beginning
by MARGARET FARRAR

In the beginning—until 1913—there were no crossword puzzles.

It was on December 13, 1913, that the first of its species, called "Word Cross," arrived on the "Fun" page of the *New York World Sunday Magazine.*

This was the brainchild of a newspaperman, Arthur Wynne, and was based on a word game he remembered from his English childhood. The world had been full of puzzles since Oedipus solved the Riddle of the Sphinx—but they had not gone Across and Down in the Wynne style.

The first Word Cross was small and simple, with two numbers for every word, but evidently it attracted puzzlers, because Arthur Wynne discovered he had a weekly feature to be carried on. It soon became Cross-Word, and later Crossword (it attained a place in *Webster's New International Dictionary* in 1934).

The puzzle went through many changes in those early years, often at the behest of the vocal solvers or increasing numbers of crusading constructors. Its popularity tided it over the grim years of the First World War, when there was little space for such diversions as puzzles, and it was a strong and steady feature in 1921.

How did I get into puzzles?

There were plenty of jobs for college graduates in the early 1920s, and my first was a dull chore in a bank figuring out percentages for bond salesmen. The chance to change came the easiest way: being recommended by my college roommate, Elsie Finch (we were Smith 1919), to her stepfather, who needed a new secretary. He was John O'Hara Cosgrave, Sunday editor of the *New York World,* a humane, humorous, fair-minded man who hailed from Australia.

I had taken a quick course in something called the Boyd Syllabic System, and was a passable typist. I hoped I was adequate to the interesting doings on the top floor of the old World Building overlooking City Hall, under the Gold Dome, and with the Brooklyn Bridge looming nearby.

J. O'H. told me that, in addition to secretarial duties, I was to inherit the job of crossword editor. Arthur Wynne had moved along to the Bell Syndicate, and the job was being passed around. A desk drawer was crammed with hundreds of contributions, and since I was not really acquainted with the crossword, this was the place to begin to explore.

The experts on the staff were a brilliant writer and opera buff, Prosper Buranelli, and an all-round feature writer and editor (out of Hill School and Yale), F. Gregory Hartswick, who was to run the "Red Magic Section," a popular feature. The crossword already had a large and articulate following, including Franklin Pierce Adams, whose column, "The Conning Tower," had made a great reputation in the *Tribune,* and who moved over to the *World* in 1922. He used to discuss the crossword puzzle in his "Pepys' Diary" column on Saturdays.

There were changes and improvements in these early 1920s. By unanimous decision, the puzzles were set up in type a week in advance (not the last minute we had been managing with) and were carefully checked over in time to be sure they were right. Around 1923, again at the suggestion of an anonymous and wise solver, we dropped the two-numbers-per-definition because one number sufficed, a great step in advance, lessening the danger of error.

F.P.A. (curmudgeon *extraordinaire* and a very kind man) became a good friend and counselor. (I even tidied up his office now and then and got away with it.) And it was early in January 1924 that he brought two young men into the Sunday room under the Gold Dome and introduced them to Miss Petherbridge (my maiden name) and Mr. Buranelli and Mr. Hartswick, surely a formidable trio of proper nouns. The visitors were Richard L. Simon and M. Lincoln Schuster, Columbia graduates, intending to go into publishing. Their motto was "Quality, not quantity," but they were fired with a new idea, a book of crossword puzzles. There had never been a book of crosswords and Dick Simon's aunt had suggested one. (Dick later admitted to me that this was all a joke, even unto the framed memo up on the office wall noting this earth-shaking idea.)

The advice F.P.A. had to offer was "Discourage 'em."

But there was that drawerful of unpublished puzzles, and the three young editors could share the work and the then-munificent advance of seventy-five dollars.

With the speed possible in those halcyon days, the *Crossword Puzzle Book* was published on April 10, 1924. For Simon and Schuster it was a risky venture; after all, it was their first book into the marketplace. Dick and Max did camouflage their precious imprint by publishing under the name Plaza Publishing Company, a title borrowed from their telephone exchange. (Their small first office was on West 57th Street, and when their names were painted on the door, "Simon & Schuster, Publishers," some wag scribbled underneath, "Of what?")

Six weeks before publication, the young publishers put a small advertisement in the

M. Lincoln Schuster (left) and Richard L. Simon holding copies of the first Crossword Puzzle Book. The date was probably the summer of 1924, and the place was the small first office of Simon and Schuster, Publishers, on West 57th Street, where it all began.

World: "Attention, Crossword Puzzle Fans...By mail only. Your money back if not 100% satisfied."

Extravagantly, they ventured another ad two weeks before publication: "Ready at last! Why wait? Order today."

The price quoted was $1.35, with Venus pencil and Venus eraser slipped into an edging slot, and the first edition was 3,600 copies. The surprise was that a couple of days later Dick and Max had some difficulty in opening the door to their office. A huge pile of letters was blocking the entrance under the mail slot.

We were all amazed and thrilled, and Dick and Max felt encouraged enough to venture a second printing of 3,600 copies. Then a third and fourth printing, which went up to 5,000. The buildup in the next editions tells the story.

The fifth edition was 6,000, the sixth 10,000, the seventh 15,000, the eighth, ninth and tenth 25,000.

It was still 1924, and it seemed right and proper to prepare what no one had expected, a Second Series. This one sold 110,000 copies. First printing of the Third Series was 40,000, in time for the 1924 Christmas market. On a single December day, over 150,000 books were sold. Something had happened, almost unbeknownst to Cal Coolidge, the speakeasy crowd, the flappers, the singers of "Yes, We Have No Bananas."

But of course the stage had been set for something dramatic. The "Fabulous Twenties," as they would come to be called, were full of excitement, and no wonder the new word game flourished, crowding out the mah-jongg aficionados who were then in the forefront.

To choose one memory from a host of them, picture Dick and Max and the three puzzle editors crowding into a barouche at 59th Street on a summer Saturday and riding down Fifth Avenue, then up Fifth Avenue, stopping at every bookstore to admire their window display, while one of us rushed in to the conspicuous front table to inquire how many thousands of crossword books they had sold that day or week.

All the earmarks of a big craze began to appear. Soon crossword puzzle jewelry was for sale. Garments appeared made in black and white squares. The cartoonists had a field day. F.P.A. had given us a friendly couplet on April 10:

> Hooray! Hooray! Hooray! Hooray!
> The crossword puzzle book is out today!

Gelett Burgess, who was well known for the famous rhyme "I never saw a purple cow," was a crossword fan, and when the *New York World* started to run daily puzzles in November 1924, he constructed a puzzle for the occasion and wrote a little rhyme that many people remember as a parody of his famous

> The goops they lick their fingers,
> The goops they lick their knives,
> They spill their broth on the tablecloth,
> They lead disgusting lives.
>
> The fans they lick their pencils,
> The fans they beat their wives,
> They look up words for extinct birds,
> They lead such puzzling lives.

Crossword puzzles were soon appearing in daily and Sunday newspapers across the country, as a number of syndicates sprang up. In London they started by reprinting puzzles from our early books. The introduction to a later Penguin book states:

> On 9 December 1924 a correspondent in the U.S. reported in one of our newspapers that the crosswords have dealt the final blow to the art of conversation, and have been known to break up homes.

Later on, this commentator says:

> The epidemic crossed the Atlantic so swiftly that already in the early
> months of 1925 it was a subject for serious newspaper comment...the
> Prime Minister made jocular reference to the development in an after-
> dinner speech: "I should think that 90 percent of the people believe that
> there was but one Roman emperor, and that his name was Nero."

During the next five years the British crossword developed into the cryptic baffling game it still is today, and by 1930 the [London] Times fought it out with its conscience and decided to include a daily puzzle.

The puzzle spread very quickly all over Europe and to some parts of Asia. The Romance languages offered enormous opportunities for the puzzle constructor, which turned out to be not so true in some other languages, and of course Chinese and Japanese made the crossword puzzle process impossible. Russian newspapers found ways of using the crossword as a propaganda vehicle. Their definitions were often loaded with political meanings.

Was it Bea Lillie who said, "The Beatles are here to go"? There were many predictions that, since it was the latest craze, the crossword was to be a "flash in the pan." If so, it has been the longest flash in the pan in history.

The overexaggerated phase of the craze abated, but the newspapers could not drop their daily and Sunday offerings. Enormous demand was still there, or maybe it was now a habit, as Gelett Burgess predicted, not to be denied. The Simon and Schuster books rolled on, at least two per year. There was even a *Celebrities Crossword Book,* and many of the puzzles were actually made up by enthusiastic celebrities. By accident, trying to see if a mislaid pattern could be reproduced, F. Gregory Hartswick discovered that a puzzle could be solved without the diagram, and so the diagramless puzzle was born.

Greg Hartswick, an adventurous constructor (one of his feats was to include the entire Greek alphabet in a 15 x 15 puzzle) who ran the famous Old Gold contest and wrote several books, died in 1948. Prosper Buranelli, who worked brilliantly as Lowell Thomas's right-hand man for many years, died in 1968.

The *New York World* disappeared tragically in 1931; it was sold to become the *World-Telegram* and an afternoon paper. The *Herald Tribune,* which had started running Sunday and daily crosswords neck and neck with the *World,* carried on the standard under editors Dorothy Kiggins and Ruth Biemiller, and later William Gant, for many successful years.

Some more chronology to keep the record straight: In May 1926 I left my job on the *World,* that happy combination of secretary to one of the wisest editors in New York, and the Sunday-daily editorship of the crosswords, to marry a publisher, John Farrar. Women did leave jobs to marry in 1926.

The crossword books became most adaptable homework, shared with Pros and Greg. Even the Depression years had only mild depressive effects, because the puzzles flourished in bad times, offering accessible and inexpensive entertainment. During the Second World War, newspapers in England shrank to four pages but the puzzle held its place. It proved to be of enormous value as a lifter of morale.

It was in January 1942 that *The New York Times,* following by a dozen years the *Times* of London, reached the decision to devote a page in its Sunday *Magazine* to crosswords. The puzzle had obviously proved its staying power and was deemed respectable enough for "the good gray lady of 43rd Street." (The apocryphal story was that Arthur Hays Sulzberger realized he was forced to buy the Sunday *Herald Tribune* in order to do its puzzles. Eventually both he and editor Charles Merz contributed to the new Sunday *Magazine* page.) Someone at the *Times* phoned Simon and Schuster, still the font of puzzledom, and said, "Send us over a crossword editor." Well, my son and two daughters were all in school (and all with large vocabularies!). I was carrying on the puzzle books, two a year, with a little help from busy Greg and Pros, so there was plenty of time to get to 43rd Street once or twice a week.

The first puzzle page appeared on February 15, 1942, and a box on that initial page stated:

> Beginning today, The New York Times inaugurates a puzzle page. There will be two puzzles each Sunday—one with a flavor of current events and general information, and one varied in theme, ranging from puzzles in lighter vein, like today's smaller one, to diagramless puzzles of a general nature. . . .

The top puzzle was a 23 x 23 titled "Headlines and Footnotes," by Charles Erlenkotter, a veteran also called Charles Cross. The first definition Across was "Famous one-eyed general" (WAVELL). At the bottom of the page was a 15 x 15 called "Riddle Me This," by Anna Gram. An explanatory note said, "Here are puns and persiflage, anagrams and homonyms, all fair game for the amateur sleuth." Incidentally, Anna G. became an often-used pseudonym in years to come.

The bottom of the page specialized in variety, with emphasis on what came to be called "Puns and Anagrams," with stellar performances by Edward Buckler, Mel Taub, Herbert Ettenson, Eugene T. Maleska and other experts. Diagramless puzzles appeared every other week, and the Double-Crostic, Elizabeth Kingsley's outstanding feature of the *Saturday Review of Literature,* began as an every-fourth-week treat in May 1943. By 1953, it was appearing every other week.

Lester Markel, who was the vital editor of the Sunday *Times* (and who did an amazing job for at least a quarter of a century), was not a real fan of the crossword puzzles, which were a little frivolous for his taste, so the puzzle was in the special-features class to begin with. However, this particular special feature soon proved its value as an attention-getting page, and Mr. Markel later became its staunch supporter.

Looking back at the developments and changes that had taken place since those early *New York World* offerings, it is somewhat hard to account for the suddenness of the craze. Arthur Wynne confessed that no one was more surprised than he to find his 1913 invention the great craze of the middle '20s. "All I did," said he, "was to take an idea as old as language and modernize it by the introduction of black squares."

The first puzzle in the first book of 1924 was supposed to be an easy problem, an 11 x 11 pattern carrying fifty words, many of them very short. Two eleven-letter words crossing each other was a startling feat at that time.

Primary definitions were insisted upon, with pronouns and printer's measures and plenty of clichés intermixed. All this was leavened with some very unusual words, not at all useful in ordinary conversation but perfectly acceptable ammunition for the crossword constructor. Luckily, this method of making the puzzles difficult and unusual did not last very long. Within a few years constructors began to find different and much better ways of making the puzzles interesting.

It was in September 1924 that something called the Amateur Cross Word Puzzle League of America was formed, which proceeded to formulate some rules for construction of crossword puzzles:

1. "The pattern shall interlock all over." (Always a good rule. Earlier patterns often resulted in dividing up the puzzle into several small independent sections.)
2. "Only approximately one sixth of the squares shall be black." (Always a good rule, later revised to "one sixth or less." Earlier puzzles were overpopulated with black squares. This ruling resulted in far better patterns, more difficult for the constructor but infinitely better for solvers.)
3. "Only approximately one tenth of the letters shall be unkeyed." (This liberty was countermanded in the 1940s when unkeyed letters, so dear to the British puzzlemakers, were ruled out entirely. "Two clues for every letter" made for much better crosswords the American way.)
4. "The design shall be symmetrical." (Simply because the pattern looked prettier on the page. A rule to be broken for special purposes, but it has been adhered to all over the world.)

There were four guides on the use of words, meant to edify constructors. In general, they seem as good today as they were in 1924. Obsolete and dialectic words were allowable in moderation (anybody's guess), plainly marked and out of a standard dictionary.

(Now the tip-off may be "old style," or the old word may be defined by an equally old word.) Foreign words that are more or less familiar have gradually become an ingredient in the puzzle mix (and those few but vocal objectors to the use of anything but "American words" have luckily been given short shrift). Technical terms in the dictionary were welcome. Later they were frowned upon, but in recent years they have made a comeback. Think of all those space terms and the inviting accumulation of the computer vocabulary, much of which is going into general conversation.

As for the defining, eventually recognized as a vastly important factor in the game, the "rules" or helpful hints were disarmingly generous and broad, and suggested "great variety" with common sense as the biggest requirement. "Synonyms that are too far removed from the word and what Gelett Burgess calls 'smarty-cat definitions' should be avoided." Truly, this was a strange interdiction from a humorist who gave a new meaning to *bromide* and who coined the word *blurb*.

Gregory Hartswick had a wise hand in forming the rules, and excellent suggestions were offered by Ruth von Phul, an expert solver who won two early crossword contests. Those contests were part of the lively doings from 1924 on. They became real festive occasions and challenges of skill as the expert solvers gathered to show off their marvelous vocabularies and their speed. The phenomenon has recently gained new popularity, and there are large yearly gatherings for this unusual indoor sport, all based on words, words, words.

There was, surprisingly, no stated rule against more than one word per definition, and a few did appear in early books, but they always had the "2-words," "3-words" tip. For a long time the routine seemed to call for primary dictionary definitions. The editors made corrections but were doubtful about their freedom to change the constructor's definitions.

Again, it was a gradual process. In the early 1930s, the preferred way to make the puzzles more difficult, and possibly more interesting, was to reach out for unusual words that had been hiding in the dictionary for years. Another forward step was to banish the use of unkeyed letters, so that patterns benefited by wide-open spaces, and longer words crowded out the short repeaters. In fact, the two-letter words were eventually ruled out completely by many editors—another reason for better patterns and incidentally the finale of the sun god Ra, who had been omnipresent since early days.

In 1946, the jacket of the current book, Series 58, presented a little list of seldom-used words that might be welcomed by hardy solvers: aquarelle, byssus, cambistry, dickcissel, edaphology, frabjous, geophagy, hippogriff, ikona, juggins, kolo, lundyfoot, meglip, noctivagant, Ormus, papillote, guoin, rasceta, shadoof, twayblade, umbrette, vaticide, Wegg, xanthic, Yima, zizith.

Do not rush to add these frabjous words to your working vocabulary. The crosswords luckily took another course, which led them into much more adventurous and enriching fields, and eventually to the real gold mine of the phrases.

And another giant step was announced in "Times Talk" in 1950: "When The Times broke a 99-year-old tradition on September 11, and quietly slipped crosswords onto the Daily Book Page, it evoked what you'd expect—cross words. Oddly enough, though, the crosspatches were a minority. Most of the letters were jubilant in praise of the innovation."

Arthur Hays Sulzberger thought the book page was the proper milieu for crosswords, and they were to be the "little brothers" of the Sunday puzzles.

One of the notable variations along the way was first called the inner-clue puzzle. It was introduced by a brilliant advertising man, Harold T. Bers. The solver would find Chesterfield, Camel, Lucky Strike, etc., all with straight definitions until it would suddenly dawn that a long list of cigarettes was concealed. Similarly, Cadillac, Ford, Pontiac, etc., appeared with a number of other concealed cars. The great variety of such topical puzzles still provides extra entertainment.

Other straws in the wind had been around for a long time. The British Cryptic puzzles early used compounds, quotations, full titles and full names, with the number of words always provided; the Double-Crostic also indulged in more-than-one-word entries, giving the number of words called for. The temptation was attractive. Although hardly a concerted action, as expert constructors noted what other constructors were doing (for example, a HARD-SHELLED CRAB crawled across a daily puzzle by Eugene T. Maleska) well-chosen phrases and colorful quotations were clearly coming into their own.

Constructor Maleska started puzzling in high school, when the place to contribute puzzles was the *Herald Tribune,* and so began his development as one of the top crossword innovators and editors. He of course contributed regularly to the original series of Simon and Schuster books, and after 1942 was a regular contributor to *The New York Times,* having a great deal to do with the improvements which took place through those early years.

Constructors had found the freedom that allowed them to use word combinations that provided greater variety. The repeaters and the clichés that had troubled original-minded puzzlers could now very often be avoided. Puzzlers found myriads of new "words" at their disposal: RELEE or ELEE; EAPOE; TSELIOT to mention a few signatures; ADIN and ADOUT; ATEE and ASIS and OFOZ and countless other combinations.

A comment from Will Weng, himself a promoter of that new look, the hilarious pun, and a veteran newspaperman who filled the crossword editor's slot from 1969 to 1977: "An entry such as RELEE would have been unthinkable in the early unimaginative days of the Crossword. . . . Some people still object to the use of phrases or gimmicks, but the majority seem to find that they add an interesting and challenging new dimension."

Many people ask if there are any real taboos in puzzlemaking. The puzzles have always been synonymous with entertainment. The taboos are all mainly efforts to rule out downbeat words, the bad news that solvers do the puzzles to get away from. Finishing a good, amusing, challenging crossword gives one a feeling of elation and accomplishment. There are plenty of educational values concealed in the puzzles, but they are by-products. The basic taboo was phrased as "Death, disease, and taxes." This motto seemed to serve very well, an echo of the Benjamin Franklin saying of 1789: "Nothing is certain but death and taxes."

As a case in point, the name IDI AMIN, with its very convenient vowel-consonant mixture, was becoming a crossword cliché and appearing far too often. It was a positive pleasure for puzzle editors to do a little homework and edit out this most unsavory character.

The far greater variety which is given by the free use of phrases and quotations and combinations that were not used in earlier days has made it entirely possible to build much better crosswords than ever before.

In the 1960s, experimentation was an outstanding feature. The EMU-MOA-ROC era was gradually being ushered out, and the stage was set for fresh ideas, new ways and means of bringing the puzzlement to a high level of entertainment. Constructors made many imaginative sorties that sometimes proved too baffling for the solvers, but they always accepted the challenge and followed with enthusiasm along every ingenious path.

The 1960s brought novelties such as the "Stepquote," which was one of Eugene T. Maleska's gifts to puzzlers. The ability to interlock five or six 23-letter entries became a specialty of constructor Anne Fox, whose Christmas puzzles became a most welcome feature of the Sunday *Magazine*. Frances Hansen discovered a way for weaving hilarious limericks into a puzzle pattern. The unusual word mixtures done by Jack Luzzatto and Maura Jacobson and Herbert Ettenson, to name only a few of the stars, all contributed to the increasing popularity of the game.

Since that unheralded day in 1913 when the first "Word Cross" made its appearance, exciting developments have come about. Words have fascination without end. As we lunge into the computer age, enjoyment of this game of words will go into another age, era, epoch, time, day, date, cycle, aeon . . .

1

The Fans

Most crossword puzzle solvers, unlike Gaul in Caesar's time, can be divided *in partes quattuor:* Sleepers, Squawkers, Leapers and Gotchas.

Sleepers are my favorite group. Their attitude is that puzzles are merely a pastime and no big deal. With stoic indifference they accept whatever comes along. If the puzzle happens to be an easy one, they give themselves a mild pat on the back for having finished it. When they tackle a "stinker" and can't get anywhere with it, they shrug and put it aside without a murmur. They say to themselves, "Oh well, tomorrow is another day!"

To the Sleepers, the constructor and editor are demigods who can't possibly be wrong. They have implicit trust in the Olympians who put the puzzle into print. If Bambi is defined as a doe, then the Salten-Disney deer *must* be a female. Of course, it's conceivable that some Sleepers actually spot an error now and then, but they never write in about it. Usually their letters are brief and complimentary: "I'm enjoying the puzzles. Keep up the good work!"

Squawkers don't concentrate on mistakes either, but they take their puzzles seriously. When they can't finish one they regard it as a personal affront. Since blows to their egos cannot be tolerated, they write bitter letters venting their frustration upon the editor or constructor. They threaten to cancel subscriptions, call a solvers' strike in their area or induce all their friends to demand that the publisher fire you-know-who.

Offsetting the baffled Squawkers, who are usually flailing in waters over their heads, is a group of experienced solvers. These sophisticated Squawkers complain that the puzzles are "too damn easy." They long for the "challengers" of yesteryear or they compare the puzzles pejoratively with those appearing in some other publication. One such Squawker recently complained that he always looked forward to curling up with the Sunday *Times* puzzle for an entire afternoon. "Now," said he, "I finish the puzzle in an hour and don't know what the hell I should do with myself for the rest of the day." Another fan hinted that there may be two sides to the problem. "Are you getting simpler," she asked "or am I getting smarter?"

That Squawker probably hit upon one of the truisms applicable to solving: Proficiency increases with experience. However, it is also a fact that the puzzles vary in difficulty. To meet the objections of the "too hard!" and "too easy!" Squawkers, I deliberately publish about four rather easy puzzles in the Sunday *Times* each year and about four mind-boggling creations.

A third category of Squawkers includes the people who send in their blurred copy of the puzzle and blame me rather than the printer. Sometimes they complain that the definitions, numbers, boxes and solutions for daily puzzles are so minuscule that they produce myopia, strabismus and other optical disorders. Such Squawkers do not realize that I have no control over such matters except to squawk along with them to the powers that be.

Nor can I control the layout bigwigs who, for complicated reasons known only to themselves, occasionally place the continuation of an article on the other side of the Sunday puzzle. This arrangement causes consternation in thousands of homes, especially when an avid solver tears out the puzzle page and holes up someplace with it.

The position of a puzzle on a page can cause dissatisfaction, too. Left-handed people complain about the placement of a daily *Times* crossword in the bottom left corner of the book page. They say that it causes their palms to be out in space as they write. Others object when the puzzle is placed in a different section of the newspaper or printed at the top of the page. Again I sympathize but plead Not Guilty.

Diagramless fans can be Squawkers, too. Once, Will Weng got discombobulated and failed to publish the diagramless puzzles on the Sunday usually allotted to them. He was bombarded with angry letters. Many of the fans told him that they buy the paper only on "Diagramless Sundays."

I was subjected to a strafing when I published one very large diagramless puzzle instead of two smaller ones. The aficionados accused me of depriving them of their accustomed double feature.

Puns and Anagrams devotees got into the act when their favorite type of puzzle was replaced by a Cryptic on the Sunday *Times* puzzle page in 1980–81. It was a shock to me. In the previous three years of my editorship, I had received only two letters in praise of Puns and Anagrams. Then a Cryptic was published and about forty ecstatic letters poured in from people addicted to the British-type puzzle. This response seemed to indicate that the day of the Cryptic had arrived and the era of the Puns and Anagrams had become moribund. I was wrong. As more and more Cryptics appeared, the trickle of squawks from P.&A. fans gradually became a flood. My Solomonic decision was to alternate the two in 1982.

In contrast to *Times* fans, solvers of crosswords in puzzle books seldom indulge in cross words. One exception occurred when Margaret Farrar and I decided to publish a mixture of five P.&A. puzzles and Cryptics in the *Simon and Schuster Crossword Puzzle Book*. An incensed gentleman accused us of robbing him of five pages of regular puzzles.

□

Leapers are a surprisingly large group. Until I became an editor, I had never realized how many solvers are impulsive people, ready to take pen or typewriter in hand at the drop of a word. Many of them are gleefully arrogant; their letters usually start with "For shame!" Then they go on to describe an alleged error and pummel me for perpetrating such a crime.

The trouble with Leapers is that they fail to look before they lash. What bewilders me is why many of them rush in with criticisms when they have access to reference books that will correct their misconceptions. In contrast to the Sleepers, why do they assume that a mistake has been made?

One of my first encounters with Leapers occurred in a correspondence with some English professors at a renowned New England college. The institution shall be nameless, lest the prexy decide that one of his faculties had lost theirs.

The bone of contention was the word *Astrophel,* which I had defined as a "Spenserian work." The profs all signed their names to a letter stating that *Astrophel* should be attributed to Sir Philip Sidney, not Spenser. They were flabbergasted when I cited several reference books showing that Spenser had written an elegy called *Astrophel* on the death of Sidney, who had been his friend. What confused the profs was that Sidney had written a sonnet sequence called *Astrophel and Stella.* Apparently not one of them had ever studied Spenser.

A Spanish professor in New York became my next Leaper. I had defined the *Ebro* as "the longest river in Spain." He got into deep water when he claimed that the Tagus was longer. True, but the Tagus flows into Portugal, while the Ebro remains entirely in Spain, and its length in that country surpasses that of the Tagus. Subsequent to my reply, the professor has informed me that he is now sharing his new knowledge re *rios* with his students.

Returning to literature, let me cite the Pope misapprehension on the part of a solver in Braintree, Massachusetts. Alexander Pope was called "The Wicked Wasp of Twickenham" because of his acerbic personality and his satiric denunciations of his critics in *The Dunciad.* The disparaging nickname was eventually shortened to "Wasp." In a daily *Times* puzzle, I defined *wasp* as "epithet for Alexander Pope." My Bay State slater assumed that I meant White Anglo-Saxon Protestant — an acronym unknown in Pope's time. He chided me for changing the writer's religion and said, "Let's call old Alex a WASC." It did my heart good to reply with a couplet from Pope's *An Essay on Criticism*:

> A little learning* is a dangerous thing;
> Drink deep, or taste not the Pierian spring.

Another Massachusetts solver, this time a woman from Newton, also did some leaping recently on a religious basis. I had defined *primate* as "archbishop," and she was incensed. She wanted to know why I was so anticlerical and she berated me for indoctrinating our youth against men of the cloth by equating an archbishop with an ape. Like many other Leapers, she apologized profusely after I had urged her to consult any good dictionary.

A similar apology came from a Leaper in Pennsylvania who seemingly had good credentials. "My husband is an engineer," she wrote, "and I have consulted him on your definition for *berm*. You describe it as the 'shoulder of a road,' but he says you are all wet! It's a ledge! You should print a retraction!"

When I gently explained to my critic that there are seven or eight definitions for *berm,* including her husband's and mine, she sent me a red-faced reply.

Sometimes a definition touches a sensitive nerve, thereby causing a solver to berate me in a petulant paragraph before consulting a good dictionary. The wife of a son of Old Eli displayed such tender feelings when I defined *Yale* as a "mythical beast." Maybe she knew about my Harvard background. In any case, she protested my sly derogation of the New Haven university and demanded that I print a retraction. I referred her to *Webster's Third* and she subsequently apologized.

Using a new clue for a familiar puzzle word often causes a horde of Leapers to attack. Take *Ariel,* for instance. The usual definitions refer to the Shakespearean sprite or the Arabian gazelle. One day I defined the word as "rebel angel in *Paradise Lost*." A number of fans erroneously took me to task. They were sure I meant *Uriel*—another Miltonic being whom the poet called "the sharpest-sighted spirit of all in heaven."

Similarly, *arete* is usually called "alpine crest" in puzzles. Tired of that definition, I once used "valor or virtue" as the clue and received a dozen letters suggesting that I get my act together. Incidentally, those two *aretes* are interesting because they come down to us from entirely different sources. The more familiar one is derived from French and originally meant "fishbone" in Latin. (Ridges do look like bones of fish.) The other *arete* comes from a Greek verb meaning "to please."

Another coincidence caused me to become involved with a score of Leapers. Botanists, zoologists and puzzle addicts are probably the only people who know that *seta* is a bristle or bristlelike organ. To get away from that bit of crosswordese, constructors sometimes define the entry as "___ trap" or "___ precedent." But even those clues have become hackneyed. And so I was elated when I discovered that an Italian film director

---

*This line is often misquoted. People who are not alliterative supply "knowledge" for "learning."

bore the name *Vittorio de Seta*. A few weeks later when *seta* reared its ugly bristle in a puzzle, I rushed my director into print. Simultaneously, I made sure that all the crossings were easy, so that nobody would write *Sica* into the four boxes.

As might be expected, twenty letters arrived. A typical one derided me as follows: "Your answer to 'Director Vittorio de ___' is *Seta*. I'm *Sica* your mistakes!"

Topi is another puzzle favorite. This alternate spelling for *topee* is usually defined as "pith hat" or "safari headgear." When I learned that a topi is also an African antelope, I gave the animal due recognition and was told by a New York City fan that I had earned a dunce cap.

As indicated by the previous examples, Leapers often expose the narrowness of their knowledge by assuming that *their* definition for a word is the only one in existence. I empathize because I once thought that *ravel* merely meant "to entangle." What a surprise I received later when I learned that the same verb can mean "to untangle"! Another instance of a word with far different meanings, by the way, is *cleave*. It can be defined as "adhere to" or "divide into two pieces." And let's not forget *scan*. It means "look at searchingly" or "glance over quickly."

This elasticity of our language, vis-à-vis the rigidity on the part of some solvers, is the prime reason for letters accusing editors of taking liberties with definitions. To some people, a nun cannot be anything but a woman dwelling in a convent. To define the word as "type of buoy or pigeon" is to cause them to regard you as some sort of kook. Similarly, a nib must be "the point of a pen," according to these Leapers. One of them chided me sarcastically for defining the word as "bird's beak." Her letter declared, "You mean a *neb!* Be more careful!" Had she practiced what she preached, she would have discovered that an avine bill is spelled as *nib* or *neb*.

Neb is very close to *Ner* in spelling, and that biblical character provides another example of many Leaper letters. Whenever I define *Ner* as "Saul's grandfather" (1 Chr. 8:33), some fan who has read another section of the Old Testament is sure to chastise me for altering the relationship from "uncle" to "grandfather." Apparently there were two men named Ner in Saul's family.

Leapers are often good for a laugh. When *Porthos* was described as a "Mousquetaire," a woman from the Bronx wanted to know where we found that Disney character.

One faction of this group of solvers cannot be bothered to wait to see the answer in print. These fans get stuck by rash decisions on crossing words and stubbornly assume they are right. For example, in a recent puzzle the third letter of FALL crossed with the fourth letter of POLLO. The latter was defined as "trattoria offering" (Italian word for chicken) and the clue for FALL was "be overthrown." A solver from Medford, Massachusetts penciled in the word FAIL. She then wrote to ask what connection POLIO had with a trattoria!

And from a Nova Scotia neophyte came the following. "Some of your offerings are sloppy. *Mauve* is not a shade of yellow." With all the tact at my command I informed my Canadian critic that the answer was *maize*.

A really hilarious letter recently arrived from a woman in Westbury, New York. She had confused *careen* ("to lurch") with *career* ("to rush wildly"). When the definition called for *career*, she chose the other verb and came out with ABIE'S IRISH NOSE as the crossing phrase. Her letter asked why I was making jokes about Abie's proboscis.

Sometimes, however, the Leapers have a good point. Since all my dictionaries give "hypocrite" as one of the definitions for *Pharisee*, I once used that clue and received a flood of indignant letters from Hebrew scholars who castigated me for perpetuating a slur on a scholarly ancient Jewish group. I apologized and promised never to use that definition again.

But apologies do not seem to be in order when some fans accuse me of rearranging the order of the Hebrew months. For instance, I once defined *Adar* as "sixth Hebrew month" and was taken to task by people whose religious calendars indicate that Adar is the last of the twelve. In this case, my critics and I are both right. My reference was to the civil year and theirs was to the ecclesiastical year.

To avoid such confusion, I have recently elected to eschew my usual penchant for specificity. *Adar* is now merely a "Hebrew month" or "Jewish month."

Rosalind Moore, executive editor of Dell Crossword Publications, was once accused by a leaping solver of being anti-Semitic, because he had not looked into the back of one of her magazines to see the answer. The word *Navaho* crossed with *hew*, and the verb was defined as "chop down." Unfortunately her castigator had written NAVAJO and had come out with JEW for the three-letter word. In raging prose, he charged her with perpetuating a vicious slur concerning dickering.

In connection with the above, several Christians once assailed me about a Mitzvah definition. Most people know *Bar Mitzvah*, the ceremony celebrating the arrival of a thirteen-year-old Jewish boy into religious responsibility. But when the rites are performed for a girl in Conservative and Reformed congregations, *Bat* or *Bas* replaces *Bar*. Seeking a new definition for *Bas*, I chose "___ Mitzvah"; some Gentiles were far from gentle in their letters. I guess I should have defined *Bas* as "Oh, what a relief it is!"

Folk usage is another problem for Leapers. When thousands of educated people spell *lodestone* as *loadstone*, lexicographers succumb and equate the two. But when *loadstone* is defined in a puzzle as "magnetic attraction," solvers possessing outworn dictionaries take up epistolary cudgels.

My most recent skirmish with linguistic tories came when the clue for *fortuitous* read "bringing good luck." That definition appears in many modern lexicons including the excellent Webster's *New World Dictionary–Second College Edition*, for which I have great respect. Like me, however, many fans have been taught that the only definition for *fortuitous* is "accidental." They jumped at the chance to tell me that at last they had discovered a mistake. As a Latin major, I am delighted that *fortuitous* has broken away from its former shackles. After all, it has the same Latin origin (*fors, fortis*) as *fortunate!*

Speaking of Latin, the most sarcastic letter I have ever received came from an anonymous solver who sneered at me for using *iters* ("brain passages") in a puzzle. He or she imperiously gave me a Latin lesson. To wit, the plural of *iter* ("Roman road") is *itinera,* whence we derive *itinerary*. It was frustrating not to be able to reply. Whoever you are out there, I hope you are reading this passage. For centuries, Latin words have been Anglicized, especially in the plural. As just a few examples, let me cite:

> *forums* or *fora*
> *cerebellums* or *cerebella*
> *cactuses* or *cacti*

Similarly, we have altered Greek diphthongs. Consider the following:

> *esthete* for *aesthete*
> *Etna* for *Aetna*
> *ether* for *aether*

And yet, a solver from Florida blasted me for "liberality." She insisted that the only spelling for *amebas* was *amoebae*. Resistance to change seems to be a common characteristic of one brand of Leapers.

The alterations we make when foreign words are transposed into English are also evident in the English spellings of words from other modern languages. For instance, a fan of Teutonic background from Tenafly, New Jersey, chided me for the use of *yager* as an accepted variation of *jaeger* (German rifleman). Furthermore, she lectured: "*Jagen* means 'to go hunting' and a *jaeger* is simply a hunter." Well, Madam, isn't it possible that many hunters own rifles?

My Hispanic friend Carlos Muñoz from New York City became a Leaper when he declared that I had misspelled *Rosinante* (Don Quixote's steed). The Spanish word is *Rocinante,* but in English it has undergone a "c" change. Also, the fourth letter of Quijote has achieved an X rating.

Lexicographers must keep up with alterations caused by folk usage, and so must a crossword puzzle editor. For example, a *pom-pom* is an automatic weapon and a *pompon* is a chrysanthemum, among other things. Maybe because of the "m" in "mums" the cheerleaders at football games are now called *pom-pom girls* by most writers. Hence, new dictionaries grudgingly accept the change in spelling. But the Leapers don't! When I used *pom-pom girls* in a puzzle last year, I received a number of satiric letters asking if the beauties who lead the cheers are now cannoneers.

Incidentally, I wonder how many readers are aware that the original spelling of *apron* was *napron,* from the same French source that gave us *napery* and *napkin*. But because of the constant use of "a napron" in oral communication, the initial letter of the noun was pushed forward to become part of the modifier. Folk usage is indeed a powerful force in altering our language.

Another area that brings Leapers out in droves is geography. For example, I once referred to Tripoli as "a city in Lebanon." A physician from Brooklyn was among the many solvers who rushed to their typewriters and informed me that the city was located in Libya. Had the good doctor consulted his atlas first, he never would have written. There are two Tripolis—his and mine.

Similarly, there are two groups of Leeward Islands. The lesser-known chain is part of the Society Islands in the Pacific and includes Bora Bora. When I chose to define that volcanic spot as "one of the Leeward Islands," I knew I would evoke from many Leapers a raft of letters scolding me for moving the island eastward from the Pacific.

Duplications in names often fool the solvers. There are two edifices in Italy that are called Doria Palace. One is in Rome; the other in Genoa. When I chose the latter a woman in New York City wrote, "I'm disappointed in you!"

Also, my favorite among Michelangelo's masterpieces is the pietà in the Duomo at Florence. When I referred to it, another New Yorker asked, "Since when was the Pietà moved from Rome to Florence?" Apparently she knew of only the one at St. Peter's. Actually there are three famous Michelangelo pietàs: the third one is located in Milan.

☐

Now let us turn to that elite group of fans that I call the Gotchas. They are a mixture of cool customers who know their onions, their literature, movies, geography, foreign languages, sports, music and other fields in which I occasionally reveal my humanity by making an error.

About 99.9 percent of my flubs occur in the definitions. I can recall only four that appeared in the diagrams. In one case, the word was *cittè,* and my clue was "Napoli e Milano." Lo and behold, a score of Italian scholars came out of the woods and wrapped me in their nets. They declared correctly that the plural of *città* ("city") is *città*. It's an exception to the rule. *Mamma mia!* My reply to some of my critics was

> I wish I were a polygot —
> Something I'm, by golly, not!

Please note the accent mark over the last letter in *città*. I often get irate letters from fans of Teutonic background who insist that the printed answers should contain umlauts when certain German words appear in the puzzles. I see their point, but invariably the crossing word is an English one that would look silly with an umlaut.

The German language tripped me on my second error in the diagram itself. The entry was ESELS, which I defined as "Bonn beasts." Bill Anderson, a librarian at the *Times,* convinced me that I had made an ass of myself. He wrote, "I remember my German professor saying that plurals are formed any way except by adding s."

By the way, if you ever see *nenes* in a puzzle and the clue is "Hawaiian geese," the editor was napping. The plural of that state bird is the same as the singular.

My third non-definition mistake occurred partly because the constructor of the puzzle was one of the top ten in the business. One of his entries was THE LADY AND THE TIGER. Trusting him, I let it slip through. Strangely enough, only one letter arrived to remind me that Frank Stockton's short story was entitled "The Lady or the Tiger." Having once taught that tale, I felt like jumping off the nearest bridge. When I told the constructor, he vowed that he would accompany me.

The fourth error within the diagram was called to my attention by only one person, the wife of Fred Foy. Who's that? Well, he was the one who announced "Hi Yo Silver Away" for twenty years in radio's Lone Ranger programs and in the film. Mrs. Foy gently reminded me that "Hi *Ho* Silver Away" was incorrect.

But most of my boo-boos are minuscule ones which compassionate solvers probably assume to be typos. Here are a few examples:

Clue	Answer	Proper Answer	Better Clue
Actor Estrada	ERIC	ERIK	Sevareid
Actress Hedy	LAMAR	LAMARR	Truman's birthplace
Presley's middle name	AARON	ARON	Home-run king

Names do plunge me into trouble occasionally. In that respect, my worst gaffe involved the noted New York City newscaster Liz Trotta. I called her "Trotter," and she sent me a reply that was a bit sulky. Who could blame her?

In that same vein, I called the track at Aqueduct a "raceway" and was informed by a sports fan that the appellation applies only to harness racing.

Some other rather minor mistakes that elicited Gotcha responses are as follows:

Clue	Answer	Proper Clue
Buy a horse after a race	CLAIM	Buy a horse before a race
Undev. film	NEG.	Opposite of pos.
Put through a strainer	RICE	Prepare potatoes, in a way
America's Cup challenger	INTREPID	America's Cup defender
Cannon or Luger	SENATOR	Cannon or Lugar
Suffix with suffrage	ETTE	Suffix with major
Comparative ending	IER	Ending with cash
Pfc. or cpl.	NCO	Sgt. or cpl.

Clue	Answer	Proper Clue
Initials for Elizabeth II	HRH	Initials for Princess Anne
Violin feature	FRET	Ukulele feature
*Biblical queen	SHEBA	Biblical land
*____ Angelica	FRA	____ Angelico

Sometimes the movies are stumbling blocks, too. Early in my career as *Times* editor, I defined DEEDS as a "Jimmy Stewart role." Of course, I'd mixed up Mr. Deeds with Mr. Smith who went to Washington. One gleeful Gotcha letter read: "It was Gary Cooper! Two years ago I caught your predecessor, Will Weng, in the same mistake!"

My latest flub in the film field came on a Sunday when I defined PINK PANTHER as a "Sellers role." A score of solvers let me know that Sellers was a bumbling inspector named Clouseau. One of the fans, a law professor at Loyola University, explained that the original panther in the series was a gem. He went on to say, "The challenge of looking for minor errors is every bit as exciting as the puzzle itself."

That Sunday puzzle will live in infamy because it contained a terrible total of two mistakes—neither attributable to the constructor. The second error involved Fran Allison. I called her a "puppeteer" and was immediately informed by the cognoscenti that she is an actress. I discovered that the real puppeteer in the *Kukla, Fran and Ollie* show is Burr Tillstrom.

As you can see, editing crossword puzzles is a learning experience. I am constantly amazed by the knowledge fans possess, not only with regard to trivia but also in more important matters. For example, I once described Abba Eban as "the first Israeli ambassador to the U.S." and was inundated by Gotcha letters enlightening me to the fact that Eban was preceded by Ambassador Elath. In another case, my reference book stated that Tyrone was a county in Ireland. I should have consulted a more up-to-date source. The Irish had made some administrative changes; Tyrone, I found out from the fans, had been replaced in the 1970s by a number of new districts.

Similarly, the Gotcha crowd gave me an education in astronomy. Saturn no longer has nine satellites, as my old encyclopedia states. A recent discovery has increased the number to ten. Also, the ancient constellation that Ptolemy called "Argo Navis" is no longer recognized by authorities. It has been divided into smaller constellations, including Vela and Carina.

Sports is one of my fortes. Hence, overconfidence can lead to little lapses of memory in lazy moments when I fail to check with some authority. I owe apologies to Terry

---

*These are two of several errors called to my attention by Monsignor A.V. McLees, whom I have designated as the president of my Gotcha Club. His corrections, by the way, are always couched in clever verses.

Bradshaw for calling him "Bradford," to Larry Bird for making him into a relative of Admiral Byrd and to golfer Ed Sneed for confusing him with Sam and J. C. Snead. And I'm mortified to say that I accepted a misspelling of Rabbit Maranville's name in a sports encyclopedia. When I was a boy, Rabbit was one of my heroes; apparently lots of others idolized him, too. At least ten old-time baseball fans objected to the "Moranville" clue.

Another area in which I feel confident is Shakespearean literature. Here again, carelessness was my undoing. What were Caesar's last words? Not "Et tu, Brute" (as I stated) but "Then fall, Caesar!"

Another Caesarean fluff occurred when I defined *Anglia* as "England, to Caesar." Erudite solvers gave me a lesson in history. *Anglia,* they explained, is a medieval Latin word which came into being subsequent to the invasion of Britain by the Angles and long after Caesar was dead. His term for the island was Britannia.

England seems to be a jinx for me. Like Pussycat in the well-known rhyme, I've been to London — not once, but several times. As usual, a combination of sluggishness and overconfidence led to my downfall when TRAFALGAR SQUARE appeared in a daily *Times* puzzle. In a bleary-eyed moment, I decided on the following clue: "Where to see Eros." Somehow that egregious error escaped my wife, who had accompanied me on my trips to London and who always acts as the first test-solver of the puzzles. It also eluded my eagle-eyed proofer, Harriett Wilson, and her backup spotter, Judy Spindler.

But the goof did not get by over a hundred fans who had been used to seeing EROS defined as "statue in Piccadilly Circus." Their letters ranged the gamut from sneering denunciations to pleasant needling. A few transmitted their curses in verses, rhyming *Circus* with *irk us* or *statue* with *catch you.* Others just couldn't believe that I had blundered so badly. Several solvers asked naively when Eros had been moved to Trafalgar Square. Some suspected me of trickery. "You're a sly guy," wrote one fan. "You probably mean that if I climbed the statue of Lord Nelson and peered through binoculars, I could see Eros at Piccadilly."

Incidentally, the letters from the aficionados often reveal their individual personalities. But I must point out that very few missiles are aimed at me in their missives. If all members of the human race were as nice as crossword fans, this would be a far better world. Let it be noted, too, that most Squawkers, Leapers and Gotchas append appreciation and congratulations when they write. They understand that even though I have a Polish name, I cannot join Pope John Paul II in claiming infallibility. They also seem to recognize that pitfalls loom before me each time my editorial pencil is activated or held back. How many times? Well, I edit about 40,000 definitions per annum for the *Times* alone and I average about seven mistakes each year. The same ratio applies to the crossword puzzle books I edit or co-edit for Simon and Schuster.

Facing me on my desk is a card on which I have written the following verse:

> Maleska, you gotta
> Watch out for errata;
> Don't sleep at the switch,
> You son of a gun!

The euphemistic coda takes into account the fact that occasional visitors may be ingenues, toddlers or little old ladies in tennis shoes.

Since most puzzle fans love quizzes, this chapter concludes with a true-false test based on letters from Leapers and Gotchas. Give yourself 4 points for each correct response. The answers, along with your rating, are on page 181.

T 1. Onega is a Russian lake.

F 2. A proverb states, "Money is the root of all evil."

F 3. A scene can be defined as a stage set.

T 4. Anthony Tudor is a London-born choreographer.

F 5. Louis XV said, "Après nous le déluge."

6. "And" is a song in *A Chorus Line*.

T 7. Spads fought Fokkers in World War I.

F 8. Aeneas led Dante through Hades.

F 9. "The Little Engine That Could" is about a male locomotive which lent a helping hand.

F 10. Handel wrote *The Messiah*.

F 11. A rat can be defined as a mongoose's prey.

F 12. The U.S.M.A. and U.S.N.A. freshmen are called plebes — not plebs.

F 13. Churchill and J.F.K. each wrote a book called *While England Slept*.

F 14. A consoler may be defined as one who sits Shiva.

T 15. Lima beans have always been an ingredient of succotash.

F 16. The rand is the official currency of Botswana.

F 17. Cho-Cho-San is the heroine of a Puccini opera.

F 18. *Printemps* is a symphonic suite by Debussy.

F 19. Erato can be defined as a dryad.

F 20. Lehr was a noted comic: 1896–1950.

F 21. "Hallowe'en" is the only accepted spelling for All Hallows Eve.

T 22. Some lichens are mosses.

T 23. Whoopers are cranes — never swans.

T 24. Phintias was Damon's friend.

F 25. The pika is a rodent.

2

Facts, Figures, Questions and Answers

It has been estimated that approximately 50 million people solve crossword puzzles. If that figure boggles your mind, consider it this way: The solvers would fill all the seats at Fenway Park in Boston for more than thirteen baseball seasons. Admittedly the illustration is incongruous; it's ridiculous to think of 37,000 aficionados with crossword puzzles in their laps while the Red Sox swing away. But the point is that the puzzles do fascinate legions of people. Such games as bridge, chess, checkers, bingo and poker take a back seat to the world's most popular leisure-time activity.

My educated guess is that more than one million fans solve the daily *New York Times* puzzle. And a recent survey reveals that almost one-third of the 1½ million people who get the Sunday *Times* are interested in the puzzles. My fan mail indicates that many of them buy the newspaper merely because they want to tackle the crossword. In some homes, where several people are fanatical about the black and white squares, more than one copy is purchased.

It's a bit frightening to contemplate the vast numbers of solvers. Each time I make a decision about a definition, I visualize hordes of mavens peering over my shoulder. If I should make a mistake, heaven forbid, a nightmarish feeling sweeps through my bones. Suppose all those millions catch the error and send "for-shame!" letters.

Another problem that bothers an editor when faced with such figures is the realization that no puzzle will please everybody. The range of solvers includes neophytes who have ventured into deep waters too soon and experts who become bored when the puzzles are somewhat easy. In that connection, a coincidence occurred a few years ago. A retiree in Miami sent me a bitter letter complaining that I was a show-off whose puzzles were impossible to solve. He threatened to establish a boycott throughout his area. In the same mail, a Park Avenue resident stated that the puzzles had become too simple ever since I had succeeded Will Weng. After deleting the names and addresses, I sent the New Yorker's letter to the Miamian and vice versa. I never heard from either of them again.

A question often asked of me is Why do people tackle crossword puzzles? Obviously there is no single answer, because of individual differences. Margaret Farrar points out that puzzles are relatively inexpensive forms of entertainment. Will Weng notes that lots of people in our leisure-oriented society get bored and do the crosswords to kill time. And some psychologists believe that the puzzles are popular because they present orderly problems in contrast with life's complexities.

Nature abhors a vacuum and so does human nature. To some, the blank spaces seem to cry out, "Fill us in!" These fans are like explorers venturing into the unknown. Many of them seek the satisfaction of meeting a challenge successfully. Others claim that the puzzles have expanded their vocabulary and their scope of general knowledge. Of course, a portion of such lore is esoteric or trivial. That aspect of puzzles will be dealt with in the chapter called "Crosswordese."

In my opinion, the chief motivation for thousands upon thousands of people is the need to escape from personal troubles or "the jungle out there" where criminals roam, politicians squabble and nations take up arms against each other. For this reason I have always tried to follow Mrs. Farrar's dictum that the puzzles should not be cluttered with offensive or downbeat words like *entrails, ulcers, offal, sot, lice, nits,* etc. I even attempt to expunge such words as *war, blood* and *strangle*. Naturally it is not always possible to eliminate every unpleasant entry and I try not to be obsessive about the matter, but most of the time crossword fans are not exposed to the seedier side of life.

Another question that frequently arises is Who are the fans? Again, there is no simple answer. If my mail is any indication, women outnumber men by a 5-to-3 ratio. But those figures may be deceiving since it is possible that women have more time or have a greater predilection for writing letters. The mail also reveals that most solvers have at least a high school education and many are college graduates.

A great number of fans are retirees. It amazes me how many octogenarians are skilled in solving puzzles. On the other hand, multitudes of university students have taken up the hobby. Will Weng and I have been guest speakers at Yale, and a Maleska Fan Club sprang up at Cornell during the late 1970s. Some college professors use the puzzles as teaching devices; one even asked me to send him a *Times* puzzle, along with the answer, prior to publication so that he could impress his class with his brilliance.

Lawyers and doctors abound among the fans. The former love the legal terms that puzzlers use. *Torts, res judicate, oyer,* etc., are their favorite entries. The physicians gloat over the anatomical terms. They get a head start when an *ulna*, a *tibia*, an *aorta* or a *pia mater* appears in a puzzle.

Teachers seem to love crosswords, too. In one New Jersey high school they keep records on the time it takes them to solve a *Times* daily 15 x 15 challenge. In a New York City junior high school the principal passes his answer around to a group of addicts on the faculty. My photograph is exhibited in the teachers' room at another school. When the puzzle is too hard, darts are thrown at the smiling countenance. A bull's-eye is a shot on the proboscis.

Office workers, from the executives down to the steno pool, are hooked on puzzles. In several New York corporations the crosswords are Xeroxed each weekday and during the coffee breaks contests of a sort are conducted to see who can finish first.

Many inmates of prisons are avid solvers, fulfilling the need to kill time, and some of them have become adept constructors who have been published in the *Times*, Simon and Schuster puzzle books and several crossword magazines. In at least one penitentiary, the monthly house organ contains an excellent puzzle and a contest is conducted to see which convict can complete the crossword accurately and quickly. The "prize" is praise in the next issue.

Many patients recuperating from surgery or illnesses find crossword puzzles to be therapeutic. Part of a nurse's job these days is to be able to answer a question such as What's a seven-letter word for kneecap? I am reminded of the time I was hospitalized for a hip injury. An intern woke me up at 6 A.M. for two reasons: he needed the answer to 17-Down and he wanted me to autograph the puzzle.

But probably the solvers who outnumber all other groups are the women who call themselves "average housewives." I spend an eight-hour day each week sending replies to their letters. But as the old song states, "Bless 'em all!"

Finally, it should be noted that many celebrities have been and are crossword puzzle fans. Columnist F. P. Adams was among the first when the fad hit its peak in the 1920s. Also, Stephen Vincent Benet and Heywood Broun prided themselves on their solving skills.

Speaking of F.P.A., here's a quote from his book *The Diary of Our Own Samuel Pepys* (Simon and Schuster, 1935):

> Sunday, March 26, 1922. Late up and felt low-spirited, so to solve a cross-word puzzle, which I did in less than half an hour, which restored my confidence, till I said to myself, Bring on your problems. And that, methought, is why these puzzles are so popular, as the ability to solve them is mistaken by the solvers for intelligence. Lord, for a few minutes after I solve a puzzle, I am as vain as any peacock, and strut about the house till my wife takes my vanity away by calling me silly or some such thing. But she's away this day in Orange, so my inflation endures for an hour.

My first fan letter from a famous person was written by Ben Hecht during the

1930s. He noticed that I had often chosen his first name instead of Franklin's in the puzzles I was publishing. Later Joseph Cotten and I became pen pals because he liked my Stepquotes, and Frank Sinatra's secretary proudly informed me that her boss does the *Times* puzzles in ink.

Among the other stars who enjoy crosswords are Greer Garson, Van Johnson, Julie Harris, Eli Wallach, Henry Morgan, Walter Matthau and Ellen Burstyn. Incidentally, Miss Burstyn claims that *Times* puzzles were the catalysts that spurred her on to complete her education.

Beverly Sills is a fan, too. One day her secretary called me up and asked if Ms. Sills could have a set of puzzles in advance because she was scheduled for a tour of the boondocks where the *Times* would not be available. Naturally, I obliged. In return, Ms. Sills sent me "hugs and kisses."

Although Tom Seaver has never written to me, sportswriters have passed the word that he is a crosswords addict. I wonder what his reaction is when I define *slider* or *curve* as "one of Seaver's deceivers."

Writer Rex Stout has stated, "If I were bound for a desert island, the ten books I would want along would be ten crossword puzzle books edited by Margaret Farrar. Then I wouldn't bother to look around for footprints."

And Noel Coward once declared, "When I make 1-Across fit with 1-Down, my day is made."

Sir Noel's statement reminds me to mention lyricist Sammy Cahn. He wrote to say that he could hardly "Cahn-tain" himself when he discovered that he was 1-Down in a daily puzzle. My reply stated, "I'm so glad you care"—in reference to one of his hit songs, "I Should Care." Incidentally, songwriter Stephen Sondheim not only solves puzzles but has published a book of Cryptics.

Presumably there are scores of other celebrities who do the puzzles regularly or occasionally but do not reveal their interest. I have devoted entire 15 x 15 "birthday" puzzles to such people as Irving Berlin, Bob Hope, Luciano Pavarotti and Jackie Gleason but have never received acknowledgment. Their silence is understandable; correspondence must be a prime problem for one in the limelight.

In that connection, during 1982 a Sunday *Times* puzzle was called "Katharine the Great." It featured the films of Katharine Hepburn. Several fans asked if such tribute had ever been paid before to any other celebrity in a large *Times* crossword. The answer was "To the best of my knowledge, no." Did Hepburn say thanks? No, but who can blame her?

Where do people solve puzzles? Mostly at home, of course. But as indicated above, a great deal of brain power is expended in educational institutions, offices and hospitals. Nor should we ignore the thousands who scratch their heads on buses, subways, airplanes and trains. Apropos of those commuters, the story has been bruited about that George S. Kaufman used to astonish his fellow travelers on the Long Island Rail Road by finishing the daily puzzle in two minutes. But one day he left his newspaper on the seat as he detrained. Another passenger grabbed it, turned to the crossword and discovered that every open square was marked with an X.

My first encounter with a "subway solver" occurred in the 1930s on a morning when one of my puzzles was published in the *Herald Tribune*. A middle-aged man in the seat next to me was having an awful time moaning and groaning over my puzzle. After his fourth harrumph, I couldn't resist any longer. "Pardon me, sir," I said. "I see you're having trouble with that puzzle. Maybe I can help you. I'm the one who made it up."

The harried solver gave me a quick, frightened look and then marched to the other end of the car. He got off at the next stop.

Since then I have sat alongside dozens of people struggling over puzzles that I have constructed or edited, but I have resisted all temptations to introduce myself. To paraphrase Will Weng, puzzles are private matters to many people. Let no intruder disturb the concentration!

Lunch hour is a time when many workers choose to solve puzzles. On a warm, sunny day visit any park or mall and you will see people bending over a crossword as they munch on their sandwiches. And when the toilers take their summer vacations and head for the beaches, thousands of them take the puzzles along.

Some breadwinners rip out the puzzle and take a stab at it later in the day. One such solver is Pat Clark, a union shop steward in a Glasgow shipyard. When his foreman caught him filling in words and ordered him "in a dictatorial manner" to put the puzzle away, he flung some cross words at his boss for interrupting his train of thought. As a result, he was fired. But 300 of his Glaswegian colleagues objected to his dismissal and went on strike.

That episode reminds me that *fan* is derived from *fanatic*.

Coffee and crosswords seem to go together like bagel and lox or apple pie and ice cream. Innumerable addicts have told me that they can't start their day without a cup of java and a puzzle. What utensil do they use? For most, it's a pencil; but in recent years the pen has become more popular. One reason is the advent of the pen with erasable ink. Another reason is that pencil markings are often so light that the solver becomes confused as to what letters he has previously entered. Personalities must be considered, too. Some egotists like to flaunt their skills by showing their inked-in answers to others — somewhat like the boy on the bicycle who cries, "Look, Ma, no hands!" Incidentally, an optimist has been defined as "one who uses a pen when trying a Sunday *Times* puzzle."

To use or not to use reference books has been a subject of controversy among fans since the dawn of crossword puzzles. Is it "cheating" to consult a dictionary, almanac or encyclopedia? My advice is not to worry. Constructors and editors employ such books regularly. Why not the solver?

Pride appears to be a factor in this matter. Solving a puzzle "on one's own" is certainly an ego builder, but while examining hundreds of puzzles completed by fans who have not depended on outside sources, I have found scores of errors. In other words, those solvers have fooled themselves and have indulged in mislearning.

A middle-of-the-road policy is to leave blank those words that require some kind of minor research and to scrutinize the answer thereafter. In the course of the years, I have used that method myself and have constantly gained new knowledge.

An editor must take into account whether or not solvers have access to authoritative sources. When I succeeded Will Weng at the *Times,* he let me in on a system he had been using for daily puzzles:

> Monday—easy (people recovering from weekend)
> Tuesday—still easy, but a bit harder
> Wednesday—middling
> Thursday—a bit harder
> Friday—hard (people can finish it on the weekend)
> Saturday—very hard (people can use reference books).

I have followed the Weng System, and some fans have noticed the gradual increase in the challenge. A few complain that the Monday puzzle is too simple, while others thank me for giving a boost to their self-confidence. As for Saturday's toughies, the expert solvers relish them. On the other hand, those who refuse to resort to reference books become irate. Author William Slattery recently wrote, "The Saturday puzzles are bitches! I've given up on them!"

I am often asked if there is any correlation between intelligence and the ability to solve crossword puzzles. As far as I know, authoritative studies on that subject are nonexistent. My personal guess is that I.Q. and solving expertise are not mutually reciprocal. There are many bright people who find crosswords impossible to do. On the other hand plodders with normal intelligence often acquire the knack. Among them are the ones who memorize crosswordese—when the clue reads "Irish freedman" they immediately write LAET. Similarly, they know all the lizards, sloths, foreign coins, medieval toilers, etc.

There is a high correlation between mathematical reasoning and intelligence. Since most crossword puzzles require very little ability in math, engineers and physicists may be at a disadvantage when they venture into the world of the black and white squares. Conversely, the correlation between spelling prowess and I.Q. is rather low. Any solver or puzzlemaker knows how important orthography is in crosswords.

The high correlation between intelligence and sense of humor makes me feel that people who zip through Cryptics and Puns and Anagrams puzzles probably are a cut above the crowd.

Education appears to be a factor in solving success. However, there are exceptions. For example, the winner of a recent crossword contest in Dartmouth, Massachusetts, was a high school dropout who had been doing puzzles for decades. The victory buoyed her confidence so much that she went to night school and finally acquired the precious diploma.

My conclusion is that the adept-solver category includes people with high mentalities and others with normal intelligence. And those who can't get to first base when tackling a puzzle aren't necessarily stupid.

Crossword fans do possess a great deal of intellectual curiosity. They ask questions about every aspect of their hobby. Aside from the ones previously covered in this chapter, here are some typical queries along with my answers.

Q. *Why doesn't everybody solve crossword puzzles?*

A. There are lots of reasons: illiteracy; lack of ability or interest in language arts; no time for this particular hobby; work-ethic syndrome; the feeling that CWP's are a frivolous waste of time; fear of failure; force of habit.

Q. *What is the record for the fewest number of words in a 15 x 15 puzzle?*

A. Don't know for sure. Jordan Lasher published one with only 58 words (S & S Pocket Book #18). The average number of entries is 74.

Q. *What is the record for the fewest number of black squares in a 15 x 15 puzzle?*

A. Again, don't know. Jack Luzzatto once published a *Times* daily puzzle with only 24 black squares. The average is about 36.

Q. *Is there an average time for solving a 15 x 15 puzzle or a large Sunday-type puzzle?*

A. Probably a half-hour for the former and about two hours for the latter. The range is tremendous, depending upon the skill and experience of the individual solvers. Contest winner Stanley Newman has allegedly solved a *Times* daily puzzle in three minutes. Others claim that they have completed Sunday puzzles in ten minutes. But quite a few people take an entire week. Many tell me that answers come to them in their sleep!

Q. *Do you have any tips as to how to solve an ordinary puzzle?*

A. Let your eyes run down the clues. When you discover one for which you have a "sure-bet" answer, start there. Then work on the crossing words. When stuck, find another easy clue in a different part of the puzzle and proceed along the same lines.

Place an ED at the end of all words for which the clue calls for past tense. The same applies to plural definitions that usually signal an S at the end of the word. But watch out for traps. If the clue is "intended" the answer might be MEANT (no ED) and if the definition is "antitoxins" the probability is that SERA is required (no S at the end).

Don't be ashamed to consult a dictionary or other reference book, especially if you're a tyro.

When you're quite confident about a word you have entered but you're getting nowhere, take a second look. You may be wrong. In other words, cultivate flexibility rather than obstinacy.

See methods used by contest winners in the chapter called "Crossword Contests."

Q. *Why do you use words that I can't find in my dictionary?*

A. You probably own an abridged or "desk" dictionary. Constructors of puzzles use unabridged lexicons. My own favorites are:

> *Webster's New World Dictionary — Second Edition*
> *Webster's New International Dictionary — Second Edition (W-2)*
> *Webster's Third New International Dictionary (W-3)*
> *The Random House Dictionary of the English Language*
> *American Heritage Dictionary of the English Language*

Q. *I have heard that constructors start with the clues and build the puzzles around those definitions. Is that correct?*

A. Absolutely not! The clues are the last items in the procedure, but they are very important. See my chapter on "The Fine Art of Defining."

Q. *How long does it take a constructor to create a 15 x 15 puzzle? How long for a large Sunday-type puzzle?*

A. The time varies according to the experience, personality and general ability of the constructor. My first 15 x 15s took me six or eight hours to complete. Now I can put one together in less than two hours, counting the time it takes to type the clues. Similarly, I used to consume about sixteen hours in the process of constructing a 21 x 21 puzzle. Now I can finish the job in four hours, but I must confess that it sometimes takes twice that long to come up with a new idea for a theme and then research it.

Q. *Please tell me the difference between a combining form and a prefix.*

A. Combining forms usually occur in compound words and are mainly of Greek origin. They have more strength than mere prefixes. An example of a word which consists of two combining forms is *odontology.* The first part, *odont,* means "tooth" and the last part means "science of." A synonym for the entire word is "dentistry."

Q. *I know that crossword puzzles are popular, but I wonder to what extent. Can you give me some round figures as to how many newspapers carry the crossword? And what about puzzle books and magazines?*

A. There are about 1,800 newspapers in the United States. Almost every one of them publishes a crossword puzzle. Simon and Schuster is the leader in publishing books of crosswords — sometimes as many as seven each year — but several other companies have recently provided stiff competition. The average hardcover puzzle book sells about 10,000 or more copies a year, whereas paperback sales have been known to reach as high as 750,000.

Dell Publishing Company is the acknowledged leader in the crossword magazine field. There are about twenty-five puzzle magazines on the market. They vary greatly in quality, but most are good sellers. In a few cases more than 100,000 copies of each issue are bought by fans all over the world.

Q. *My daughter and I compete via long distance to see who can finish the Sunday puzzle first. Are we unique?*

A. Your game is not really unusual. In many communities neighbors compete or trade answers. In some households husbands and wives compete or form a team to solve the puzzle. Scores of variations of partnerships have come to my attention. These instances seem to belie Will Weng's conclusion that puzzle solving is a solo flight, but in most cases he is correct.

Q. *Sometimes when I solve a Sunday puzzle or one in a Simon and Schuster book, I don't understand the theme. Can you help?*

A. Yes. Scrutinize the title. It will give you a hint. In the case of S & S puzzles, the blurb will often provide a clue.

Q. *I've been solving crosswords for thirty years and now they bore me because I finish them so fast. Do you have any suggestions for relieving my ennui?*

A. Yes, indeed! Father Ronald Knox in England used to try to finish a puzzle by consulting only the horizontal or vertical definitions. Go thou and do likewise. If still bored, graduate to Puns and Anagrams, Cryptics or diagramless puzzles.

Q. *I've attempted to do your puzzles but I can't get anywhere. Why don't you make them easier for people like me?*

A. You're probably in the wrong league. Try the puzzles at the beginning of most crossword magazines and books. After practicing on the simple ones, you may be ready for the big time.

Q. *I'm an octogenarian and have been solving puzzles for more than fifty years. My brain is as sharp as ever. Do you think it's because of the crosswords?*

A. Possibly. At any rate your hobby hasn't been a deterrent. Dr. James Fries of the Stanford University Medical Center says that mental agility in old age comes from giving the brain regular workouts. Your letter seems to prove his point.

Q. *Do constructors ever make up words just so they will be able to complete the puzzle they are creating?*

A. Sometimes, but a good editor sends them a rejection. I turn down many puzzles that contain concocted phrases such as "was in session" or "a hotel." I call them "forced expressions." But I must admit that some editors who have loose standards occasionally allow a made-up combination of words to slip through, much to their discredit.

Q. *I have heard that you sometimes recycle old puzzles. Is that true?*

A. Not on your life! That rumor started when I published a puzzle that had apparently been copied from one that had appeared in Mrs. Farrar's day. A fan detected the similarity and informed me. By the way, plagiarism in this field is a rarity.

Q. *In my opinion, crosswords help to subdue anger and anxiety. What do you think?*

A. Could be. But sometimes the opposite occurs when I publish a very difficult puzzle. You should see the irate letters I get!

Speaking of letters, some of the most fascinating I receive are sent by Ms. Betty M. Pringle. Each week she reviews the Sunday *Times* puzzle with a check sheet. A sample of one of her less critical evaluations appears below.

Any Monday, 1982

Mr. Eugene T. Maleska
Crossword Puzzle Editor
The New York Times Co.
229 West 43rd Street
New York, New York 10036

Dear Mr. Maleska:

In regard to last Sunday's Crossword Puzzle,

- ☐ go to hell!
- ☑ you're a genius!
- ☐ what school did you walk on?
- ☐ how dumb do you think I am?
- ☐ how smart do you think I am?

The puzzle, for which I give you total

- ☐ blame
- ☑ credit

was, without a doubt,

- ☐ sophomoric.
- ☑ a work of art.
- ☐ a ten-letter word meaning absurd.
- ☐ impossible.
- ☐ sadistic.

In addition, I would like to say that because of you I

☐ spent $20 in long-distance phone calls to get the answers.
☐ ignored my husband all day.
☑ expanded my mental horizons.
☐ am covered with newsprint smudges.

☐ Very truly yours,
☑ Sincerely yours,
☐ Up yours,

Betty M. Pringle

cc. Arthur Ochs Sulzberger
The Honorable Ronald Reagan
Dr. Joyce Brothers

Sometimes I stoop to doggerel when I reply to fans. To Ms. Pringle I wrote:

There is a *Times* solver named Pringle,
Whose messages give me a tingle;
Her letters are ever
So cryptic and clever —
Unlike my inelegant jingle.

In the previous chapter, I assigned the solvers to four categories — Sleepers, Squawkers, Leapers and Gotchas. Perhaps a fifth classification should be added. I call them the "Bewildered." Consider the following questions and answers.

Q. *We are confused! Please put us out of our misery and explain how "Some cod-carrying Communists" turns out to be* NETTERS.
A. Sorry! "Cod" was a pun on "card." But apparently you haven't heard about the brouhaha raised by New England fishermen who claim that the Russians are invading our waters and throwing out their nets to catch codfish.
Q. *Your clue for 25-Across reads, "First name of the 18th U.S. President." The answer should be Ulysses but there are only five boxes. Can you explain?*
A. Yes. President Grant's first name was really Hiram. He never used it but never officially disclaimed it.
Q. *How can* SEX *be defined as "VI." Was it a typographical error for "V.D."?*
A. *Sex* is the Latin word for "six."
Q. *The clue for 36-Across was "a title for R.W.R." The answer was C.I.C. Who is R.W.R. and what does C.I.C. mean?*

A. Ronald Wilson Reagan — Commander in Chief.

Q. *At 11-Down in yesterday's puzzle the clue was "letters before cee." The answer to-day is* A BEE. *How could a plural definition result in an answer that is singular. And what does an insect have to do with letters?*

A. The letters A and BEE precede CEE in a spelled-out alphabet.

Q. *How can KUE be defined as "ar predecessor?" My wife and I have consulted various dictionaries and encyclopedias but can't find the word* KUEAR. *Is it some small place that you have dug up for your own convenience?*

A. KUE is the letter Q spelled out. AR is the letter R spelled out. Q does precede R. Sorry I confused you. By the way, I never break up words in a puzzle.

Q. *What is the relation between* SACK *and "*FIRST, SECOND *or* THIRD.*"? Is it some kind of doubletalk used by dockworkers?*

A. The three bases around the infielders are called sacks in baseball parlance. The term is extended to the players, too. For example, a man who is stationed at second base is called a "second sacker."

Q. *How can "whipstitch" come out* SEC? *Until I know, I'll be a wreck! For all the needlecraft I know I thought that "whipstitch" meant* to sew.

A. Sew sorry! You're correct and so am I,
But my clue was rather sly.
A sec's a second, which you knew;
The term applies to whipstitch, too.

Q. *With utmost chagrin I must ask you why ENS is defined as "quartet in* No No Nanette.*" What connection is there between printers' measures or a U.S.N.A. grad and a Broadway show?*

A. ENS is N's spelled out. There are four N's in the title of the musical comedy.

Q. *Claudia Alta Taylor Johnson? Who is she? I looked up all the Johnsons in my encyclopedias, and there are plenty — but no Claudias. Please relieve my headache.*

A. Male chauvinism obviously rears its ugly head in reference books, too. Mrs. Johnson is the widow of President Lyndon B. Johnson.

Q. *Your clue reads: "They report for. news" and the answer is* CORRS. *Something's amiss, or did I miss something?*

A. You did miss something. The clue contained a period after *for,* indicating an abbreviation for foreign. CORRS. is a shortened form of *correspondents.*

The Bewildered are flanked by a sixth group, which I call the "Offended." Feminists have rightfully berated me for calling Millay a *poetess* rather than a poet and for defining *female* as "the tender gender." But some people lead with their emotions. Here are some examples.

"It's bad enough to include *gold diggers* in a puzzle, but to define the term as 'Their daddies have lots of sugar' reveals your callousness with regard to women. You are perpetuating a biased view of females by concentrating on those whose only object is to snare a rich man."

I wonder how that fan would react if *gigolo* appeared in a puzzle.

"Your definition for *aborts* in the Puns-Anagrams puzzle exceeds the bounds of good taste. I understand how 'Bachelor scraps' can become *A.B. orts,* but it's quite insensitive to refer to abortions as 'scraps' and to have it refer to bachelors."

The writer went on to lecture me on the pro-life principles. Another solver objected to using the word *abort* in any context whatsoever, including the cancellation of a space trip.

Years ago a solver accused Will Weng of "racism" when *patsy* was defined as "fall guy." Now either the same fan or one of his cousins has jumped all over me for the same reason. He claims that the name is derived from a trick used upon the Irish by British troops and is an insult to St. Patrick. Maybe he has a point, but my Irish mother used to tell me not to be anybody's *patsy*. Maybe she would have eschewed the word if she had known the alleged source. At any rate, at least one of my dictionaries relates *patsy* to *pazzo,* the Italian word meaning "crazy."

In 1982 I published a puzzle called "Split Personalities." The constructor had linked names—a favorite ploy in recent years. One of the entries was THOMAS JEFFERSON DAVIS, defined as "relative of Angela?" Well, that clue evoked two angry letters from opposite sides of the fence. One asked me where I got the gall to connect Thomas Jefferson and Jefferson Davis with a "Commie." The other berated me for allowing a constructor to unite two slave owners with "an eminent black leader like Angela Davis."

But most fan letters do not emanate from irate people. Often the solvers will thank me for teaching them new words, such as *battologize* for "iterate" and *diaskeuast* for "editor." In one case I actually taught a fan a new meaning for his own name. Mr. William T. Saltus of Medford, New Jersey, was doing a Sunday puzzle in 1981 when he came across a clue that read, "Logician's boo-boo." To his amazement, the answer was SALTUS.

During a long newspaper strike, I learned a lot about the importance of puzzles to people who called themselves "addicts needing a fix." Their letters filled my heart with compassion, but it was encouraging to hear from some who heeded my advice and found therapy in various Simon and Schuster crossword puzzle books. Also, the strike proved to be efficacious for some who needed to kick the habit. Family members who hadn't conversed or shared activities for years were suddenly discovering one another. A typical letter arrived from Lawrenceville, New Jersey: "I was horrified Wednesday morning when no newspaper was delivered because of the strike. No crossword! However, my husband and I actually talked at breakfast and watched the birds from our window."

Another fan, Mrs. Alice Spalding, sent me this anecdote about her visit to the local pharmacy during the strike.

> A.S.: "You must be really suffering without all your Sunday clients who buy the *Times* only because of the crossword."
> Pharmacist: "Not a bit! We have them all on tranquilizers."

My favorite letter came all the way from South Carolina just after the strike was terminated. It reads: "Now that we can have our fix again, I hope you've reformed in the meantime. Please don't tax us little old ladies whose minds can't remember where our glasses are, where we have stashed the food money or in what section we parked the car at the shopping center."

Such good-natured wit seems to be a common characteristic of the CWP aficionados. The ultimate example comes from Mr. James C. Murphy of Cos Cob, Connecticut. His latest letter closes as follows:

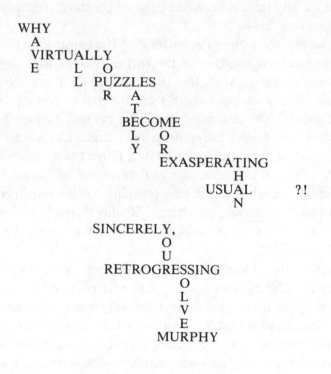

```
WHY
  A
  VIRTUALLY
  E   L   O
      L  PUZZLES
         R   A
         T
         BECOME
         L   O
         Y   R
             EXASPERATING
             H
             USUAL        ?!
             N

    SINCERELY,
         O
         U
    RETROGRESSING
         O
         L
         V
         E
    MURPHY
```

3

Crosswordese, Criteria and Craftsmanship

If you have never solved a crossword puzzle, the chances are you can't tell an *asse* from an *eland*. The former is a South African fox and the latter is a large antelope. Like the *lar* (small ape), *urial* (wild sheep) and those infamous *ais* (two-toed sloths), these animals are familiar denizens of the Land of Black and White Squares.

Another quadruped that rears its ugly head in puzzles is the *anoa*. Margaret Farrar has conducted a lifelong campaign to extinguish that wild ox of the Celebes, but the creature has all the persistence of a Hydra. As soon as it is eliminated from one puzzle, it crops up in the next two. The same is true of the *gnu*. To an editor, the presence of no *gnus* is good news, but those kin of the *elands* have been roaming around puzzles ever since that day in 1913 when Arthur Wynne created the first crossword.

Neophytes are flabbergasted by such beastly entries as *urus* (another wild ox — but extinct), *tahr* (wild goat) and those two lizards called *uma* and *uran*. However, veteran solvers welcome their appearance. Similarly, they salute such salamanders as the ubiquitous *newts* and *efts*.

Willy-nilly the CWP addicts have become bird watchers, too. Their favorite feathered friend is the *ern* or *erne*, which has such rivals as the *emu, roc, arara* and the extinct *moa*. The *ani* may drive a tyro cuckoo, but the experienced fans embrace it lovingly. They may have no idea as to what a *ruff* looks like, but they are aware that the female of the species is a *ree*.

Botany is no problem for the old hands, either. They know that an *aril* and a *testa* are seed coverings; the *sepal* is part of the calyx of a flower; the *itea* and *osier* are willows; the *oca* is a wood sorrel; and the *ule* is a rubber tree.

Perhaps the most fascinating aspect of crosswordese is the "education" that fans receive concerning parts of the body. Solving puzzles is like taking a course in *anat*. (a crossword repeater). The devotees discover that a *rete* is a neural network and soon learn that the plural is *retia*. If they had studied Latin, they already knew that *iter* was a Roman road, but while tackling a puzzle they are surprised to find that the highway is also a brain passage. As a bonus, they come across brainy membranes like the *dura mater* and the *pia mater*—to be stored in the cranium along with cousin Alma.

Bones are omnipresent in puzzles, too. The most popular one is the *ulna* in the forearm, closely followed by the *talus* in the ankle. The latter usually appears in the plural form, *tali*. The *costa, femur, fibula, radius* and *tibia* get a fair share of the action, often in definitions.

Clues for words in the puzzles have also taught solvers synonyms for familiar parts of the body. A toe can be a *hallux,* a thumb is a *pollex,* the heart is a *cor,* the knee is the *site of the patella,* the hips are *huckles* or *coxae* and the nape of the neck is a *nuque* or *nucha.*

If the M.D.'s have a head start in the CWP stakes, consider the numismatists. Coins of the past and present are sprinkled through the puzzles day after day. Here is just a sampling of some of the clinkers and their homelands.

AES (Rome)	DURO (Spain)	LEV (Bulgaria)
ATT (Siam)	ECU (France)	OBOL (Greece)
AVO (Macao)	LAT (Latvia)	ORA (Old England)
BAHT (Thailand)	LEK (Albania)	REI (Brazil)

Foreign weights and measures have also found their niches in the puzzles. The *tael* of China, the Turkish *oka* and the Indian *ser* are among the entries that cause heavy going for many solvers. Distance measures are led by the *stere* (cubic meter) and dry ones feature the Hebrew *epha(h)* and *omer*.

Hebrew is a favorite of puzzle constructors, not as a result of any religious preference but because the language offers such enticing months as *Adar, Elul, Iyar, Nisan* and *Tebet* as well as letters of the alphabet like *aleph, heth, teth, mem, ayin* and *resh*. Only the Greeks can surpass that lineup. They have supplied a host of goodies for puzzlemakers. Consider *eta, beta, phi, chi, psi* and *omega* as just a few examples.

Tribes of all sorts are another source of crosswordese. From Nigeria alone we get the *Aro, Edo* and *Ibo,* and from other parts of Africa the *Efik, Egba, Ikwe* and *Tshi*. Among our American Indians, *Utes* and *Otos* or *Otoes* have made reservations for at least one puzzle in every ten that are published. The *Eries* would outdo them were it not for the canal, lake, city and county that bear their name. If you were a *Hopi, Cree* or *Wea,* you might expect to see yourself ensconced in a crossword puzzle every month. Your chances as a *Ree* are lessened by that "female ruff"; as an *Osage* you might have to yield to the orange or the apple named after you or even to a river in the Midwest. But as a *Seri* from Sonora or an *Auca* from South America, you would have no competition.

Gods and goddesses provide a Lucullan feast for people who have devoured puzzles through the years. Babylonia offers *Abu* or *Anu* (sky and sun), *Adad* (wind), *Erua* (mother), *Irra* (war) and *Etana* (eagle rider). Egypt has a delicious assortment, too. Here are a few.

Apet (maternity)	*Keb* (earth)	*Mut* (wife of Amen)
Bes (evil, pleasure)	*Maat* (truth)	*Ptah* (Memphis)
Geb (earth)	*Min* (procreation)	*Sati* (queen)
Isis (fertility)		

The deities of the Norsemen have also invaded the puzzle world. Most crossword aficionados are familiar with *Odin* and his Valhalla comrades. *Loki,* who raised *Hel,* is a frequent visitor horizontally or vertically. The same is true of *Thor,* the thunder god for whom the fifth day of each week was named. His wife, *Sif,* and his stepson, *Ull,* step in occasionally, as do *Tyr* (war hawk) and *Ymir* (primeval giant, slain by *Vali* and his cronies).

Teutonic gods that are closely related to the Norse crowd often get into the boxes. *Tiu, Woden* and *Frigg,* who can also claim weekday fame, appear in various orthographic forms. *Hler,* whose alias is *Aegir,* gets a play once in a while along with *Hoth,* the blind god who competed with *Balder* for the hand of *Nanna. Hoth,* by the way, is a character in the *Eddas* — mythological collections of songs that are immortalized by puzzlemakers. Finally, the foregoing pantheons loom up in crosswords as the *Aesir* — a perfect "out" for a constructor who is stuck with a word beginning with AE.

But the divinities that shape our ends in puzzles are usually of Greek and Roman origin. The most popular Olympians are *Ares, Ate, Eos, Eris, Eros, Gaea* and *Hera.* Lesser lights are represented by such characters as *Idas* (killer of Castor), *Iole* (Hercules' captive), *Leda* (mother of Clytemnestra, et al.), *Leto* (mother of Apollo and Artemis) and *Maia* (mother of Hermes).

Among the Muses, *Erato* wins hands down. Sappho's inspirer is occasionally rivaled by *Clio* (history), *Thalia* (comedy) and *Urania* (astronomy). Titans like *Atlas, Rhea* and *Uranus* also appear frequently.

Another source of grist for the puzzlers' mills is the Bible. Along with people like Adam and Eve, the solver is often confronted by lesser characters like *Adah* (wife of Esau), *Asher* (Jacob's eighth son), *Enos* (son of Seth), *Ittai* (one of David's generals). *Obed* (son of Boaz and Ruth) and *Omri* (a king of Israel).

Eden is the most popular biblical locale but constructors sometimes can't fit it in. They must resort to one of the following: *Edar* — "a tower in Genesis" or *Edom* — "Idumenea or Esau's land."

The above are only two of the scores of spots that only a Bible student would know, but puzzle addicts become familiar with most of them over the years.

The same is true of non-biblical geographic places. Among the constant repeaters are *Aar* (or *Aare*), *Aden, Agra, Aral, Arno, Ede, Eder, Elba, Elbe, Enna, Erie, Etna, Iola, Iran, Oahu, Oder, Ohio, Orel, Oslo, Ossa, Ural* and *Utah*.

One aspect of crosswordese that irks many solvers and delights the polyglots is the presence of foreign words. Thirty years ago non-English entries were frowned upon by many puzzle editors, and contributions containing such words were sometimes automatically rejected. Today a plethora of foreignisms can still cause the return of a puzzle to a constructor but editors have relaxed the standards a bit, partly because more and more solvers are college graduates possessing a reasonable knowledge of Latin, French, Spanish and/or German.

At any rate, regardless of their individual backgrounds, inveterate fans soon learn the continental words. For instance, every daily solver knows that *enero* is the Spanish word for January, *été* is a Parisian's summertime and *août* is a month in that *saison*.

Note the French spelling for "season." In recent decades a favorite device of constructors and editors is to use a relevant foreign word in the clue for the non-English entry. Some examples of definitions for *été* are the following:

> Period after *printemps*
> Season before *automne*
> *Juillet, août,* etc.
> *Saison* in Sedan

Puzzlemakers who enjoy punning define *été* as "Nice summer"—a clue that sparkled when it was introduced but has become tarnished by overuse.

Foreign spellings of numbers crop up often. Italian gets the most coverage in this category: *uno, due, tre, sei, sette,* and *nove* constantly appear. Here again, the clue may play on the language. For example, *sette* might be defined as "*uno e sei.*"

The constructors' favorite French number is *huit* whereas *drei* wins the Teutonic prize. Spanish repeaters are *tres, seis, siete* and *ocho.*

The Latin numerals come in handy when constructors need to extricate themselves from difficult situations, usually involving a succession of consonants such as DCV, MDC and MCCV. Combinations like those cause the puzzlers to scour their encyclopedias for suitable definitions. Thus, solvers are frequently confronted with relatively trivial information concerning the year in the reign of some ancient emperor or Vatican dweller.

A second method for defining Latin numerals is to give the fans a mathematical exercise. LVI might be defined as "Half of CXII" or "Twice XXVIII" or even "VIII x VII."

Most constructors are unhappy when forced to employ Latin numerals. They welcomed the success of actress Liv Ullmann; her first name provided a new clue. Rarely these days is LIV defined as "Half of CVIII."

Non-mathematical Latin words and phrases are regularly seen in puzzles, partly because of their use in such fields as medicine, law and philosophy. *Esse* ("being") is a prime example of our philosophical inheritance from the Romans. That four-letter word is one of the most familiar repeaters between the black squares. Finding new clues for it gives headaches to constructors and editors. What experienced solver does not know that "Esse quam videri" is the motto of North Carolina?

The outstanding scion of *esse* in puzzledom is *erat,* usually defined as "part of Q.E.D." and sometimes clued as "Quod ____ faciendum." One wonders how many inexperienced solvers know that the word literally means "it was, he was or she was."

Each member of the Latin I trio — *amo, amas, amat* — is given more than its proper due in the crosswords. And probably the most hackneyed of all Latin-derived entries in puzzles is "*Dies Irae*" (an ancient hymn). Two other hymns that continually loom up are "*Agnus Dei*" and "*Ave Maria*." And any puzzle fan can testify to the omnipresence of *nota bene, rara avis, Anno Domini* and *id est.* Latin pronouns and demonstratives roll along from year to year in puzzle after puzzle. But constructors must be credited for attempting to be fair. When they use such words they usually attach them to phrases that have become part of our language. Consider the following favorites:

Clue	Answer
____ dixit (dogmatic statement)	IPSE
____ facto (by that very fact)	IPSO
____ generis (unique)	SUI
____ culpa (my fault)	MEA
"____ Brute"	ET TU

Ille was eschewed by puzzlemakers for years and on the few occasions when it appeared the definition read, "River at Rennes." But grateful kudos were bestowed upon Alexander Lenard after he wrote *Winnie Ille Pu* in glorification of Milne's beloved bear.

Ego, on the other hand, has never been a problem, largely because of Freud. It might be surmised that some puzzle fans do not know that the word means "I" in Latin. Constructors seldom resort to that definition since so many easier ones abound. Examples are: "self," "personality," "kind of trip" and "psyche component." Incidentally an unusual non-Latin clue for the word is "playwright O'Neill's monogram."

Speaking of monograms, for many years the only definition for *aes* was "Roman bronze." Then creative craftsmen recalled that those three letters formed the initials of Alfred E. Smith (loser to H.C.H.) and Adlai E. Stevenson (loser to D.D.E.).

In general, constructors and editors studiously avoid regular use of long, unfamiliar foreign words but feel little or no remorse when tiny pronouns, articles, verbs and adjectives are used as fillers between main entries — especially if such minuscular words are familiar or if the crossings are easy. Hence, the puzzle fan is bound to come across a *las* or *los* from Spanish; an *ils, les, une* or *ces* from French and an *ein* or *ich* from German.

As noted earlier in this chapter, the main contributions of the Greeks to the foreign-words category in crosswords are the letters of their alphabet. Words like *agora* and *stoa* appear often in the puzzles, but it must be remembered that they have been incorporated into our language. The same is true of Hindu nouns such as *rama, rani, rana* and *sitar*—all members of the crosswordese clique.

Portugal and the Balkan countries have hardly made a dent in the puzzles. Ireland has provided a few "strangers" such as *arrah,* a war cry, and the ever-present *Erse.*

Disregarding coins and proper names, the Mideast and Far East have stayed out of the picture except for an occasional sally. *Emir* (Arab chief), along with its many variations, is a constant repeater. The *aba* (desert coat) and the *agal* (Arab's headdress) appear now and then, as do the *obi* (Japanese sash) and the *tao* (Chinese pagoda). Others, of course, will occur to fervent solvers, but throughout this section the purpose is merely to serve up a soupçon of examples.

Hawaii can hardly be called a foreign land, but its Polynesian idiom has been a boon to puzzlemakers. Instances of semi-crosswordese pop up in such words as *poi, luau, taro, lei* and *aloha.* The state has also given the crossworders at least two exotic fish—the *ahi* (tuna) and the *aku* (relative of a mackerel). Both of those sea creatures apparently must beware of the *akia,* a shrub having a bark that is used as a fish poison. The *nene* needn't worry; it's the state bird and is carefully protected from extinction.

If the Scots do not head the list as the purveyors of the most crosswordese of foreign extraction, they come mighty close. Constructors get away with *gae, hae, tae, ain, sma* and other words of that ilk by quoting Robert Burns. But sometimes even that worthy poet is no help. Hence, the solver is liable to be assailed by one or all of the following in any given month.

Clue	*Answer*
Snow in Scotland	SNA
Glaswegian's uncle	EME
Odd, to Scottie	ORRA
Knead, in Edinburgh	ELT
Urge, in Aberdeen	ERT

Foreign words aside, here is a sampling of three-letter words that almost every puzzle addict knows by heart. Would all these words be familiar to an educated person who has never solved a crossword? The answer is a capitalized NO!

AIT, islet	IVA, Marsh elder
EAN, to lamb	OBE, Laconian clan
ECU, small shield	ODA, harem room
ELA, Guidonian note	ULE, rubber tree
ERG, C.G.S. unit	UVA, grape

By this time, the reader has probably noticed that crosswordese features an inordinate number of words beginning with vowels. The very nature of the medium causes this phenomenon. A glance at the Across words on the top of the answer to any crossword puzzle will reveal that at least one-third of the letters are vowels. This means that about 30 to 40 percent of the Down words in that area will begin with vowels. In contrast, such words consume only one-sixth of the total number of pages in the average dictionary.

The strictures of the craft are also responsible for the prevalence of crosswordese. A prime regulation for American CWP's is that "unkeyed" letters are taboo. In other words, every letter that occurs in an Across word must also fit into a Down word. This rule, by the way, evolved from the recognition that the "blind" letters in early puzzles were unfair to the solvers.

Some of the other limitations imposed by most editors today are:

    a. no two-letter words
    b. maximums for numbers of entries
    c. no artificial or concocted expressions
    d. preference for puzzles with themes.

Partly as a result of the above restrictions, only about 600 people are capable of constructing a really good crossword puzzle, and a mere handful can be classified as "professionals."

Amateurish creations abound in the puzzle world. Such CWP's contain a plethora of esoterica and crosswordese. This fact is the chief reason that millions of copies of crossword puzzle dictionaries are sold in America. One mark of a superior crossword puzzle is a paucity of crosswordese. But because of the factors previously cited, it is virtually impossible for the best of constructors and editors to eliminate all the repeaters and the strange little words that help to complete otherwise impossible corners.

Thus, the wings of Amor (*alae*) will continue to flutter between the black squares, the ornamental case for needles (*etui*) will stick new solvers, the curved molding (*ogee*) will not molder and the feudal serf (*esne*) will gain immortality. However, dyed-in-the-wool fans who carry such baggage in their heads will probably revel in the constant reappearance of old standbys.

In addition to the four criteria mentioned several paragraphs ago, editors of legitimate American crossword puzzles have other touchstones for accepting or rejecting a contribution. An interesting one that has evolved through seven decades is diagonal symmetry for black squares. For example, if a black square appears in the upper left corner, its counterpoint must be inserted in the bottom right corner. The same balance must be preserved throughout the diagram.

How did this rule come about? Margaret Farrar modestly waves off the credit and attributes the regulation to members of a league of crossword puzzlers that sprang up in the 1920s. But obviously, as the first bona fide editor to preside over the craft, she was in a position to enforce or disregard the advice. She says she liked the idea because it made the diagrams "look pretty." At any rate, all the pros among the constructors applaud the stipulation because it presents a barrier that rank amateurs cannot surmount. Tap Osborn, a noted puzzlemaker, says that the rule reminds him of Robert Frost's comment re composing free verse: "It's like playing tennis with the net down." Mr. Osborn, by the way, is a New Englander and an avid tennis player.

But the diagonal-symmetry standard has had a rival — namely, lateral symmetry for the black squares. In this case, a black square in the upper left corner must be complemented by another in the upper right corner, and so on throughout the diagram. This method, also sanctioned by the early solons, is still used in an occasional diagramless puzzle and is rarely employed in other American crosswords. The principal reason for its decline seems to be the fact that laterally symmetrical black squares often produced wide-open spaces in a rectangular grid; hence, most constructors shy away from such a design. But the outcome is just as "pretty" as diagonal symmetry.

On page 55 an example of a 15 x 15 puzzle with lateral symmetry appears. Note the unusual pattern and the juxtaposition of long words at the top and bottom.*

One more word about the pattern. It should be an open one, and the more outlets the better. Some inferior diagrams contain labyrinths walled in by black squares, with only one opening in each maze. The solver who cannot figure out the key letter at the end of the passageway is hopelessly stumped. Worse yet, some neophytes create puzzles in which the black squares actually divide the diagram into three or four separate parts. In such cases, the fans are really being asked to solve several small puzzles instead of one larger crossword.

How many black squares are allowed? Well, the traditional role is that they should add up to about one-sixth of the total number of boxes in the entire grid, but this regulation is sometimes waived if a puzzle is otherwise superb.

□

Ideally, a puzzle should not contain abbreviations, prefixes, suffixes and combining forms. But this consummation, however devoutly to be wished, is very difficult to achieve on a regular basis. Therefore, editors must often accept contributions that are a little less than perfect.

Fans do not object to common abbreviations such as C.I.A., etc., R.A.F., and lbs.

---

*Grateful acknowledgments are due to Ms. Rosalind Moore, executive editor of *Dell Crossword Puzzle Magazine,* for permission to reprint this puzzle.

ACROSS

1 Susa
14 Proverb for a cynophile
16 *The ___ of Edward Bok*, Pulitzer Prize autobiography
17 Femme fatale
18 ___ hand (aid)
19 Nobel product
20 Of the summer
26 Inquired in Dogpatch
27 Bellhop's beat
28 Spa in New York
38 Soprano Galli-Curci
39 Prufrock's creator
40 Rolled cubes at a casino
41 Skater Babilonia
43 Herbert ___ Hoover
44 Estimates based on facts
47 Fire-engine adjuncts
48 Group for whom a sea was named
52 Neat ___
57 Thessalian's ancient neighbor
59 Living
60 Jimmy ___ , Hall of Fame golfer
61 Secured firmly
62 Board of education purchase
63 Emperors; dictators

28 *Vic and ___* , old radio program
29 Surrounded by
30 René's receipt
31 Pianist Templeton
32 Hazard for mariners
33 Opposite of dominant, in genetics
34 Escapees from Pandora's box
35 Island off Sumatra
36 Author Vidal
37 Wall St. certificates

42 Say further
45 Winery employee
46 Muse for Hipparchus
48 Yield
49 Mimic
50 *Green Mansions* girl
51 One of Cleopatra's maids
53 College town in Iowa
54 ___ -cake (tots' game)
55 Highway for Hadrian
56 Buntline and Rorem
58 French connectives
59 Rainbow

DOWN

1 "I Feel a Song ___ On"
2 Ward off
3 A Dumas
4 Ammonia derivative
5 Gumshoe
6 Chicken ___ king
7 Actor Chaney
8 Egg: Comb. form
9 Turk's topper
10 "Bless ___ ," 1941 song
11 "Abide with Me" hymnist
12 Soprano role in *L'elisir d'Amore*
13 Indicative, subjunctive, etc.
14 Endure
15 Midge
21 Jigger
22 Dignified, as a judge
23 Give ___ whirl
24 Trace
25 Dolomites or Pennines

But they become rightfully indignant when the abridgment of an obscure term in physics, chemistry or some other special field is thrown at them. Even if the abbreviation emerges via the crossing word, the solvers are still perplexed and annoyed. They say to themselves, "What in heaven's name do those letters stand for?" In some crossword puzzle magazines, editors manage to forestall the complaints by placing an explanation of the weird abbreviation under the answer to the puzzle at the back of the issue.

The problem of prefixes can sometimes be skirted by constructors and editors by the use of other definitions. Here are a few examples:

Clue	Answer
Oppositionist	ANTI
Underworld god	DIS
Scale notes	MIS
Slammer occupant	CON
Grand ____, Evangeline's home	PRE

Dabblers in the craft sometimes fail to realize that prefixes, unlike suffixes for verbs or nouns, cannot be pluralized. Editors occasionally find a word like *transes* in a newcomer's contribution, accompanied by "Across: plural prefix" as the clue!

One overused prefix that appears as part of a longer word is *re*. Sophisticated solvers who find *retake, resee* and *readmit* (or others of the same genre) in a single puzzle realize that the constructor was inept and the editor was lax. Even worse are concoctions like *redrown*.

As for combining forms, the same standards as those applying to abbreviations are used by competent redactors. Some combining forms are fair: *mega* means "large," *micro* means "small." Others are so obscure that the editor should change the entry or reject the puzzle.

Another reason for rejection of a puzzle is the constructor's overdependence on plurals ending in S. This cop-out eases the problems of the contributor but afflicts the solver with a bad case of boredom.

Cockneyisms provide a similar way out for puzzlemakers whose skills are unequal to the task. In this case, a quotation from Kipling can sometimes save the day. For instance, "The ___, he knows..." might be the clue, and the answer will be ORSE. But if fans find UNTED in a puzzle and the definition is "searched for in Soho" they should know that standards have been thrown out the window.

In connection with the above, the use of dialect is a no-no except in cases that are easily recognizable by an average solver. *Agin* (defined as "opposed to in Dogpatch") is an example of an entry that will not stump most Americans but will probably bewilder Englishmen. In contrast, dialectic words from Wales, Yorkshire and other places are anathema to U.S. fans.

Obsolete and archaic words have no place in puzzles, but a few exceptions creep in now and then. They take their place as egregious examples of crosswordese. The most notable among them is *erst*. This ubiquitous intruder regularly enters under three separate disguises that are readily seen through by the mavens:

1. Formerly formerly
2. Once once
3. Whilom

Obscenity, lewdness and bad taste are also taboo in the Kingdom of Puzzledom, where almost every prospect pleases and no man is vile. When *sex* rears its ugly head in the diagram, the word is mildly defined as "gender," but on occasions a daring editor will try some new clue like "Kinsey topic" and hope no letters of protest will arrive.

Certain legitimate nouns that have been seized upon by the vulgar do appear regularly in puzzles. The definitions in one case refer to an onager, a burro or a dunce. In a second three-letter instance, a small bird beginning with T is cited. The ultimate avoidance of licentiousness appeared in a recent magazine puzzle. The clue read: "The ____ mightier than the sword."

As stated elsewhere in this book, puzzle fans do not like to be reminded of diseases and unpleasant parts of their bodies. Therefore, constructors shun *ulcers, entrails* and the like.

Variants once presented a problem for conscientious editors. When *align* was spelled as *aline,* the definition would read: "Straighten: Var." But many modern dictionaries recognize that second spellings are commonly used for multitudes of words and consequently substitute "same as" in place of "variation of" when defining the word in which changes in orthography have taken place.

In those cases involving a British spelling, clever constructors and editors have found a new way to eliminate "Var." as an appendage to the clue. Here are some recent examples:

Clue	*Answer*
Pigment for Gainsborough	OCHRE
Canterbury headdress	MITRE
Examine in detail, British style	ANALYSE
What Lovelace loved most	HONOUR

Because editors do not wish to appear to be favoring one company or product over another, puzzlemakers are asked to avoid trade names, except those that have become part of our language (e.g., *saran*) and others that are no longer on sale (e.g., *Reo*). But this proscription is often honored in the breach. Entries like *Amex, I.T.T.* and *I.B.M.* have been appearing more and more in modern puzzles.

Apropos of the above, *Estee* is a word that fits easily into a puzzle because its letters are so common. Constructors resort to that proper noun occasionally and define it as "cosmetician Lauder." On a Sunday in 1981 the word appeared in a *Times* puzzle, and MONO ("howling monkey") was also entered. The vice president of a cosmetics company headed by a woman named Mono subsequently sent in a humorous verse asking for "equal time." His good-natured complaint seemed to have merit. And so, the next time MONO cropped up in a puzzle the clue read: "Noted cosmetician"—much to the delight of the v.p. and his comely boss.

Back in the 1930s, editors frowned on the use of proper names in the crosswords. Puzzles weren't necessarily rejected on that account, but contributors were urged to adhere to words in the dictionary. They were also admonished about the use of plural names, such as *Saras* and *Amys*. Today that stricture has been relaxed but not entirely forsaken. Editors remind constructors not to overload their puzzles with names of people and places. Also, if a person's given name is used, the custom is to make it refer to a celebrity. Thus *Ava* is usually defined as "actress Gardner" and *Erle* as "writer Gardner."

Sometimes neither the constructor nor the editor can find a famous individual to attach to a first name. For instance, the appearance of *Edwina* in a puzzle will cause brains to be racked for a suitable clue. Resorting to "girl's name" is considered to be unfair to the solver. Hence, editors equip themselves with books that give the literal meanings of first names. *Edwina* happens to be "valuable friend," from Anglo-Saxon. Incidentally, one resourceful constructor recently got around the problem by defining *Edwina* as "U.S. painter Abbey." But that clue is misleading; the artist is Edwin A. Abbey.

Unusual first names like *Derissa* or *Elwyn* are not acceptable, and the same rule is frequently applied to surnames. Stuck in a corner, some contributors delve into encyclopedias and find an obscure individual who has earned a few lines in a reference book. "Voila!" they cry, and submit their creations, only to receive a polite rejection.

One last word on people's names. In the last few decades constructors have been bombarding the fans with themes that revolve around celebrities' names. Puns on *Ball, Cotten, Caine,* et al. are rampant. Linkages of names (*Alexander Pope Pius*) loom up constantly, and all kinds of other tricks with stars' monickers are employed ad nauseam.

Somewhere out there is a new constructor who thinks he has a bright idea for a theme. He'll use the original names of movie stars. Won't the solvers be surprised when they learn that Natalie Wood was *Natasha Gurdin,* Cary Grant was *Archibald Leach* and Judy Garland was *Frances Gumm!* The poor fellow doesn't realize that his brainchild had a debut in the 1950s and has been foisted upon the fans over and over again. The puzzle will probably be rejected on the grounds that the theme is hackneyed.

To avoid such calamities, many contributors submit to editors a list of proposed thematic entries before attempting to put the puzzle together.

Admittedly, themes that are fresh and clever are hard to dream up, and the difficulty increases with every passing month. But the resourcefulness of pros and some tyros is amazing! Just when editors and fans begin to surmise that there really is nothing new under the sun, along comes a superb original creation.

Realizing that ingenious blockbusters are rare, editors sometimes reluctantly publish themes that are repeaters. In such cases, the fact that the constructor has not borrowed old words but has mustered up a group of new ones for the theme is enough to salve the editor's conscience.

Aside from the problem of triteness, other considerations concerning themes come into play. Let us say that the title of the puzzle is "Spectrum" and the contributor has used ORANGE RIVER, BLUE SKIES, RED HERRING, etc. If one of those colors is repeated in the theme, a stringent editor will return the puzzle.

Similarly, if puns are used, some editors will demand consistency. Suppose that the title is "Fish Story" and the entries include PRINTS OF WHALES, DOVER SOUL and WHOLLY MACKEREL. The middle entry does not belong, because the spelling of the fish itself (*sole*) has been altered; whereas the other two retain the original spelling.

Too finicky? Perhaps, but the best craftsmen do not allow minor flaws to mar their puzzles. Incidentally, punning is a rather difficult art which most constructors fail to master. They settle for outrageous distortions that frustrate the fans.

Speaking of outrageous, a female constructor who shall be nameless included *phallic cymbal* in a punny puzzle submitted to the *Times*. Her definition was "crashing male instrument"! Obviously, the puzzle was rejected.

Another problem relating to themes stems from the vast difference of preferences among solvers. In 1980 a Sunday *Times* puzzle entitled "Gallup Poll" appeared. Every thematic entry contained the word *horse*. If memory serves correctly, HORSE CHESTNUTS, HORSE FEATHERS and GET ON ONE'S HIGH HORSE were some of the featured phrases.

Fan reaction was startling. Examination of the letters that poured in revealed the delight of inexperienced solvers who pounced gleefully on the deliberate repetitions. But the sophisticated set protested vehemently; they called it a "fill-in" puzzle in which *horse* is automatically inserted.

Relevant to the above is the editorial tradition that different forms of the same root should not appear in a puzzle. For instance, if *pose* is an entry, the constructor should eschew *dispose, depose* and *repose,* unless he or she is striving for a theme similar to the controversial *horse* puzzle. Recently, a new contributor submitted a 15 x 15 crossword containing TURNS and IN TURN. The puzzle was on the verge of rejection when a way out was found. TURNS was changed to BURNS.

A time-honored regulation is that no entry should be repeated unless it is part of a theme. This editor inadvertently broke that rule once in a *Times* daily puzzle. XAT, at the bottom of the puzzle, was changed to RAT. But the same word had already appeared at the top of the puzzle! Somehow the repetition eluded the eagle eyes of test-solvers and proofers. At least twenty fans, however, caught the violation. The reply they received was terse and to the point: "Aw rats!"

One of the marks of a good craftsman is the avoidance of bad crossings. When an Across word is abstruse, the pro makes sure that its vertical crossers are all easy words with relatively simple clues. Also, the definition for the esoteric word must never be hard to understand. An example of a violation of this rule recently occurred in a puzzle published by a small-town newspaper. The definition was "Nymphalid" and the answer was IDALIA. Only a zoologist would be able to comprehend such gibberish. The clue should have been "type of butterfly."

In the beginning, many crossword puzzle editors forbade the use of slang, but today they are more liberal because they recognize that today's slanguage is often tomorrow's accepted language. Also, if not overdone, a slangy entry can add zest to a puzzle. Words like *snafu, kook* and *pizazz* are welcome.

In an effort to be fair to the fans, editors usually require that a slang word be matched with a slangy clue. Here are some examples:

Clue	Answer
Hollywood flicks	PIX
Opposite of "Nah"	YEAH
Lalapalooza	LULU

Incidentally, a concomitant problem when using slang is orthography. For instance, there are at least four ways to spell "lalapalooza." As time goes by, one of them may win out over the others. Hence, constructors and editors take the risk of choosing one of the losers.

Another ban that was imposed upon constructors for many decades was the use of phrases. Every entry in every puzzle was a one-worder. Contributors chafed under this restriction and besieged editors with requests to let down the barriers. Finally, Margaret Farrar decided to take a chance. As related in her introductory chapter, she allowed this writer to cross the threshold in a daily *Times* puzzle, but she warned that only one entry should be a two-worder. For some strange reason I chose HARD-SHELLED CRAB and placed that 15-letter phrase across the center of the diagram. The clue carefully indicated that the answer contained two words.

Mrs. Farrar sat back and waited for the flak from conservative fans. When no protests filled her mailbox, she published a few more puzzles containing phrases like *once in a blue moon* or *one in a million*.

Gradually she realized that most fans were greeting this innovation with delight. When some of the solvers complained that they were being "babied" by clues that indicated the number of words in the phrases, she belled the cat once more and took away the crutches. The kudos from the fans exceeded the boos. Most *Times* aficionados enjoyed the challenge of guessing where one word in the phrase ended and another began.

The idea caught fire in other newspapers and in puzzle magazines, although some editors still prefer to specify in the clue how many words are present in the phrase. At any rate, Mrs. Farrar's bold pioneering opened up a whole new world for constructors and solvers. Long entries became the rage from the 1950s until today, and her leap in the dark eventually led to puzzles featuring themes.

One insidious side effect resulted from the lifting of the phraseology embargo. Some constructors failed to distinguish between legitimate phrases and the concocted or forced expressions previously mentioned in this chapter. Editors became bombarded with made-up entries like *had an awful time* or *was threatened*. Other amateurish contributors seemed unable to see the difference between an acceptable phrase like *A Place in the Sun* and a silly one like *a place to rest* (defined as "bed").

In my career as an editor, I have found forced expressions to be the chief reason for rejection of contributions. Sometimes I can find a loophole to save the puzzle. For example A RACE (defined as "Run ___") appeared in a 15 x 15 sent to me several months ago. I discovered that a poet named Young had written "___ without a goal." Reluctantly I published the puzzle, using the quotation as a clue.

But the above example illustrates another of the abuses of phrases—namely, an overdependence on partial quotations, especially obscure ones. In this case and in the use of concocted phrases, standards seem to vary widely; some editors are very strict while others are lenient. Since judgment is part of the picture, it is doubtful that the matter will ever be resolved to the satisfaction of all concerned.

In connection with the above, would-be constructors should write to crossword puzzle editors for their guidelines or style sheets. Such statements list not only the rules but also the proper methods for preparing and submitting puzzles.*

Finally, a word to solvers who have no intention to make up a crossword puzzle but enjoy doing them. If you have read this chapter carefully, you are now cognizant of some of the functions of an editor and many of the rules and nuances that distinguish a good puzzle from a poor one. Also, you have probably discovered how difficult it is to construct a puzzle that follows all the regulations, contains a minimum of crosswordese and captures the interest of the solver while being simultaneously fair and accurate.

But, to quote Rabbi Ben Ezra, "the best is yet to be." The next chapter on "The Fine Art of Defining" may open your eyes to the most important aspect of the craft.

---

*The *New York Times* style sheet is quoted verbatim in "How to Construct Crossword Puzzles"—a chapter in my book *A Pleasure in Words* (Simon and Schuster, 1981).

4

The Fine Art of Defining

If the entries in the diagram of a crossword puzzle are its body, then the definitions are its soul. To put it another way, constructing a puzzle is like building a house. The words in the diagram are its bricks and mortar. But the clues provide the interior decoration. Definitions that are dry as dust and repetitive produce a dull or shabby atmosphere in the construction, whereas those that sparkle and stimulate interest result in delight for the solvers as they travel from room to room.

Strangely enough, for two solid decades constructors and editors gave short shrift to definitions. There were two basic reasons for this neglect: laziness and timidity. With regard to the first, even today many puzzlemakers consider the creation of clues to be a tedious chore; they feel they have done their job when they have entered all the words into the diagram. When confronted with contributions from such constructors, modern editors who are worth their salt have a choice: either reject the puzzle or change most of the definitions.

Fear of upsetting solvers also played a large part in the old-timers' conservative approach to clues. The theory was that if the constructor used a primary definition that could be found in any dictionary, no complaints would arrive from the fans. Thus, *tree* was always defined as "woody plant" and nest as "bird's home."

Here are some other examples, taken from puzzles in the 1920s and early 1930s:

ORE	Native mineral	SUM	Total
EAR	Organ of hearing	DOOR	Portal
STY	Pig's home	HEN	Chicken
NAP	Short sleep	HAT	Head covering
OAT	Cereal grass	DIET	Regimen

The upshot of that unimaginative and pusillanimous tradition was knee-jerk solving. Asked to fill in a three-letter word for "stinging insect" the fans immediately wrote in *bee*. If four letters were called for, they inserted *wasp* quicker than one could say "vespiary denizen." For many years, the stimulus-response practice pleased the majority of solvers. As they gained experience in memorizing repetitive definitions, their speed and facility increased. Furthermore, they could show off to their friends, relations and colleagues. A non-solver, watching a veteran fan zip through a puzzle, would say, "Gosh! How do you do that? You must be really smart!"

But during the late 1930s, dissatisfaction began to set in. Ennui caused many solvers to kick the habit, and the popularity of crossword puzzles declined. Meanwhile creative young constructors chafed under the unwritten law that definitions must be taken bodily out of the lexicons and repeated ad nauseam. Led by such constructors as Jack Luzzatto, Herb Ettenson, Jules Arensburg, Harold Bers and this writer, a minor revolution took place. One of the first breakthroughs was Luzzatto's "nectar inspector" as the clue for *bee*. Yours truly chimed in with "nutcracker's suite" for *nest* and the daring "when both hands are up" for *noon* (previously defined as "midday" or the now obsolete "meridian").

The reaction of bored fans was a three-letter word for "delight." Their joyous response encouraged editors like Margaret Farrar to congratulate constructors who demonstrated originality in defining and to chip in with their own innovative clues. Little by little, the old order changed. Puzzles had received a shot in the arm that made them more exciting and a bit more challenging. Of course, some of the knee-jerk crowd complained because now they were forced to use their imagination here and there. But most editors did not go whole-hog for the offbeat clues, nor do they today. A good modern puzzle should be a sort of feast for the fan. Unusual, creative definitions should be sprinkled around like pepper and salt but should never be so omnipresent that the banquet is spoiled. The exceptions, of course, are gimmicky puzzles like Cryptics or the Puns and Anagrams type. In such cases, the devotees expect every clue to be tricky.

Now let's take a look at some definitions that no editor dared to print fifty years ago. Jack Luzzatto's "nectar inspector" was the forerunner of the *rhyming definition*. Here are some examples taken from recent puzzles.

Clue	Answer
Greek peak	OSSA
Raven's haven	NEST
Sound in a round	TRA
The scourge of serge	LINT
Man in the van of a clan	THANE
Scar on a car	DENT
Support is his forte	AIDE
Track of a yak	SPOOR
Song for the Met set	ARIA
His chief had a fief	ESNE
Tale on a grand scale	SAGA
Short snort or light bite	NIP
Look of a rake on the make	LEER
Ferry or wherry	BOAT

An offshoot of the above is the alliterative definition. A few examples are:

Clue	Answer
Foiler of forty felons	ALI BABA
Party popper	CORK
Calaveras County contest competitor	FROG
Churlish child	BRAT
Jeremiah, Joel and Jonah	PROPHETS
Feed feasters for a fee	CATER

Prompted by the popularity of rhymes and alliterations in the clues, constructors and editors with chutzpah have occasionally inserted *devilish definitions*. Again, some examples:

Clue	Answer
The longest sentence	LIFE
Norman who invaded TV	LEAR
He picked on the Britons	PICT
Their meal is a mess	NAVY MEN
Article appearing daily in English newspapers	THE
Man with vested interests	TAILOR
Item stolen while thousands cheer	BASE

The reader will note that the above clues feature hidden puns but are simultaneously fair to the solver because they literally mean what they say. The late Ted Shayne, who for many decades was a featured constructor of Dell Crosswords, pioneered in the creation of "Daffynitions." His continual popularity attests to the fact that many puzzle fans possess a great sense of humor and like to have their funny bones tickled now and then.

With that in mind, here are some additional *Clues to Amuse* which have been published in the *Times* or in various recent volumes of the *Simon and Schuster Crossword Puzzle Book*. This time the reader is asked to guess the answers to the flights of whimsy. If stumped, please turn to the last page of this chapter.

1. Cause of many a strike   __ __ __ __ __
2. He fails to pass the bar   __ __ __ __ __
3. "Icicle built for two"   __ __ __ __ __
4. He may be wrong but he's always right   __ __ __ __
5. Place for a loafer   __ __ __ __
6. They made a star trek   __ __ __ __
7. Poem about a rich man's red boat?   __ __ __ __ __ __ __ __ __
8. He never should rub people the wrong way   __ __ __ __ __ __ __
9. This place has a lock on New Haven   __ __ __ __
10. Girl in a pool   __ __ __ __ __

11. What Goliath got   __ __ __ __ __ __
12. Roads scholar   __ __ __ __
13. Man of sound mind   __ __ __ __ __
14. Scull session   __ __ __ __ __ __ __
15. The high cost of leaving   __ __ __ __

In the same genre are *Clues to Confuse*. When appearing in regular American cross-words, such diabolical definitions should always be crossed by easy words to give the solver a fair chance. Again, the answers to the examples appear on the last page of this chapter.

1. The skipper's hands   __ __ __ __ __
2. He crashed with a Ford in 1976   __ __ __ __
3. Man in a box   __ __ __ __ __ __
4. Chair person   __ __ __ __ __
5. Mailed   __ __ __ __ __
6. Quaker in a grove   __ __ __ __ __
7. Trunk in a trunk   __ __ __ __ __
8. Where to get good marks   __ __ __ __ __ __ __
9. Edible submarine   __ __ __ __
10. He's never out of butts   __ __ __

Once more, it should be stressed that the above definitions and answers are not the same as distortions found in Puns and Anagrams puzzles or others that feature puns as a theme. In contrast, here are some examples of changes in spelling via puns concocted by constructor John Prosser:

Clue	Answer
Dowery	MATRIMONEY
Lumberman's folly	AXE DENT
Honeymooners	SUITEHEARTS

In a straightforward puzzle, that trio would be out of place because the answers are made-up twists on the original words. But to define *Gable* as "Butler in a 1939 film" or *essays* as "Bacon pieces" is now considered fair game in a regular crossword as long as the trickery is not overdone.

Another innovation, encouraged by editor Will Weng, is the clue that requires a solver to put words together. The definition usually begins with "kind of" or "type of." Two examples are:

Clue	Answer
Kind of yard or room	COURT
Type of billing or board	STAR

Sometimes the clue is shortened to such an extent that it leaves the solver up a tree. A fan who comes across "potato or heart" in a regular puzzle is usually befuddled and rightfully indignant. What five-letter word will rightfully fit? The answer is *sweet*. Now if the definition had been preceded by "kind of," the solver would have had a chance to figure out the intention of the clue.

In current puzzles a definition similar to the "kind of" clue is the "predecessor" one. Thus, *pot* can be defined as "predecessor of luck or shot." A relative of the above is the "follower" definition. In this case, *sale* might be clued as "follower of yard or garage." Most "follower" definitions, however, are used to define suffixes. If *ite* appears in the puzzle the constructor might type "Follower of Jersey or Wisconsin" as the clue.

The mention of "relative" in the foregoing paragraph brings up another favorite ploy of today's constructors. Tired of defining *eland* as "African antelope," they often resort to such clues as "relative of an impala." Sometimes "cousin" or "kin" is used instead, but the point is that puzzlemakers are constantly seeking indirect ways to present new information to solvers. For instance, some of the fans may not have known that the familiar *eland* is related to another antelope called *impala*. Other "cousins," by the way, are the *bushbuck, dik-dik, topi, kudu* and *wildebeest*. What an advance from the trite definition repeated over and over in old puzzles!

Imparting information via definitions is one of the main goals of today's constructors, much to their credit. Examples of this aim abound in most daily and Sunday puzzles. But let's go back to the ten words cited at the beginning of this chapter and see what a variety of clues have evolved since the ice of tradition was broken. In each case, only a sampling is given:

ORE (Native mineral)

Mesabi Range product	Bauxite or malachite
Pittsburgh intake	Prill or mispickel
Shipment to Bethlehem	Magnet material
Small change in Denmark	Galena or cinnabar
Vein's glory	Prospector's quest
Pay dirt	Contents of a certain hutch
Miner's find	School of Mines topic

EAR (Organ of hearing)

Concha or pinna	Front-page box for weather reports
Sound receiver	Cob
Grain spike	Crossette
Musician's sine qua non	Pitcher handle
Abalone shape	Site for a drum
Matador's trophy	Favorable attention
One of Dumbo's "wings"	Lug of a jug
Audience	Corn unit

OAT (Cereal grass)

Pilcorn
Kernel of a grain
Kind of grass
Pastoral pipe
Word with cake or meal

Feedbag item
Morsel for Dobbin
___ Willie of comics
Avena sativa
It won't fill a filly

SUM (Total)

"Cogito, ergo ___"
Aggregate
Epitomize
Present briefly (with "up")

Bottom line
"Non ___ Qualis Eram": Dowson
Partner of substance
Terence's "Homo ___"

DOOR (Portal)

Wicket, e.g.
French window
It's in a jamb
Revolving item

Updike's "The Same ___"
Spot for a slot
Place to give a rap
O'Keeffe's "Farmhouse Window and ___"

STY (Pig's home)

Hordolum
Swine's confines
Unkempt abode
Piggery or swinery

Pen
Duroc's dwelling
Den of iniquity
Barnyard unit

NAP (Short sleep)

Siesta
Forty winks
Pile
Fabric feature

Suede surface
Feature of baize
Lose concentration
Part of a baby's day

HEN (Chicken)

Biddy
Grown-up pullet
Rhode Island Red
Billina in the "Oz" tales
Creature with no sweat glands
Guinea or pea follower

Brooder
Gossipy woman
Female lobster
Plymouth Rock
Dominique
Layer

HAT (Head covering)

Londoner's trilby
Gibus
Pillbox or porkpie
Busby or kepi
Bowler or sailor
Dicer or skimmer

"The Cat in the ___": Seuss
Hockey player's ___ trick
Oft-passed item
Cloche or toque
Medicine ___, Alberta

DIET (Regimen)

Mind over platter	Watch calories
Bant or bantingize	Scarsdale ____
Sitology subject	"Never Say ____": Simmons
Legislative body	Fare
Practice girth control	____ of Worms

As the reader can see from the above sampling, today's solvers are presented with a mixture of information, vocabulary building and humor via definitions that are repeated less often than they were four decades ago.

In that connection, let me tell you my *ort* story. When I became editor of the *Times* crosswords, one of the first puzzles that lay on my desk contained ORT. It was defined as "table scrap." I started to change the clue to "fragment for Fido." Then I remembered that an international group sponsoring vocational education was called Organization for Rehabilitation and Training and bore the initials O.R.T. Happy to have found a new clue for an old example of crosswordese, I penciled in "Noted service group, for short"—or something like that.

What a surprise awaited me! More than fifty letters and thank-you cards arrived from members of the organization. One of them stated, "Hooray for you! At last we're no longer a leftover morsel!" Later I was made an honorary member of the group.

But the opposite happened when I defined RNS as "doctors' aides." The chief of the nurses' organization in New York berated me for demoting her colleagues to candy stripers. Red-faced, I wrote an apology and asked for some better clues. She sent me about five or six, which I use to this day.

The above incident underscores the prime criterion for definitions—namely, accuracy. A clue must not only be factually correct, but it also must observe the principles of grammar and spelling. Most constructors are good spellers, but an astonishing number have little or no grammatical sense. Nouns are defined as adjectives; words are split up in violation of their etymological configurations; all sorts of errors in diction crop up. Thus, it behooves an editor to have an excellent background in morphology, syntax, phonology and semantics.

Another consideration that an editor must take into account when dealing with definitions is the type of "audience" for whom the puzzle is intended. It may astound some readers to learn that a puzzle containing all simple words can be made very difficult merely by making the clues somewhat abstruse or offbeat.

Let us hypothesize that the following entries appear in the diagram of a puzzle:

1. ROAM	4. AGED	7. CACTUS
2. ODE	5. FLUTE	8. MOTORIST
3. OWL	6. TIP	9. COMET

All easy words—right? But watch how the definitions can transform them into brain teasers:

1. Spatiate
2. Parabasis
3. Boobook or ruru
4. ___ P, Dickens character
5. Goffer

6. Lagniappe
7. Saguaro
8. One for the road
9. It has a tail and a fuzzy head

The last two clues are the devilish type mentioned earlier in this chapter. Numbers 2 and 4 require knowledge of literature. All the others are ten-dollar words that are not part of the average solver's vocabulary.

Is it fair to use such definitions? The answer to that question depends on whether the puzzle is intended as a superchallenger such as many that appear in crossword puzzle tournaments. For general purposes, esoteric or diabolical definitions should be used sparingly and the crossings should be relatively easy.

Blanks were rarely used in definitions for early puzzles, but today they have become commonplace. An example is "Grand ___ Opry"—the solver is asked to write in OLE. When examining a contribution, an editor must make sure that the clues are not overloaded with blanks. This same principle applies to allusions to literature, history, mythology, music and other subjects—unless a theme is involved.

For example, suppose that EROS, MARS, MUSES, AMOR and ORION all appear in the same puzzle but the theme happens to be something other than mythology. The constructor or editor would do well to find non-mythological definitions for most of that quintet.

EROS	Friend of Marc Antony	AMOR	Don Juan's emotion
MARS	Planet (or Botches)	ORION	Constellation
MUSES	Ruminates		

Some other do's and don'ts for defining that are kept in mind by most editors are:

1. Try as hard as possible to avoid annoying cross-references such as "See 41-Across and 52-Down."
2. Never define a *re* word (like *restore*) with another *re* word.
3. In the clue, don't repeat any word or words in the entry. For example, "on a toot" is not a good definition for *on a spree*. Similarly, "treaty org." is a bad clue for *NATO* because you are giving away half of the acronym.
4. If you have used a certain technique for one definition, try not to employ the same technique again in that particular puzzle. For instance, if *force* is defined as "part of A.E.F.," don't define *parent* as "part of P.T.A."

5. When defining a celebrity's name, be specific. If *Allen* is in the puzzle, "Ethan" is not a good clue. The answer could be *Frome*. "Patriot Ethan" would be acceptable. Sometimes resort to two first names. In this case, "Steve or Woody" would be okay.

6. The same goes for geographical entries. "River in Europe" is a poor definition for *Oder*. "Stettin's stream" zeroes in on the proper river.

7. Avoid vague definitions. For example, "be remembered" is a terrible clue for *inherit*. "Receive a relative's property or title" is much better. As for "become an heir," that definition suffers from being too close to the last two syllables of *inherit*.

8. Eschew verbosity. Definitions that take up four lines are usually boring. Also, they may cause an overrun on the page. On the other hand, terseness throughout is abominable. Behind every puzzle that contains all one-word clues is an indolent or unimaginative editor.

9. Watch out for blind definitions like "word with in or out" for a 4-letter entry. The answer could be *take, shut, pull* or any number of other words.

10. Use "e.g." when necessary. For example, "cattlemen, e.g." is a proper definition for *breeders,* because there are all kinds of other *breeders*.

11. Try not to repeat endings of words. "Loftier" is an inferior definition for *higher*. A better one is "homophone for hire." Similarly, "stimulater" or "stimulator" is not a good clue for *bracer*. Instead, use something like "a shot at the bar." This standard applies to adverbs, too. Defining *lastly* as "finally" presents the solver with two letters on a platter. "In conclusion" would be preferable.

The above list could go on and on, because there are so many pitfalls and nuances in the fine art of defining. As intimated previously, a large number of puzzle constructors are either too lazy or too careless about the key factor in every crossword—*definitions*. Therefore, the task often must be tackled by the editor. The reader who has scrutinized this chapter and the previous one should now have a good idea as to the role of the editor. He or she not only approves or rejects contributions while using a large number of criteria for such decisions, but each editor must then make whatever changes in the diagram are necessary to eliminate esoterica and other faults. Finally comes the all-important job of providing a variety of accurate, interesting, informative clues interspersed perhaps with a bit of humor. To this editor, the struggle to reach such goals is a labor of love. The fact that complete success is not always possible makes the challenge more exciting.

Answers to CLUES TO AMUSE (pages 64–65)

1. PITCH	5. FOOT	9. YALE	13. TUNER
2. TOPER	6. MAGI	10. STENO	14. REGATTA
3. IGLOO	7. RUBAIYAT	11. STONED	15. FARE
4. TORY	8. MASSEUR	12. HOBO	

Answers to CLUES TO CONFUSE (page 65)

1. CREW	6. ASPEN
2. DOLE	7. AORTA
3. BATTER	8. GERMANY
4. CANER	9. HERO
5. ARMED	10. RAM

5

Crossword Contests
and Contestants

Solving crossword puzzles is essentially a solitary activity. But two of mankind's proclivities have sometimes turned a loner's hobby into an instrument for rivalry. The first is the human propensity to strive to be *numero uno;* the other is the profit-making motive. Hence, the organization of contests for puzzle solvers was bound to happen sooner or later.

The "sooner" part took place in the 1920s when the crossword rage was at its height in America. Probably the most famous of the early contests took place in the ballroom of New York City's Roosevelt Hotel in 1925. It was called an Intercollegiate Crossword Puzzle Tournament and was arranged by the music department of Bryn Mawr College as a fund-raising gimmick.

Several thousand spectators looked on as Yale, led by alumnus Stephen Vincent Benét, eked out a victory over Wellesley in the final round. With erudite contestants like Heywood Broun and Robert E. Sherwood, Harvard barely missed out. Other participants represented Princeton, Smith, C.C.N.Y. and Bryn Mawr.

After that, a rash of puzzle contests burst upon the scene. Newspapers in search of greater circulation capitalized on the fad by offering cash prizes totaling as high as $25,000. But the tournament that excited the most interest was the one held by the National Puzzlers' League, also in 1925, at the Robert Treat Hotel in Newark. Strictly for eggheads, the contest featured strange words of Hindu and African origin.

The advent of the Depression put a damper on such "frivolities" as crossword puzzle contests. One tournament initiated by the *Chicago Herald and Examiner* attracted thousands of participants in 1932, but subsequently the interest in cruciverbal competition faded away like a nova. Newspapers took another stab at contests in the postwar period by offering big prizes for people who could complete pseudo crosswords in which unkeyed letters abounded. The clues were usually sentences containing blank areas for the words to be entered in the puzzle. However, to make it look easy, in each case every letter of the puzzle word was already filled into the grid except the important one. An example of a definition is "A ___ is likely to leave his wife." In the diagram the entry read: -OVER.

Which answer is correct? LOVER? ROVER? MOVER? Your guess is as good as mine. But the possibility of chicanery occurred to me when I was invited to construct such puzzles. The sentence that aroused my suspicions in the instructions to me was "Submit at least two plausible answers—one for each logical choice." I envisioned the use of a computer by the entrepreneurs. All the solutions sent in by the fans would be run through the machine and the one chosen by the fewest number of people—or by nobody—would later be published as the proper answer, along with the specious explanation. Wary of becoming an accomplice to a hoax, I turned down the offer.

Apparently thousands of contestants in the get-rich-quick game gave up in disgust, because those puzzles soon disappeared. Once again it looked as if the opportunity for solvers to pit their skills against one another and experience the joy of victory or the agony of defeat had been extinguished.

The British, however, kept the light burning. In 1977 their annual contest reached the attention of the manager of the Marriott Motel in Stamford. He called me to ask if it would be feasible for him to run such a contest during a weekend in March. Encouraged by the reply and the recommendation that he seek out Will Shortz (a budding young word expert who then lived in Stamford), he revived crossword puzzle contests in America. Nancy Schuster, a puzzle constructor and part-time editor of crosswords, was the winner. The event at Stamford has become an annual affair attracting nationwide attention and superb solvers. Margaret Farrar makes an appearance each year to present the prizes.

A newspaper publisher in Ridgewood, New Jersey, then got into the act for two years with less success. But Grossinger's in the Catskills took up the idea in 1980. Their tournament, offering a first prize of a weekend for two at the resort, has continued each winter.

In the late 1970s the most unusual contest of all was conducted for two successive years by a bookstore in Cleveland. The store, located in a sheltered mall, placed a score of tables in the arcade for the convenience of approximately seventy-five participants and handed each person an almost impossible puzzle created by constructor Jordan Lasher. For the next twelve hours, contestants were allowed to enter the bookstore and delve into the reference books (including a Hungarian-English dictionary) for the answers. The winner of this first marathon contest was Mike Donner, at that time editor of *Games*. In the second event, the laureate was conferred on none other than Will Shortz.

In 1982 a postal worker in Chicago concluded that there must be big money in crossword tournaments. He and his friends rented a large room at the Conrad Hilton Hotel and invested their hard-earned money in advertising the project. To their surprise, only thirty aficionados chose to pay twelve dollars apiece to participate. Organizers lost $500 on the venture.

In the small town of South Dartmouth, Massachusetts, just outside of New Bedford, probably the most intimate and friendly puzzle contests in America have been conducted annually since 1979. Sponsored by the Friends of the Dartmouth Library, this event does not make or lose much money but gains a great deal of good will. The fifty to seventy-five regular contestants from nearby areas in New England donate whatever they please as they enter. After struggling through the puzzles, which are constructed gratis by Bay State pros, they enjoy a box lunch together. Prizes are little silver-plated bowls supplied by Reed & Barton Silver Company.

Radio stations in such cities as Rochester, Manchester, Boston and Hyannis have also caught the puzzle-contest fever. In each case a professional is hired to construct a crossword featuring programs and personalities associated with the station. The diagram, sans clues, is then distributed at various stores and potential solvers are told to listen in each day for the definitions. A typical first prize is a brief trip abroad or a Caribbean cruise.

All of the competitions described above are regional, including those that occurred four or five decades ago. But in the summer of 1982, *Games* magazine sponsored the first U.S. Open crossword puzzle contest at New York University. A total of 250 experts from twenty-five states and two Canadian provinces matched wits and speed against one another. They had survived a qualifying round that had eliminated 40 percent of 7,770 entrants, and they had subsequently triumphed over four tie-breaker puzzles baited with snares.

After this elite coterie had tackled five semi-final puzzles, the group was narrowed down to three, who were then ushered up front to a stage for a sudden-death playoff. Devices on the stage enabled the audience to watch the progress of the trio. Oohs and aahs were heard as the spectators marveled at the quickness and accuracy of the finalists.

The winner was Mr. Stanley Newman, a middle-aged Brooklynite, who had triumphed at Grossinger's the previous winter. Margaret Farrar presented him with a check for $1,500. Rumors that he cried, "Evoe!" and the losers muttered, "Eheu!" are untrue. However, Mr. Newman's victory was savored by many fellow amateurs in this Open tournament. Although he had never created a puzzle, he had defeated a goodly number of pros—including some crossword constructors and editors.

How did Mr. Newman reach the pinnacle? I wrote to him and here is his reply:

> I credit my success in crossword solving to several factors—one, a broad base of general knowledge and trivia which I possessed before I became a serious solver—two, I have for some time looked up every word I have encountered in puzzles. Thirdly, I possess fast recall of

these facts and words—which enables me to solve them quickly. Also the ability to write fast and legibly should not be overlooked in a tournament.

I feel reference books are essential to learn "puzzlese." I own five sets of the *Encyclopedia Britannica,* four unabridged dictionaries, five foreign language dictionaries, five sets of Grove's *Dictionary of Music,* etc., etc. I use them *after* I have solved puzzles and corrected my solutions, to reinforce new facts and words in my head.

Mr. Newman also informed me that he actually trains for contests, somewhat like a boxer before an important bout. He shuts himself up in his room and tackles scores of puzzles.

Recently I persuaded the U.S. Open champion to try his hand at constructing puzzles. After a few false starts his efforts have made the grade and will eventually appear in the *Times* and in Simon and Schuster crossword books.

Nancy Schuster, winner of the first Marriott contest, lives in Rego Park, New York. She states that she began solving puzzles on her daddy's knee and got into constructing when her two children were babies and she was housebound. When Dell crosswords hired her as a part-time editor, she became knee-deep in reference books—a factor which she credits as most important in developing her skill as a fast and accurate solver.

In later Marriott tournaments, Mrs. Schuster finished second, sixth, fifth and ninth—thus becoming the only contestant to finish in the money every year. In the 1981 Ridgewood Newspapers Competition, she placed second to constructor-editor Henry Hook. She attributes his success to the fact that instead of nails "he has lead growing out of his fingers."

As for tips to other solvers, Mrs. Schuster suggests:

1. Solve plenty of puzzles from many different sources, to become familiar with the wide range of styles that exist, from straight dictionary definitions to plays on words.
2. Read the puzzle title so you know what you might expect as a theme.
3. Stay cool and relaxed. I can't.
4. Use a pencil—who are you kidding?
5. Work quickly without panic and fill in as much as possible in the grid before going back to trouble spots. Half your problems will be solved by the time you go through both Across and Down. When you get completely stuck, run quickly through the alphabet in your head in search of a reasonable letter. Rethink some entries, particularly multiple-word answers, to see a different division place of the words. Remember that words in the clue are carefully chosen, and a term that may sound odd is there on purpose, not because the editor didn't know how to phrase it correctly.
6. Finally, take an extra minute even if it kills you, to scan the grid for

omissions and illegibility. Sixty seconds is amazingly long under contest stress and is ample for this purpose. The point loss on a less than perfect answer is enormous.

Joel W. Darrow, a founding partner in an investment advisory firm, is another prize-winning contestant who began to solve crosswords at an early age. As a ten-year-old, he attempted his first puzzle, and when he was thirteen his father regularly bought two copies of the Sunday *Times* so that young Joel and he could solve the puzzle separately.

Now in his forties, Joel Darrow can solve a Sunday *Times* 21 x 21 in twelve to fifteen minutes and a daily puzzle in about five minutes. He does the crosswords in ink because it makes him concentrate more. Knowing he cannot erase makes him feel like a high-wire walker with no net below. In tournaments he prefers to use Schwan-Stabilo fine-line markers. "They don't smear," he says, "and they let me write small letters, which means less hand motion—hence greater speed."

Some of Mr. Darrow's techniques are as follows:

1. First read the title (if any) and orient your eyes to the grid's topography; i.e., placement of numbers and clues.
2. Look for soft spots in the first half-dozen Across clues; then attack the first dozen Down.
3. Use the left hand as a place marker.
4. While entering an answer, look for other clues.
5. It helps to have a retentive memory, an extensive vocabulary and an off-beat sense of humor.

About two weeks before a tournament, Mr. Darrow works on eye-hand coordination and mental alertness by solving two or three puzzles a day in the *Crossword Book of Quotations*. He spends less than twenty hours in preparation for a contest and wishes he could find more time. Aside from his business activities, he's a husband, father and member of the school board of White Plains, New York. "Someone once told me," he says, "that I solve fast because I have too little time to solve slow."

In six tournaments, Mr. Darrow has won prizes five times. He missed out by one letter in his debut as a contestant.

Philip M. Cohen of Aliquippa, Pennsylvania, doesn't seem to fit the mold of other tournament winners. Ordinary American puzzles bore this consultant to computer programmers; he prefers Cryptics and verse puzzles. As for techniques, he begins with 1-Across and moves along from there as fast as he can. When he enters a word, he checks the crossing word immediately to make sure his answer is correct.

Mr. Cohen was an avid solver of Dell crosswords in his high school days. He gave up the hobby for a few years but returned to it when he discovered Cryptics. He prefers to use a pencil, because "anything easy enough to do with a pen isn't worth doing."

Another champion who starts with 1-Across is Miriam Raphael, a teacher of English as a second language in Port Chester, New York. Like many other tournament winners, she started solving as a child and acquired the hobby in emulation of her parents. Later she discovered Acrostics—her favorite type of puzzle to this day.

For ordinary solving, Mrs. Raphael uses a Flair pen, but in competition she prefers a freshly sharpened #1 pencil and always keeps spares on hand. Her "training" method is to go through crossword puzzle books. She also times herself on daily and Sunday puzzles.

Mrs. Raphael cites her own experience as a rebuttal to those who claim that puzzle constructors and editors have an advantage in contests over the "amateurs" who merely solve the puzzles. Not long after she had won several tournaments, she became a puzzle editor for a new book of "Championship" crosswords published by Simon and Schuster. Thereafter, her speed decreased in the contests—a logical consequence, because editors are forced to proceed slowly lest errors go unnoticed.

Vivian Gomes of New Bedford, Massachusetts, has won first and second prizes in the annual South Dartmouth tournaments. As mentioned in a previous chapter, her success encouraged her to go back to school to obtain her high school diploma. She is now studying computer programming.

Ms. Gomes employs an unusual technique for solving vertical entries. When she has filled in some of the letters via the crossing words, she copies them horizontally on a separate piece of paper and leaves blanks for the missing letters. She finds that the word is easier to see if it is written from left to right.

Her general method is to fill in the first easy word she can find, starting at the top, and then branch out from that spot. If a puzzle has a theme, Ms. Gomes uses logic to guess what was in the constructor's mind for each thematic entry. For example, if the title is "Child's Play" and she has worked out *tic* as the ending of a long entry, she uses her brain plus the clue to come up with *Toys in the Attic*—a reasonable choice, considering the title of the puzzle.

Ms. Gomes points out that she has always been a good speller and that she has acquired a large vocabulary (including crosswordese) by solving puzzles for several decades.

Prizewinner Joseph R. Clonick from New York City is a young songwriter. When queried about his solving techniques, he replied as follows:

I truly wish I could explain my relative success at CWP-solving. Nothing mysterious, as far as I know. I've always had an acuity for the *look,* the *shape,* of words, if you will. And often, when the plain old memory fails me, the presence of one or two letters in the grid will suffice for me to *see* the rest of the word. Also, I've a fair ability to concentrate pretty hard on what I'm doing. Also, as soon as I fill in the given word or phrase, the given solution immediately leaves my mind, often without a trace. People will ask me what I thought of last Sunday's puzzle, which I may have completed in fifteen minutes, and which may have taken them hours to complete. I give them a blank look, and often have to be reminded what the theme of the puzzle was. I can't explain this. All I can tell you is that I *do* enjoy the puzzles — *while* I'm working on them.

One more thought: To me, a successfully constructed puzzle is one in which two obviously obscure words do not cross. Of course, one solver's "obviously obscure" word may be another's piece of cake. But my general feeling is that a solver, faced with some piece of obscurity or another, ought to have a reasonable shot by going the other way. In this sense, I feel that the Stamford puzzles, including the one where my mind turned to curds and whey, were totally fair and well constructed. That is why I have never had a great enthusiasm for Scrabble, wherein it is necessary to make one's mind a compendium of ridiculous two-letter words that have virtually no life beyond the confines of the Scrabble board. Not everyone shares that view, but that's the way I feel.

All of the above is just a sampling of the crossword puzzle tournaments and leading contestants. Any reader whose appetite for more information has been whetted should consult *Contest Crosswords: Celebrating 60 Years of Crossword Puzzle Championships* by Will Shortz (Simon and Schuster, 1983).

Finally, let me give my personal reaction to organized crossword puzzle competition. Although I have been the guest speaker at some of the contests and although I helped the Marriott manager to arrange the tournament in 1979 that revived the rage for pitting fan against fan in a moneymaking scenario, I have misgivings. In my opinion, solving a crossword should be a private matter. If you complete it, your ego gets a boost; if it stumps you, no problem: you can blame the constructor or the editor. And if you blame yourself, nobody else need know how inept you feel.

Relatives, neighbors and friends who feel the urge to compete have my blessing provided they can suffer defeat gracefully or enjoy a victory without gloating. One of my fans recently related an experience apropos of the above point. She and a close friend would each purchase the Sunday *Times* at 8:A.M. and proceed to fill in the answers. The one who finished faster would call the other. It so happened that the friend was a speedier solver who always rang first. So far so good, but after a while the friend became an obnoxiously triumphant winner. The loser felt crushed. In a tearful letter, she reported to me, "I hadn't realized what a mean person I had befriended. I'll never speak to her again!"

Some husbands and wives tell me they compete. Well, I hope they are good sports whose marriage can survive the "I-win, you-lose" syndrome that permeates rivalry of any sort. At least they have a common interest—unlike the Chicago woman who obtained a divorce on the grounds that she had become a "crossword widow."

Contests, it seems to me, exacerbate the loser's problem. In many tournaments, the rank order of the competitors is posted. Let's say there were 400 entrants and you ranked 400. What effect would that news have on your psyche?

Even the top contestants feel terrible anxiety, which is contrary to the main purpose of crossword puzzles. Listen to a prizewinner who participated onstage in one of the major tournaments and who wishes to remain anonymous.

> After what can only be described as a grueling day and a half of puzzling, I found myself in third place, which qualified me for the final playoff round. This required that the top three finishers sit at special lecterns placed at the front of the room. The contestants write on a transparent sheet which is powerfully illuminated from below. The writing is then projected onto large screens behind the contestants, so that every machination and perturbation of their minds is made available to public scrutiny. It is obvious that I must have been doing *something* right to have reached the playoffs, but you never would have known it to have observed me in action (or rather *in*action), on that final puzzle. All I can tell you is that whatever mental acuity or flexibility I once had deserted me with a vengeance, and the fifteen minutes I spent staring foolishly at a half-empty grid seemed interminable. Instead of being relatively pleased to finish third, I felt like a damn fool. This kind of thing can certainly put a crimp in the sense of leisurely enjoyment that one comes to associate with the solving of crossword puzzles!

6

The Constructors
and Editors

Young children in elementary schools tend to look upon their teachers as out-of-this-world creatures who are let down from heaven each morning on invisible strings —or, in some cases, are magically pushed up from the floor by the Prince of Darkness. Similarly, many addicts of crossword puzzles find it hard to comprehend that the people who delight or torture them every day are actual human beings. On rare occasions when they meet a puzzlemaker, they seem to be looking for haloes or horns —or both. Their typical reaction is "You're Mr. X! Oh, my God! I don't believe it!" This burst of incredulity is accompanied by a searching look that combines reverence with bewilderment. Finally, after they are convinced that Mr. X is the real McCoy, they let loose with a barrage of questions, such as "Where do you get all those words?" or a flood of compliments or complaints.

Yes, Virginia, there are living, breathing puzzle constructors. They do not come from the North Pole or planet Krypton in another galaxy, but they grew up not far from you and perhaps they even attended your school or one nearby. As children, nearly all of them excelled in spelling and most of them were avid readers. They ranged from fair to excellent in high school and many of them went on to college.

Do they make up crosswords for a living? In the vast majority of cases, the answer is a resounding "No!" The recompense is too small; the number of outlets is meager; the competition is fierce. Only a few who become editors can count on the crosswords for subsistence, and even then the stipends are modest at best. To the average constructor, the craft is a challenging and enjoyable hobby.

How and when did the hobby develop? A questionnaire sent to top puzzlers reveals that most of them liked word games as young children. In many instances, one or both of their parents were solvers of crosswords and excited their interest in that particular word game. Almost without exception, the constructors began as preteen or adolescent solvers and after a time developed such skill in filling in the words that the pastime became somewhat boring. Hence, they decided to "graduate" to creating puzzles. Some of them, it should be noted, took up the craft after retiring from time-consuming occupations.

A large number of the constructors are homemakers. Professors, teachers, lawyers, doctors, architects and engineers are well represented. A few businessmen and stenographers have recently joined the ranks. Two well-known actors, a Hollywood scriptwriter and about four successful authors contribute once in a while. Among the more affluent are a TV network executive, a vice president of a silver company and a Texas millionaire who employs a secretary just for the crosswords. Musicians, too, get into the act. One of them is a conductor; another is a recently retired violinist for the New York Philharmonic Orchestra. Probably the most eminent of the constructors is a state supreme court judge in the Southwest. A few of the wrongdoers that he and his colleagues send to jail occasionally send in puzzles.

Where do the constructors come from? New York City and the rest of its state take the prize. The silver medal goes to other Northeastern states such as New Jersey, Massachusetts, Connecticut and Pennsylvania. Florida and California come next, but it must be added that many of their representatives grew up in the Northeast. The Midwest and the South can claim a scattering of puzzlemakers but there are vast regions of the West from which few, if any, constructors have emerged.

Note the word *constructors*. Margaret Farrar and her colleagues were the ones who pinned that label on the creators of the puzzles when crosswords were in their infancy. According to her, the word *composers* was too pompous; it seemed right to restrict that designation to the world of music. Nor did *authors* fit the bill—too literary, and again too pretentious. *Constructors,* while not perfect, appeared to be the proper nomenclature, because the contributors were building blocks of words within a framework similar to that of a house or other edifice. Also, the interweaving of letters was more like a craft than an art.

For some reason, British puzzlemakers turned down their noses on *constructors* and opted for *composers*. Thus, if you hear a crossworder state that he or she is a *composer,* you will know that the person is either British or an American afflicted with a bad case of self-importance.

Apropos of the above, some weavers of words within the squares have recently dubbed themselves *cruciverbalists*—a term which makes the self-styled *composers* of puzzles look like the epitome of modesty.

You are about to be treated to some inside information on the premier puzzlers of today, along with a list of the best of the up-and-coming who will take over tomorrow. But first, it seems proper to pay tribute to some of the movers and shakers of the CWP world of yesterday.

Surely, if you are a veteran solver whose memory of the past has not been hopelessly dimmed, you will remember Charles Erlenkotter, Laird C. Addis, F. C. Jaschob and Elsa Gorham Baker — four of the most prolific puzzlemakers from the 1930s to the '50s. Nor have you forgotten Alvin Ashby (famed for his successions of seven-letter words) and James P. Campbell (noted for clever interlocks). Fans of Sunday *Herald Tribune* and Dell crossword puzzles will certainly recall the remarkable Elizabeth Patterson, while diagramless buffs will thrill once again to such names as Alice Vaughan, Ronald Schoenleber and Mabel C. Daggett.*

Most of the above have gone on to that Great Rectangle in the Sky (to paraphrase baseball's Tom La Sorda), but some of the names of that era still produce. They include Herb Ettenson, Jack Luzzatto, George W. Frank, Edward Buckler, Nikki Folwell, Marie West and the aging constructor whose self-made anagram is Sam Lake.

But as sure as God made green apples the old order changeth, yielding unto new. In the 1950s, records kept by this writer reveal that fewer than a hundred people in America seemed to be capable of creating a crossword puzzle that would measure up to the standards of the *Times*. Now the number is at least five hundred, and the list grows larger every week. This phenomenon probably can be attributed to a variety of factors: the greater number of young people with degrees from higher-education institutions; the recent upsurge in interest in crossword puzzles; more leisure time for most Americans; and, indirectly, the effects of inflation.

Choosing the very best current constructors from such a long and illustrious array is a difficult, rash and thankless task. What criteria should be used? Certainly versatility and originality must be considered. Consistency of excellence in word selection, minimum of black squares and maximum of accuracy and creativity in defining should also be taken into account.

First, let's take a look at those top constructors who have become editors of crossword puzzles. In alphabetical order, they are:

Herbert Ettenson	Jack Luzzatto
Henry Hook	Mel Taub
Maura B. Jacobson	Will Weng
Jordan S. Lasher	

A dazzling septet indeed! Now here are the other A-1 pros who, to the best of this selector's knowledge, have never been editors. Again the listing is alphabetical.

Louis Baron	Alfio Micci	John M. Samson
Anne Fox	Mary Virginia Orna	A. J. Santora
Frances Hansen	Tap Osborn	Elaine Schorr
Bert Kruse	Vincent Osborne	Richard Silvestri
William Lutwiniak	Bert Rosenfield	

*Readers who recall with respect a first-rate constructor from the past whose name has been omitted will please forgive this sexagenarian with a sievelike memory.

Close on the heels of the above are a number of veterans whom some other arbiter might rate among the very best. All of them have been published in the *Times*. In alphabetical order, they include the following:

Nancy W. Atkinson	Threba Johnson	Sidney Robbins
James and Phyllis Barrick	Alice H. Kaufman	Mel Rosen
Alexander F. Black	Stanley Kurzban	Louis Sabin
Anthony B. Canning	Joseph La Fauci	Ruth Schultz
Martha J. De Witt	Tom Mixon	Diana Sessions
Louise Earnest	Arnold Moss	Dorothea Shipp
Barbara Gillis	Jim Page	George Rose Smith
Stanley Glass	Marjorie Pederson	Jack Steinhart
Bernice Gordon	Jean Reed	Mel Thorner
Kenneth Haxton	Norton Rhoades	Walter Webb
Fletcher Ingalls	Kathryn Righter	Eli Wesoff
Reginald J. Johnson	Herb L. Risteem	

But the following is probably the most exciting lineup of all because it identifies some of the *most promising newcomers,* many of whom took up the game in the 1970s. These are the people to watch. As today's leaders gradually fade away, the names below are likely to be seen atop puzzles more and more. Admittedly incomplete, the alphabetical listing is as follows:

Virginia Abelson*	Harold Hollinger*	Lois Sidway
Sam Bellotto, Jr.*	Timothy Hoy	Samuel Smart*
Jeanette Brill*	William Jarvis	Peter Snow*
Emory H. Cain	Lee Jones	George Sphicas
William Canine	Robert Katz	Kay Sullivan
Barry Cohen*	Vaughn P. M. Keith*	Peter Swift*
Bette Sue Cohen*	Fred Keller	Maurice J. Teitelbaum*
Judith Dalton*	I. Judah Koolyk*	Ernest T. Theimer
Charles Deber*	Joel LaFarge	Judson G. Trent*
Richard E. Dempsey	Lynn Lempel*	Arthur M. Whelan
Joan De Rosso	Albert E. Lytle	Stanley B. Whitten
Carol Dutting*	E. J. Marchese*	Norman Wizer
Dorothy Elliott	Jim Modney*	Robert H. Wolfe*
Grace Fabbroni	Arthur Palmer	Nancy Wood*
Caroline Fitzgerald*	Rosalind Pavane	Joy Wouk*
William H. Ford*	Michael Priestly*	Kenneth Wray
Teresa Forestall	Warren W. Reich*	William J. Yskamp*
Sandra Gast*	Muriel Rigby*	
John Greenman*	Nancy Ross	

---

*Constructor has published at least one featured puzzle in *The New York Times Sunday Magazine*.

It is interesting to note that in the above list of fifty-five top newcomers, thirty-five are men and twenty are women. Since female solvers apparently outnumber males, it would seem that men are more likely to take the leap into the dark and would rather puzzle than be puzzled. Incidentally, the same male-female ratio appears in the other three lists. Perhaps a psychologist or sociologist should be called upon to explain this consistent imbalance.

Another important point about the four lists is that every one of the constructors has been published in the *Times*. Their efforts have also appeared in various volumes of crosswords put out by Simon and Schuster.

Two other rather new constructors who have never appeared in the *Times* but whose work is highly regarded are Merl H. Reagle and Mike Shenk. Top constructors of Cryptics and other varieties of crossword puzzles will be discussed in another chapter.

Now let us return to our blue-ribbon group and take a look at their lives, careers, interests and preferences. We begin with our alphabetical array of A-1 constructors who also wear an editorial hat.

HERBERT ETTENSON

Back in the 1930s, when this writer was a brand-new constructor, the puzzles I admired most were those published by someone named Ettenson. Subconsciously I emulated his efforts and I pictured him as an old codger with savvy gained by years of experience. About five years later, we met under unusual circumstances. A Cuban entrepreneur had decided to publish a new crossword puzzle magazine and he had asked Margaret Farrar to recommend a pair of co-editors. She chose Herb and me.

My mouth was agape, as we say in Puzzledom, when the real Herb Ettenson stepped forward and shook my hand. He was my age! How had he become so talented in so short a time? Later, as we labored together on a project that was doomed from its inception, I learned the answer. Herb was a child prodigy who started solving crosswords and other puzzles in the *New York World* when he was an eight-year-old. At ten he began to construct small puzzles for his own pleasure, and at fifteen he became a pro: the first puzzle he ever submitted was accepted by the *New York Herald Tribune*. From then on, he knew he had found his favorite pastime.

Subsequently the *Times* began publishing crosswords. Herb teamed up with his best friend, Jules Arensberg, and again met immediate success. The partnership lasted for about thirty years and produced some of the most fascinating puzzles that have ever appeared anywhere. Herb and Jules were not satisfied with merely crossing words haphazardly in a diagram. Taking up where Herb had left off at the *Trib,* they strove for interesting themes.

One of the team's innovations was entitled "Numerology." It featured such "Arabic" entries as ALL FOR 1, COLT 45s and ROARING 20s. Needless to say, Margaret Farrar's mail brought a mixture of kudos and protests when that daring breakthrough confronted the fans. Later, the two pioneered in the use of Roman numerals as a theme, with similar results. Mrs. Farrar's minister jokingly threatened her with excommunication.

For many years, Herb worked in his family's clothing-manufacturing business and moonlighted as a part-time sports reporter and lexicographer. At one time he even tried his hand at supervising workers in the New York City transit system, but eventually he found his true vocation as a teacher of English at Roosevelt High School in the Bronx.

Herb had expected to continue his teaching career until he reached retirement age. But one day he received a phone call from the Chicago Tribune–New York News Syndicate. They needed a crossword puzzle editor, and Herb had been highly recommended by everyone whom they had contacted. "Such flattery," he says, "was irresistible. I accepted the contract."

Luckily for solvers, Herb continues to create puzzles because he enjoys the hobby so much. In his own words, "there is more originality in composition than in emendation." But as an editor he derives satisfaction from pepping up definitions in a bland puzzle to transform it into an exciting opus. Two of his favorite original clues are "meter man" for POET and "master of ledger domain" for CPA.

As a constructor of long experience, Herb can now create a 15 x 15 puzzle in about an hour. Putting together a 21 x 21 consumes an average of four hours and a 23 x 23 a bit more time. Most of Herb's contemporaries will envy those figures.

HENRY HOOK

The winners of CWP tournaments were recently asked by this writer to name a constructor whose puzzles they admire most. Henry Hook received far more votes than anyone else. He is "the contestants' constructor"—young, daring, versatile, unpredictable and strikingly original.

Henry's surge to the peak of Puzzledom is a source of great satisfaction to me, because I was his discoverer in the early 1970s, when he was a student at Fairleigh Dickinson University. The story is an example of serendipity, beginning with a jigsaw crossword that I had created for the Springbok offshoot of the Hallmark Company. The executives had instructed me to feature a Stepquote containing the following immodest message: "You have just finished the world's most remarkable crossword puzzle."

A few months after the jigsaw hit the market, an overstuffed envelope was forwarded to my home in New Jersey. Inside was a crudely prepared puzzle from someone named Henry Hook. I was about to return it unsolved when I noticed that it contained a Stepquote. Intrigued, I sat down and tackled the puzzle. The message that evolved was "What makes you think your puzzle is more remarkable than mine?"

The temptation to dismiss the crossword as the work of a rash egotist was easily set aside when I scrutinized the definitions. Original! Unusual! Exciting! A picture of Henry Hook formed in my mind: he was a mature man who had probably been solving puzzles for thirty or forty years and had recently retired from some high post in the business world. I decided to put the curmudgeon in his place while offering him an encouraging carrot. That night I whipped up a small Stepquote stating, "Hook wins by a nose."

While mailing the puzzle, my attention was drawn to the address. Mr. Hook lived only ten miles away from me! Shortly thereafter, I found his number in the phone book and decided to make a call in apology for my foul pun. A woman answered: "Henry's not here. He's at school." (Ah, he's a teacher, I reckoned.) "Who is calling?"

When I gave my name, I could hear her catch her breath. "Not Eugene T. Maleska!" "The very same."

"Well, I'm Henry's mother. (Shock!) Would you give me your phone number? I'll have him call you back when he gets home."

Thus our acquaintance began. I invited Henry to my home and showed him my reference books and notebooks on words. He was most taciturn but I could tell that his bright mind was absorbing everything. We reached an agreement: he would send me 15 x 15s for analysis and criticism. After changes were made the best one would be forwarded to editors Farrar and Weng accompanied by my letters of recommendation.

Needless to say, Henry blazed across the puzzle world *ab ovo*. Looking at his success in perspective, I firmly believe that he would have reached the pinnacle without my help. All I did was accelerate the process. But my experience always reminds me of some famous lines by Keats: "Then felt I like some watcher of the skies/When a new planet swims into his ken."

Unlike many of his colleagues, Henry did not acquire his passion for puzzling from his parents. In fact, he introduced his father to the solving hobby. Picture-clue crisscrosses in children's coloring books intrigued Henry, and in elementary school he began making up little puzzles based on various lessons. Finally, one of his high-school English teachers asked him to do a series of crosswords for the school newspaper. It was at that point that he learned how typos can cause a puzzle to be unsolvable — a lesson that serves him well today as a free-lance editor.

Of course, spelling has always been Henry's forte. In 1969 he competed in the National Spelling Bee in Washington, D.C., and ranked near the middle of that precocious group. But his talent for weaving words together goes beyond mere orthography; one of his specialities is concentrating on neglected letters such as J, Q, X and Z. And he revels in the creation of punny clues. Consider the following examples:

Dead giveaway	BEQUEST
Text-aisle store	BOOKSHOP
Have an inspiration	INHALE
Pound into pieces	OUNCES

The one I'm hooked on most is "What's black and white and Red all over?" The answer is PRAVDA.

Two of Henry's hobbies are watching TV game shows (whence he collects trivia to torment solvers) and reading mystery stories. In connection with the latter, he once took an elective in the subject at college. When the professor discovered that Henry was a CWP constructor, he asked his unique student to construct a "mystery story" crossword as the final exam. Thus, our hero attained an A in the course without attending the last half of the semester!

MAURA B. JACOBSON

Here's a pro who has not only earned accolades from the fans but has also won the admiration and respect of her colleagues. In fact in a recent poll of the top constructors, Maura was chosen as their favorite. Close on her heels was A. J. Santora. Other runners-up were Henry Hook, Jordan Lasher and E.T.M., followed by such veterans as Jack Luzzatto and Frances Hansen. Honorable mention went to Anne Fox, William Lutwiniak, Alfio Micci, Tap Osborn and relatively new Merl H. Reagle. Mel Taub also received lots of praise for his specialty—Puns and Anagrams.

Naturally, such a minuscule sampling cannot be considered definitive, but it's a safe bet that Maura's name would appear very high on any list of the best and the brightest. Her creations maintain consistently high standards while being simultaneously clever and innovative. To many, she is known as a champion in "punmanship." Others marvel at her ability to turn out stimulating crosswords week after week—first for *Cue* and presently for *New York* magazine.

Maura gives credit to her father for igniting her interest in the puzzles and other word games. The embers of those early experiences remained alive during her career as a kindergarten teacher in the New York City schools and as a private piano teacher. Then one day in the 1950s when she was ill, the latent fire burst into flame. By chance, she had acquired two copies of the *Times*. She solved the crossword and then filled her own words into the second copy. With fingers crossed, she sent her "original" to

Margaret Farrar and was amazed to receive a positive answer: The puzzle would be a winner if certain corrections were made.

Since then, with the blessing and encouragement of her congenial spouse (a New York City optometrist), Maura has constructed about 500 puzzles. She constantly searches for new themes and exults when the quest is successful. For example, one of her best crosswords contained a three-line story. The clues were, respectively, "problem," "action," "result." The last, of course, was a pun.

When not puzzling people, Maura can be found on the tennis court. She also enjoys traveling to such exotic places as the Far East and Egypt. But in recent years her leisure time has been curtailed by various editing assignments, including a stint as one of the judges for a contest introducing a series of crosswords for Bantam Books. That experience opened her eyes concerning the role of the person who is eventually responsible for the publication of a puzzle. She had never realized how many improvements in clues and alterations of words in the diagram are made by an editor with high standards.

The latest time-consuming task undertaken by this Hunter College alumna has been the creation of *Crossword Puzzles with Themes,* a series consisting of four volumes.

Maura guesses that the British Cryptics might someday become the most popular crossword puzzles in America. Maybe that's because her married daughter lives in Cornwall, England!

JORDAN S. LASHER

Just when it looked as if no member of the younger generation had the ability or the desire to challenge the old-timers in the puzzlemaking crafts, along came Jordan S. Lasher. In the spring of 1970 his first published puzzle appeared in the *Times* — a result, by the way, of his being bedridden with mononucleosis. Since then he has produced more than 400 puzzles that have gained plaudits from colleagues and solvers.

A typical Lasher puzzle is a thing of beauty. First of all, it has a striking, unusual pattern; straight lines of black squares predominate, and hackneyed zigzagging ladders are not to be found. The result is a wide-open array of juxtaposed and interesting long words and phrases — a treat for any blasé fan who seeks an adventuresome challenge. The entries themselves are extraordinary, in both senses of that adjective. Finally, the clues are fresh and original. Two examples of the last point are: "Meet me ___ Louis" for INST and "Saves nine" for SEWS.

Jordan grew up in the Bronx and attended the City College of New York but now lives in Pennsylvania with his wife and two young children. As a chemical engineer for a large oil company, he is often sent to such far places as China. But such interruptions have not prevented him from accepting an eminent position as the constructor-editor of Sunday puzzles for the *Boston Globe.*

As a child, Jordan was introduced to crosswords by his father. He started solving around the age of ten or eleven and made his amateur debut as a constructor in his junior high school newspaper. Unfortunately, the opus contained a misspelled word: TOMATOS. But don't jump to conclusions. Actually Jordan won the J.H.S. 98 spelling championship for two consecutive years and would have participated in the national bee at Washington were it not for *lavender* and some other demon that tripped him up.

One of the Lasher innovations that elicited lots of fan mail was a 1972 *Times* puzzle featuring reversals such as THE MARCH OF IDES. The IDES, of course, were little fish.

In 1978 your obedient servant was asked to choose a constructor to create "the world's most difficult puzzle" for a marathon contest scheduled to be held in Cleveland. The selection of Jordan Lasher was based partly on his ability and partly on his geographical availability. He accepted the assignment with great enthusiasm and produced a blockbuster that will live in fame or infamy depending on a fan's experience and intellect. One contestant, hearing that Lasher was dining nearby, wished him a case of ptomaine poisoning; others, recognizing that they had come face-to-face with a super-puzzler, besieged him for his autograph.

JACK LUZZATTO

Most constructors are awed by the work of Jack Luzzatto. Long before the Lashers, Hooks and Reagles came along, this master of the craft was regularly turning out 15 x 15 puzzles containing only 64 to 68 words.

But only a few of the Luzzatto admirers are aware that he comes close to being a jack-of-all-trades. From 1934 to 1943 he was a professional cartoonist. He is also a fine poet and writer of numerous articles on the history of puzzles. In his few moments of leisure, he has become an accomplished netman.

Jack was the first of the top puzzlemakers to move up to an editorship and actually support a large family on his income from crosswords. As stated earlier in this book, he also pioneered in the use of colloquial and original clues in place of definitions taken bodily from dictionaries.

Like Jordan Lasher, Jack grew up in the Bronx and developed a passion for crosswords while still a stripling. He won the English medal at Morris High school and subsequently sent his first puzzle to *Liberty* magazine in the hope of earning twenty-five dollars. It was returned with a brief note: "Sorry. Overstocked." Undaunted, he tried Margaret Farrar. Voilà! A check for eight dollars. Thus, as he says, "the virus took effect." He became a regular contributor to the *Times,* starting in the 1940s, and later published about twenty books of his own puzzles—an arduous feat which he advises others not to emulate.

Jack's interest in rhymes and rhythms showed up in a 21 x 21 Mother's Day puzzle published by Will Weng. The lines each contained 21 characters:

Mother's Day a baby rang me:
"Lots o' love," my baby sang me.
Talked one hour I suspect;
Paris calling me collect.

As one of the first creators of Puns and Anagrams puzzles, Jack revealed his superb sense of humor. CHAMPAGNE was defined: "Two pints make one cavort." Examples of other Luzzatto-isms in various types of puzzles are:

Dangerous bunk	PROCRUSTEAN BED
A clash of symbols	MIXED METAPHOR
Sometimes they beat wives	MISTRESSES

Today Jack's chief interest is constructing and solving Cryptics. He predicts that their popularity will continue to spread in America. He has a pet peeve, too: new constructors who think he owes them a free correspondence course in how to become one of his rivals. Not to worry, Jack. You'll always be unrivaled.

MEL TAUB

Now recognized as the premier Puns and Anagrams puzzlemaker, Mel Taub took a devious and bumpy road to that high station. In his undergraduate days at Brooklyn College he was the kingpin among a large crowd of students who tackled the Sunday *Times* puzzle every week. So why not make one up? He labored for days and days over the creation of a "straight" crossword and finally sent his crude effort to the *Times*. The inevitable rejection caused him to turn to another phase of puzzlemaking—the Acrostic. In that medium he met with immediate success. Over the years he sold more than 1,200 acrostics to various puzzle magazines.

After a tour of duty in the army, Mel took a few more stabs at constructing a "straight" CWP and hit the jackpot on the third try. Now his passion for wordplay, which had been somewhat inhibited in the Acrostics, could come to the foreground. In a puzzle with a literary theme, solvers got the first glimpses of the now-famous Taub touch:

Author needing repentance	CORNELIA OTIS SINNER
Riotous poet	EDNA ST. VINCENT MELEE
Aaron at first base	HENRY FIELDING

In another puzzle, HOURGLASS FIGURE was defined as "a waist of time" and the clue for RH FACTOR was "Max's blood brother."

Meanwhile, Mel had been dabbling in the creation of Cryptics; hence it was natural for him to gravitate toward Puns and Anagrams puzzles. He came to that genre at just the right time. For one reason or another, the P.&A. output of members of the Old Guard had dwindled in the 1950s. Constructors like Buckler, Ettenson, Kelly and this writer were no longer supplying Margaret Farrar with the punny 15 x 15s for the lower area of her Sunday page. Mel filled the vacuum so well that one would think he had invented P.&A.'s. Actually, he brought his unique style to that type of puzzle and devised new gimmicks for tricky definitions. Just two of many examples are "1,658 cheetahs": CATS and "Tell it t' porter": T'ALE.

In 1979 Mel joined up with Maura Jacobson and Jack Luzzatto in judging entries for a Bantam Books contest for crossword puzzle constructors. Then in 1981 Bantam offered him the editing job for three books of large-sized crosswords. He gets a thrill out of changing a so-so puzzle into one that is interesting and challenging.

In one respect, Mel is probably *sui generis* among constructors. He actually enjoyed math in school! His penchant for figures led him to his present occupation as an executive for a life insurance company. Mel commutes by subway to Manhattan from his home in Brooklyn. His wife, Phyllis, holds an executive post at Brooklyn College and shares his fondness for paronomasia. Witness her statement: "Mel doesn't play on words; he preys on them." One wonders what kind of pun-ishment this pair has visited upon their two grown sons through the years.

WILL WENG

If Mel Taub is the king of the punsters and Maura Jacobson is the queen, then Will Weng rules over the princedom. That analogy has its flaws, because Will is older than the other two. But his predilection for bits of wit is well known in the crossword puzzle world. Even before he succeeded Margaret Farrar as crossword puzzle editor of the *Times* (January 6, 1969), his own puzzles reflected his philosophy—namely, that crosswords are purely for pleasure, just another word game, albeit one of the best of the lot. And so, it was only natural for Will to encourage purveyors of *jeux de mots,* rebus puzzles, linkages of celebrities' names and all kinds of other gimmicks.

As editor, Will was the perfect man for the era. Sometimes deliberately and sometimes willy-nilly, Margaret Farrar had unlocked the gates throughout the 1960s. Her fan mail and her own interest had prompted her to allow more range to the constructors and to give the humorous and the unexpected their proper place in what had heretofore been a relatively staid hobby for word-lovers. Will Weng merely opened the gates a little wider, while maintaining most of the standards of his predecessor. True, there were fewer esthetically pleasing diagrams with a minimum of black squares; also, a modicum of concocted phrases crept in, but the number of thematic entries in each puzzle increased dramatically, and the definitions revealed the deft touch of someone who had been trained in combining terseness with cleverness.

Will's prior job as chief of the *Times* metropolitan copy desk had given him the proper apprenticeship. He knew how to make a headline accurate, concise and ingenious. Consequently, crossword clues were his cup of tea. He found a variety of new ways to define trite words and he sprinkled the puzzles with his own brand of humor. Here are some examples:

Tailless game animal	DONKEY
Large brass container	PENTAGON
Useful picnic intruder	AARDVARK
It's fine on contracts	PRINT

Will's name has sometimes led solvers to assume erroneously that he is Chinese. One fan thought it appropriate to call his puzzles "inscrutable." On the contrary, he is candid, sometimes to the point of being blunt in his expressions of dislikes. But the adjective that describes him best is *modest*.

Standing tall and straight, this self-effacing septuagenarian looks like a fifty-year-old escapee from a Dickens novel. A bachelor, he cooks his own meals, works out regularly at the New York Athletic Club and takes long walks on Broadway every day. He has had a lifelong love affair with words—a possible result of the fact that his father was a Latin teacher. On weekends he often visits his sister, Ruth Smith, in New Jersey. Since Ruth is also a puzzle constructor, the reader can bet that they talk shop.

In the summer, Will visits his other sister, Damaros Rogers, in Lansing, and estivates at his little cottage near Mackinaw City, Michigan.

The Midwest is familiar to Will. He was born in Terre Haute and spent three years at Indiana State University. From there he went on to the Columbia University School of Journalism, where he earned an A.B. degree.

While at Columbia, Will obtained a job as college correspondent for the *Times*. This opening led to a regular position as a *Times* reporter upon graduation. His first thrill in that post came when he was assigned to cover the entire Lenz-Culbertson bridge match. With typical diffidence, Will says he was selected for that task only because he was "the only decent bridge player at the office." Actually, Will is an expert in that game; golf is his other leisure-time pursuit.

Many of today's top constructors were Will's "discoveries," but the one he feels best about is a convict whose contributions were marginal. Will managed to fix up the prisoner's diagramless and daily puzzles so that they could become publishable. Then his protégé vanished without a trace.

Will now edits crossword puzzles for Times Books and for the Will Weng Crossword Puzzle Club. He continues to construct puzzles for various magazines, crossword books and commercial ventures. His carefully wrought creations, starting in the mid-1950s, add up to about 200.

□

Now let's take a closer look at some of the premier constructors who have not become editors of crossword puzzles.

LOUIS BARON

Here's one master puzzler who doesn't fit the mold, either in his life-style or his crosswords. Born on the Lower East Side, Lou barely made it through high school and hated every minute of it. He did a stint in the merchant marine and then became chief copywriter for an ad agency. Time-Life offered him a position, but he decided against it after sizing up his probable colleagues. Subsequently, he bluffed his way into a post in the pathology lab at Cornell Medical College of New York, but once again his restless nature took hold and he joined a New York company specializing in security systems. There he found a "home" for twenty-one years until his recent retirement.

While Lou was pursuing all those disparate careers, he took up the crossword puzzle hobby as part of his self-education plan. Bored with mere solving, he turned to CWP construction as a young man and met immediate success. Between 1942 and 1953 Margaret Farrar published about twenty-seven of Lou's Sunday puzzles. His work also appeared in Simon and Schuster puzzle books, the *New York Herald Tribune,* various Air Force publications and other periodicals. "Then," says he, "I quit the game altogether and vanished."

Puzzle solvers welcomed Lou back in the late 1970s. His new contributions revealed that he had kept up with the times—and the *Times.* Today his themes and clues sparkle with humor and originality. As just one example, a 1981 Baron beauty in the *Times* featured such entries as MATHLETICS ("course for grid illiterates") and BINGUISTICS ("study of a crooner's lyrics").

ANNE FOX*

Nobody, but nobody, excels Anne Fox in crossing long phrases with long phrases. Her Christmas puzzles, which have become traditional in the Sunday *Times,* interweave lines from carols and poems with such skill that other constructors stand in awe. They wonder how much research, time and effort are required for such masterpieces. The answer is that it takes months of painstaking work. To Anne, each puzzle is like a piece of

---

*While this book was being prepared, Anne Fox passed away at the age of 72.

sculpture that must be carved out with care and polished in every detail. She favors input over output and quality over quantity. Since her first puzzle appeared in 1961, she has published 250 other gems — a small number compared with the production of many other constructors, but nothing to be sneezed at in view of the close attention given to each opus.

Anne is another of Margaret Farrar's numerous disciples. Their association was serendipitous. A teacher friend of Anne's, knowing how she liked to solve crosswords, asked her to make one up for an American history class. After laboring over a 17 x 17 for weeks upon weeks, Anne decided to send it to Mrs. Farrar for one of her S & S puzzle books. The rejection was accompanied by counsel for improvement. Anne followed the advice and resubmitted the crossword. Lo and behold, it appeared on the first page of the next S & S book! From then on, Anne was hooked.

As in many other cases, it was a parent who introduced this constructor to the crossword puzzle hobby. When Anne was growing up in Tuxedo, New York, her father encouraged her to help him solve the *Herald Tribune* puzzles. The experience apparently helped her; at the tender age of sixteen she became the salutatorian for her high school graduating class and went on to Cornell, where she majored in English (of course!) and minored in French.

When Anne was a junior in college, her sorority roommate persuaded her to go on a blind date. For the sake of her friend, Anne reluctantly agreed to complete the foursome. The event turned out to be love at first sight followed by happily ever after. Anne now lives in north Jersey with her husband, Charlie, who recently retired from a position as sales executive in the textile business.

Asked to choose her best effort, Anne selected "Free Thinking," a special 27 x 27 puzzle which appeared in the bicentennial edition of the *Times* Sunday *Magazine*. The success of that mammoth crossword led to another tradition: Since then the name Fox has appeared every year atop the Sunday Times puzzles published on or about Independence Day.

But Anne's expertise goes beyond seasonal beauties. As just one example of her versatility, "Fructification" should be cited. This puzzle, which appeared in Series #128 of the *Simon and Schuster Crossword Puzzle Book,* revealed her ingenuity in other areas. Here are some of the clues and answers:

Music by N. V. H. Alkin	THE WIND IN THE CHERRY TREE
Women's diet, à la Ogden Nash	NUT SUNDAES AND CANTALOUPE
Disney movie of 1945	THE APPLE DUMPLING GANG
1964 song	THE ORANGE BLOSSOM SPECIAL
Salinger story (with 'A')	PERFECT DAY FOR BANANA FISH

All in all, fans and editors agree that Anne is a peach who never becomes too foxy.

FRANCES HANSEN

The "Idea Fairy" leaves themes for puzzles under her pillow. She shakes the notion around until it splits up into key phrases. Then, like Mary Poppins, she rises to the occasion — and each ascension brings a new treat for her legions of fans. One week it may be a "Looking Glass" opus featuring YKCOWREBBAJ; later it is "Vacancies," presenting blank squares that are signaled by "blank" in the clue. Thus, a pop song of 1933 comes out as UNDER A   ET OF BLUE.

Sometimes the elf prompts her to recall her days as a light-verse writer for *Good Housekeeping* and *Cosmopolitan,* rhyming *baybe* with *maybe.* True to her past, she often embodies original limericks in the puzzles. Here's an example:

> A defiant old maid (pray forgive her)
> Remarked with a bit of a quiver
> "Tonight I shall smoke
> And drink 'til I choke
> And nuts to my lungs and my liver."

The Hansen pillow hides so many new slants that solvers never know what to expect next. Consider "Answering Service" (*Times:* October 24, 1982), for instance:

Clue	Answer
Chaste?	YES, BUT I RAN FASTER
Weight?	NO, I'M IN A RUSH
So?	I STITCH A BIT

Is the real Franny Hansen just as lively as her puzzles? The answer is "Si! Si!"! Born in Arlington, New Jersey, she was the first Yankee in her family (hence, her ingenuity?), but she still retains all the attributes of a Southern belle. As a little girl, with four older brothers, she was introduced to parties, dances and frilly dresses. Her clan was the most popular in town because they always found a reason to celebrate something.

On the serious side, she was educated by nuns and a grandmother who owned an extensive library. To this day, reading is Franny's favorite leisure-time activity.

Franny took up golf in her adolescent years. A bank teller admired her form when she was sixteen and gave her three years "to grow up" before he came a-courting. Daddy didn't approve, because Ernest Hansen was ten years older than his sweetheart. So Franny used her wits. Ernie was a good golfer; so was Daddy. Let them play together. But poor Ernie was so nervous that he sliced ball after ball into the woods. It looked as if the best-laid scheme had gang aft a-gley. Not to worry. Daddy understood a swain's pains and gave his blessing. Incidentally, Ernie subsequently became chairman of the board at a bank in New Jersey. The pair produced two boys, and recently our heroine announced that she had become "Granny Franny."

Among Franny's other activities is a stint as a Sunday school teacher. Her last year in that role was spent in the large bathroom of an old rectory because the dilapidated parish house was being torn down. Her seat at the head of the class was you-know-what, which she discreetly covered with velvet drapery. On her head, she wore a plastic hood to offset the leak dripping from above.

When Franny was a child, nobody in her family tackled crosswords, but the game called "Ghost" enhanced her interest in words. It was only natural that she should take up solving as she grew older. Her debut as a constructor came in 1964. Since then, she has created over 200 other beauties.

A Hansen rebus puzzle almost got this writer into a peck of trouble at the *Times,* through no fault of hers or mine. One of the first Sunday crosswords that I published after succeeding Will Weng as editor was Franny's "Scrambling Around"—an Easter opus in which fans were required to draw an egg whenever the letters E-G-G appeared in succession. Well, it seems that one of the members of the Sulzberger family tried to solve that puzzle and didn't realize it was the rebus type. She called her brother, the owner of the *Times,* and informed him that the new editor had made some horrible mistakes. For example, "Skater Fleming" was one of the clues but the answer called for a three-letter word. How could PEGGY fit into three boxes?

Mr. Sulzberger was stunned. Unfamiliar with crossword puzzles, he called the managing editor. He, too, was flabbergasted. Since he didn't know the perpetrator's address or phone number, he telephoned the editor of the Sunday *Magazine.* That official had a brainstorm—he called my assistant, Harriett Wilson. She explained the rebus idea. A sigh of relief was heard at the other end. The message was then relayed back to the owner's sister and all parties spent a happy Sunday in the realization that Maleska was not really some kind of nut.

The next day the *Magazine* editor summoned me to his office and copied down my phone number. Before I left he said, "Gene, we make occasional mistakes at the *Times* and some of them are really awful. But let's never allow a horrendous boo-boo to creep into the crossword puzzle." I promised him I'd give it my best shot. But since then I must admit I've occasionally had egg on my face.

BERT KRUSE

Iowa's one-and-only gift to superb puzzlemaking has never spent twenty-four hours on a farm and knows less about corn than the average Yankee. This Hawkeye is a Yale graduate (1933) with a B.A. degree. Predictably, his major was English.

Bert's father, in contrast, never even got to high school; but he was a self-educated, bilingual man with an omnivorous appetite for books and a wide-ranging mind. Bert and his three older siblings called their sire the "Encyclopedia" and were greatly influenced by him and their loving mother. Both parents managed to send all four children to college.

The young Kruses lost their beloved father in the 1930s, but he left them a rich heritage, including a newspaper. He had been the founder, editor and publisher of the *Cedar Valley Daily Times* in Vinton — the town where Bert grew up.

After following in his father's footsteps for many decades, Bert recently retired and now enjoys golfing, fishing, table tennis, chess, reading and inveighing against editors. But, of course, puzzling is ranked high on his list of activities.

Bert credits his wife for stimulating his interest in crosswords. She bought Margaret Farrar's S & S puzzle books and enticed Bert into helping her solve difficult corners whenever they took extensive trips. As their children reached adolescence, they caught the fever, too. The daughter, by the way, is an A.C.L.U. executive in the South and the son is a top San Francisco photographer. Recently he gave Bert a T-shirt emblazoned with one of the early Kruse puzzles published in the *Times*. Bert wore it when he was invited to give a talk on puzzlemaking. The Iowa natives, he says, were not impressed.

In the early 1970s Bert decided to take the giant step from solver to constructor. After all, he had the essential attributes. Aside from being an apt solver, he had demonstrated creativity in other verbal endeavors. Consider the following:

- □ humor columnist for the *Hartford Courant*
- □ correspondent for the *Army Times* from Tokyo
- □ editor of a General Motors house organ
- □ editor and publisher of an Iowa farm paper for seventeen years
- □ versifier for the *Wall Street Journal* and sports magazines.

As a constructor, Bert has introduced many new themes. He was probably the first to conceive of such outrageous but appropriate collectives as PRIDE OF SNOBS and NEST OF EGGHEADS. His unconventional mind has also produced "Conventional Places" (*Times,* July 15, 1979), featuring possible locales for organizations to meet. Some examples are:

Credit Managers Ass'n. site	BILLINGS, MONT.
Distillers of America site	RYE, NEW YORK
American Press Ass'n. site	NEWPORT NEWS, VA.

Krusian creativity has often been imitated in puzzles on "Inflation" (TEN AND TWENTY CENT STORE, TWO DOLLAR A YEAR MAN) or "Deflation" (NICKEL A DOZEN, THOUSAND DOLLAR BABY). One of Bert's best innovations involved malapropisms that playwright Sheridan hadn't thought of: PARTIAL POST (for "parcel post"), APOCALYPSE (for "Acropolis"), PROSPERITY (for "posterity").

Bert's most challenging *Times* puzzle is reprinted in the next chapter. In it he carries to the nth degree his penchant for word association.

WILLIAM LUTWINIAK

Some constructors are prolific; others are terrific. Both adjectives apply to Bill Lutwiniak. He has created more than 5,000 puzzles, and not one of them is a clinker. What's more amazing is that he waited until 1965 before taking up the craft seriously. Prior to that, in 1934, when he was fifteen years old, Bill had published several puzzles in the *New York Herald Tribune*.*

There were several reasons for the hiatus. After graduating from a Jersey City high school at the age of sixteen, Bill joined the work force to help support a large family during the Depression. Then in 1941 his lifelong interest in puzzle solving paid off. He was invited to join the Signal Intelligence Service. He started as a clerk, progressed to cryptanalyst and was a senior cryptologist when he retired in 1982. Was he involved in breaking down the Axis codes during the war? Bill's answer is that N.S.A. means "Never say anything."

The steps that led Bill to his hush-hush post in Washington, D.C., are fascinating. As a youthful devourer of mystery stories, he loved to read *Detective Fiction Weekly*. That magazine sponsored a solving contest, which Bill won. The prize was a subscription to the American Cryptogram Association's publication, *The Cryptogram*. Bill became a top-notch solver of the ciphers in that periodical. Then the S.I.S. offered the elite among the solvers a chance to take a correspondence course in Military Cryptography and Cryptanalysis. Our hero jumped at the chance, impressed the brass and landed a job that admirably suited his talents.

What lured Bill back to constructing crosswords was the Farrar-fostered revolution that had taken place between the 1930s and '60s. The use of phrases, themes, puns and other wordplay excited his interest. Ironically enough, however, one of his prime pleasures as a constructor today is to build a themeless puzzle around a word like RAZZMA-TAZZ and try to insert as many Q's, X's, J's, etc., as possible. Simultaneously he strives to make the crossings easy, because he feels that most American solvers don't really like a difficult challenge and eschew the use of reference books. With that in mind, Bill is not above whipping up an easy 15 x 15 in less than twenty minutes.

But when Bill aims a puzzle at the experienced upper crust among the fans, he often goes all out. Among his many innovations are "Do It Yourself," which is reprinted in

---

*One of those *Tribune* puzzles prophetically featured CRYPTOGRAPHICAL across the center.

the chapter after this one, and "Spot Announcements." Two typical clues for the latter were "AVI" and "NE"—respectively requiring solvers to fill in CENTER OF GRAVITY and END OF THE LINE. In a puzzle called "Reading Letters" he refined the idea. "CCCCCCC" was the clue for SEVEN SEAS, and "Y" turned into FOURTH OF JULY. Incidentally, it was natural for a cryptanalyst to invent such themes, and it was inevitable that many other constructors flattered him via imitation.

Behind the scenes is another bright Lutwiniak named Jeanne. She gives her husband ideas for puzzles, helps with clues, proofs his work, test-solves and saves him from many a gaffe. The couple has one child, Trina, a draftsperson living in Colorado.

As a retired sexagenarian, Bill continues to pursue several hobbies—including horticulture, reading and bowling. Like many other top constructors, he prefers to solve Cryptics. But in his opinion, the British-style puzzle will never become more popular in the U.S.A. than the American crossword.

ALFIO MICCI

Crossword puzzle editors receive continual surprises. Out of nowhere comes a super-craftsman who can weave words into wonderful tapestries. It may be a professor, a physician, a homemaker or even a convict. But who would expect a violinist from the New York Philharmonic Orchestra?

After thirty seasons, Alfio Micci has recently left Zubin Mehta and his other colleagues and is spending some well-earned years in retirement. But he was doing some fine fiddling when he submitted his first puzzle to Margaret Farrar. She found it inadequate but recognized his talent and encouraged him to try again. Alfio persisted and soon caught on to the rules and techniques. He sent five puzzles to Will Weng, who had just succeeded Mrs. Farrar, and hit the jackpot. Three were accepted!

Quite suitably, editor Weng chose a musical puzzle for Alfio's debut in 1970. It featured puns on composers' names, such as HANDEL WITH CARE, BRAHMS BURSTING IN AIR, HAYDEN GO SEEK and BIZET SIGNAL. Since then, Alfio has turned to other harmonic inspirations for his themes; however, it is hard to pin down the Micci style. While publishing over 200 puzzles he has moved around restlessly from one topic to another. His rebus puzzles have featured ¢ signs for words containing "cent" or 4 in place of words containing "for." His "Atticisms," on the other hand, converted English letters into Greek ones. Thus "bb gun" became BETA BETA GUN and "lp records" was transformed into LAMBDA PI RECORDS. Whatever the theme might be, solvers salute the ingenuity and fairness of a typical Micci opus.

Alfio now lives in northern New Jersey with his wife, Martha. She is a musician herself; in 1982 she composed musical settings for a dramatization of poems by their erstwhile family physician, William Carlos Williams. The Miccis had met at the Eastman School of Music in Rochester, where Alfio was enjoying a four-year scholarship. Their union has produced three children and two grandsons.

Born in Chicago Heights, Alfio spent his infancy in Italy. When he returned to America, he knew not one word of English. His parents loved music, especially opera, but were not musicians. Alfio was introduced to the violin at the age of ten, and that meeting developed into his first love affair.

But one of his other passions was literature. Under the influence of O'Neill, he wrote long, depressing plays and fancied himself as a budding dramatist until his English professor threw cold water on that ambition and told him to stick to the violin.

During World War II, Alfio auditioned for the U.S. Navy Band and was accepted as a touring violin soloist. When the war ended he spent two seasons with the Metropolitan Opera before joining the Philharmonic.

Today, besides turning out top puzzles, Alfio composes jingles for commercials and records sound tracks for films. Obviously, the Micci bow has many scintillating strings!

MARY VIRGINIA ORNA

Place an O.S.U. after that name. Sister Mary Virginia belongs to the Order of St. Ursula and is a professor of chemistry at the College of New Rochelle, New York. She started solving puzzles in the 1950s when she was a high school student in New Jersey. After a time she became bored by the easy puzzles in the local newspapers and turned to the ones marked "hard" in the crossword magazines. Later, in college, where she had become a Sunday *Times* puzzle fan, she wrote an article called "The C.P. Addict" for the literary magazine.

When Mary Virginia entered the convent, puzzles dropped out of her life for many years. Then a family tragedy brought her back to the hobby. Her mother had fallen into a coma as the aftermath of a stroke. During the long hours of filial vigil, some distraction was needed to prevent nail-biting. Hence, the crosswords were turned to again; but experience and maturity led to a craving for a different challenge — creating puzzles.

The new constructor was not immediately successful, but her early efforts were so promising and so un-convent-ional that sharp-eyed editors saw good reasons to help her along. She proved to be an apt pupil, and in the late 1970s three of her 15s hit the jackpot. Then in September 1979 she made her debut in the Sunday *Times* with "What's Whose?" The puzzle featured such clues and entries as:

Wonderland tearoom?	ALICE'S RESTAURANT
Where George got free drinks?	MARTHA'S VINEYARD
What Mark got stuck with?	CLEOPATRA'S NEEDLE

In the few years since that initial success, Sister Mary Virginia has published several other Sunday *Times* puzzles and about 100 in other publications. She often gets her ideas from daily experiences. For example, her superior at the convent decided to "kick the habit." This step entailed a new hairdo. An Irish nun with skills in that area was called upon for aid. She proved so adept that her superior dubbed her "my Irish setter." Zowie! That single pun caused a series of geographical jokes to pop into our constructor's head and eventuated in the publication of "What in the World" (*Times,* July 20, 1980). IRISH SETTER occupied the center of the diagram and was defined as "Belfast beautician."

A recent retreat in Italy has stimulated Sister Mary Virginia to take up the solving of foreign language puzzles. And while in Rome, she participated in a magazine contest requiring readers to construct a puzzle around the theme "Fumetti" (comic strips). She used American comics and won a prize — a game called "Parole Incrociati" which is similar to Scrabble. "Incidentally," she reports, "the Italian language does not lend itself to crosswords, since almost every word ends in a vowel."

With such proficiency in language, it was only natural for Sister Mary Virginia to come up with "Latin Rhythms" (*Times,* August 8, 1982). In that puzzle, fans were asked to substitute English words derived from Latin for the original words in song titles. Some of the entries were DANCING IN THE TENEBROSITY, YOU'LL NEVER AMBULATE ALONE and I'VE GOT YOU SUBCUTANEOUSLY.

A typical Orna puzzle is carefully researched, meticulously prepared and cleverly wrought — including the title. Usually it requires solvers to put on their thinking caps. Nor does her vocation inhibit this intrepid constructor. Recently in need of a six-letter word beginning with HEF, she blithely inserted HEFNER.

If you have an old road map that you can't use, send it along to Sister Mary Virginia. She collects them.

TAP OSBORN

Versatility is one of Tap Osborn's many fortes. Since 1972, when he successfully submitted nine crosswords to the *Times,* Tap has created about 600 puzzles — many of which reveal his penchant for variety. He has produced excellent Cryptics and diagramless puzzles and quotation crosswords of every sort.

Tap is noted for building a puzzle around one of his original four-line verses. He also enjoys telling a story via sequential horizontal entries that are titles of novels, dramas, songs or movies. An example of this invention of his appeared in June 1982. The *Times* puzzle, entitled "A Father's Day," had the following clues and answers for the main entries:

6:15 A.M.	THE SUN ALSO RISES
7:30 A.M.	CLOSELY OBSERVED TRAINS
8:45 A.M.	THE ASPHALT JUNGLE
9 A.M.	SWEET SMELL OF SUCCESS
9 A.M. to 5 P.M.	THE MIRACLE WORKER
7:15 P.M.	THE MAN WHO CAME TO DINNER
11 P.M. to 6 A.M.	HOLD BACK THE DAWN

Tap knows from experience what it's like to be a father; he has five grown-up children. Like the character in the above puzzle, he commutes daily to Reed & Barton Silversmiths in Taunton, Massachusetts. There he occupies the eminent post of vice president.

Ab ovo, Tap has known excitement. His mother lost a battle with time on her way back from a visit to his father, who was a rubber company executive in Singapore. She gave birth to Tap in France; hence, he became a traveler during his first fortnight on earth, and he's been zooming around the globe ever since. For instance, the army trained him in Chinese at Harvard during World War II and then sent him to India.

After the war, Tap finished his education as an English major at Amherst College. While there, he roomed with Tad Mosel, who later became a Pulitzer Prize playwright. Tap's "dramatic" puzzles indicate that perhaps he and Mosel should have teamed up. At any rate, he has the perfect name for a writer: Stafford P. Osborn.

A prolonged bout with illness caused Tap to take up the mantle of a constructor. When not puzzling people or selling Paul Revere bowls,* he can be found romping on a tennis court or bidding a slam in a duplicate bridge match.

Among his own crosswords, Tap's favorite is "A Gaggle of Groups," published about four years ago in the *Times.* It contained such double entendres as A BRACE OF DENTISTS and A PECK OF TYPSISTS. Most important, he managed to include twelve thematic entries—a feat seldom recorded in the annals of Puzzledom.

Two years ago, without consultation with Tap or this editor, the *Times* used an Osborn puzzle as the basis for a shower curtain. More recently, another of his puzzles has appeared on a *Times* T-shirt. Some entrepreneur at the newspaper must be among the legions of Tap Osborn aficionados!

VINCENT OSBORNE

Tap Osborn and Vincent Osborne have at least one thing in common besides the similarity of their names. Both rose to the top of the puzzle world very swiftly during the

---

*PAUL REVERE BOWLS was an entry in one of the first Osborn 15 x 15s.

1970s. But in many ways they are far different. Whereas Tap is a free spirit who rushes restlessly from one puzzle to another, Vincent is a careful researcher who takes his time and polishes each creation before submitting it. To the delight of editors, he documents almost every definition.

One would expect painstaking work from Vincent. He's a systems engineer for Bell Laboratories in New Jersey, where he and his wife, Deborah, reside. Now in his late thirties, Vincent once spent eight years preparing for the priesthood. Upon graduation from a seminary, he had a change of heart and enrolled in a trade school that specialized in training students for computer programming.

Vincent credits those years as a seminarian for reinforcing his ability to work out intellectual problems in solitude — an important asset for any constructor. But his fondness for meditation dates back to his boyhood days in Kentucky. As a seventh-grader he began solving crosswords in emulation of his mother, and he turned to puzzlemaking as a private hobby while in high school. But almost two decades passed before he summoned up the nerve to turn pro.

The immediacy of the Osborne success was topped by an amazing coup. In 1980 a PBS executive called the *Times* and asked for the names of four excellent constructors who would rotate as contributors of puzzles to *Dial* magazine. Subsequently, the *Dial* editor liked Vincent's puzzle so much that she gave him an exclusive contract.

In contrast to experienced pros like Herb Ettenson, who can whip up a 21 x 21 puzzle in four or five hours, Vincent takes about eighteen hours to complete one. "For me," he says, "the entire construction process is a matter of compromise — constantly striving for perfection, always settling for less."

Vincent specializes in "straight" themes and inner-clue crosswords, but he can compete with the best of his colleagues in punny puzzlemaking. His "Animal Cracks" (*Times,* November 7, 1982) featured clues and entries such as the following:

Sketch an African king?	DRAW THE LION
Refuge for wildebeests?	GNU HAVEN
Musts for Smokey?	BEAR ESSENTIALS

But even in a no-nonsense Osborne opus careful attention is paid to the definitions to make them unusual. Some examples are

Cannon in a movie	DYAN
It can shoot or stab	PAIN
A modern Aristotle	ONASSIS

Vincent's ambition is to form a crossword puzzle syndicate of his own, and he predicts that it will be a long, long time before computers can produce puzzles involving wordplay and other forms of human creativity. Colleagues predict that the Osborne star will continue to twinkle for many years to come—syndicate or not.

BERT ROSENFIELD

Upstate New York has contributed several superior puzzlers to the crossword puzzle world, and Bert Rosenfield ranks high among them. Formerly a purchaser for a general supply company in Albany, this bachelor, World War II vet and onetime Rensselaer student retired in 1980 to pursue with fervor the puzzlemaking avocation that he had taken up six years previously.

Bert's first crossword was published by Will Weng in 1976 in the Sunday *Times*. It had a Valentine theme, and since then its creator has won the hearts of legions of fans. His "Shakespeare on Sports" opus, which appeared in the *Times* on an anniversary of the Bard's birthday (April 23, 1978), is recognized as a classic by colleagues and fans alike. Here are the eight thematic entries in that fantastic puzzle:

1. GENTLE PUCK, COME HITHER
2. MERCY ON US! WE SPLIT
3. LET HIM NOT PASS
4. GIVE ME THE IRON
5. YOU DID BID ME STEAL
6. HEAR THE SHRILL WHISTLE
7. O MONSTROUS FAULT
8. LET ME CLUTCH THEE

The clues for each of the above were respectively:

1. w.s. on hockey (*A Midsummer Night's Dream,* II, 1)
2. w.s. on bowling (*The Tempest,* I, 1)
3. w.s. on football (*Othello,* V, 2)
4. w.s. on golf (*King John,* IV, 1)
5. w.s. on baseball (*Othello,* III, 3)
6. w.s. on basketball (*Henry V,* III, Prologue)
7. w.s. on tennis (3 *Henry VI,* III, 2)
8. w.s. on auto racing (*Macbeth,* II, 1)

Aside from the many hours of research required after the inspiration for the puzzle had struck, the wonder is that Bert could manage to fit in his octet without repeating a sport or resorting to impossible crossings.

But Bert was just the right person for that puzzle. He has been a sports buff since boyhood. Baseball is his favorite. "I like the game," he says, "because the officials don't run around waving arms and blowing whistles, and because it ends when it's supposed to — not when somebody fires a pistol." Incidentally, Bert was delighted when slugger George Foster joined the Mets; now he had a new clue for SHEA — "Foster home."

Like most other constructors, Bert was a conqueror of those spelling demons in school. Orthography still fascinates him. Recently, when he visited the Big Apple, a sign in the window of a midtown restaurant stopped him in his tracks. It read: "Today's Special — Philly Mignon." Bert wondered if the announcement was a secret message to Mets fans eager to devour Pete Rose's team.

Reading is Bert's other hobby. His favorite author is the late S. J. Perelman, whom he has memorialized in at least one puzzle. In response to fans' kudos concerning his Shakespearean classic, he published "Biblical Baseball" (*Times,* May 17, 1981) with similar results. The quotations from the Bible sounded like the story of an actual game. For example:

> WE SAW THE GIANTS
> ABSALOM PITCHED
> SAMSON WENT AND CAUGHT
> TEN HOMERS

But Bert's creative mind leaps with sprightly ingenuity from one unusual theme to another. In "Literal Translations" (*Times,* August 2, 1981) he pleased pun-loving fans with such entries as AUSTRALIAN CRAWL and CHINESE CHECKERS, defined respectively as "Perth traffic jam" and "Swatow supermarket workers." And recently he entertained the bird lovers: "Cardinal" was the clue for FUNDAMENTAL; the definition for MASTER OF SATIRE was "Swift." Altogether, fourteen of our feathered friends appeared in a 21 x 21 puzzle — a remarkable feat, but one to be expected from Bert. Too bad he waited until retirement to take up the CWP-making craft. Think of all the fine puzzles the world has missed!

JOHN M. SAMSON

In this age of specialization there are very few Renaissance men, but John McCarthy Samson deserves that classification. He is an accomplished playwright, a poet and a composer. Above all, he produces breathtaking paintings. One of his murals decorates a church in his hometown in upstate New York.

Now in his thirties and recently married, John is one of the newest and most talented of the CWP elite. With his friend David Pohl he made his *Times* debut in March 1979. The puzzle, "Expansion Teams," revealed vivid imagination, careful preparation and a lively sense of humor. Later that year the two produced "Electricks," an exciting opus with lots of spark. To this editor, it looked as if another Ettenson-Arensberg had lit up the puzzle world.

Tragedy struck when David Pohl died in a boating accident. John went into mourning for a while, but to the delight of fans, he finally took up the gauntlet on his own. One topnotch *Times* puzzle after another followed. "Human Nature" is an example. John took an old theme—usually called "Body English"—and restricted it to combinations with words pertaining to geography and the elements. Thus, the title was perfect. Some of the ten thematic entries were FINGER LAKES, ARM OF THE SEA, FOOTHILLS, HEADWATERS and TEETH OF THE WIND.

But the tongue-in-cheek type of puzzle is probably John's greatest forte. In "Typecasting" his creative brain dreamed up some appropriate vehicles for celebrities. Billy Graham starred in "Ain't Misbehavin'" and Zsa Zsa Gabor played a leading role in "A Man for All Seasons." Naturally, Bob Hope became the hero of the film "Great Expectations" and Wilt Chamberlain was signed up for "Walking Tall."

Editors welcome a Samson puzzle, because he researches every entry and documents each definition. Moreover, his clues do not come straight from the dictionary. The same linguistic power that goes into his plays and poems shows up in definitions like "They loop The Loop" for ELS and "holding the bag at Shea" for ON BASE.

Asked if he had any interesting anecdote to relate, John replied:

> A few years ago I was hired to construct a 15 x 15 puzzle for a rock group named "BLOTTO," from Albany, N.Y. Luckily I was able to include all the members of the sextet—Broadway Blotto, Sergeant Blotto, Lee Harvey Blotto, Chevrolet Blotto, Bowtie Blotto and Cheese Blotto.
>
> I sent the completed puzzle off to them and about six weeks later received their new album hot off the press. What a surprise! My diagram completely took up the front cover of the album and the clues consumed most of the back cover. But the biggest surprise came when I learned that the solution to the puzzle was sung by the group on one of the records in the album. What's more, I had been given a by-line: "Crossword Puzzle: Samson Blotto." At the very bottom of the album I discovered who was responsible: "BLOTTO RECORDS, A DIVISION OF BLOTTO INDUSTRIES, A MULTI-ACQUISITIONAL CONGLOMERATE."
>
> I had just been acquired.

Well, John, keep in mind that *acquired* rhymes with *inspired*—our word for you.

A. J. SANTORA

If there were a Hall of Fame for puzzlemakers, A. J. Santora's name would be prominently inscribed. For more than thirty years he has been entertaining crossword puzzle devotees with scintillating creations of every sort. His roving mind concocts themes that are new and daring; at other times this master puts his personal touch on a hackneyed theme and gives it new life.

To an editor, a Santora contribution is like a perfect Christmas gift. The wrapping pleases the eye, and what's inside is always a delight to receive—either something wonderfully practical or a lovely bauble that will certainly glitter on a puzzle page.

A typical crossword by A.J. usually has the following features:

1. Amazing number of thematic entries
2. Wide-open pattern
3. Paucity of esoterica
4. Sprinkling of sparkling clues.

Additionally, A.J. has pioneered in finding ways to define small entries. He was among the first to use "___ even keel" for ONAN and "Keep ___ (persevere)" for ATIT. He's an avid reader who once read three books each week as a teenager, and his sharp eye constantly catches new words that crop up in periodicals. For example, should a MIRV appear in an article on missiles, one can be sure that it will find its place in a Santora opus.

When this writer recently asked a group of top constructors to select the puzzle that they most admire, A.J.'s "Locus-Pocus" (*Times,* 1977) was constantly mentioned. What astonished his colleagues was A.J.'s ability to juxtapose pairs of phrases and words. For instance, OVER A BARREL was entered at 25-Across and defined as "where most of this is." Sure enough, BARREL appeared beneath the phrase! Similarly at 70-Down "where most of this is" became BESIDE ONESELF, and to the right of the entry the word ONESELF was duly ensconced. The feat was carried out seven times in a 23 x 23 puzzle.

Another remarkable accomplishment by A.J. appeared in Series 15 of *Simon and Schuster's Crossword Book of Quotations*. The following statement by Herbert Hoover was horizontally embodied in a 23 x 23 puzzle along with that U.S. President's full name: "Once upon a time my political opponents honored me as possessing the fabulous intellectual and economic power by which I created a world-wide depression all by myself."

That quotation, plus the complete name of the author, added up to 152 letters, or more than 35 percent of the horizontal spaces. The average in a puzzle of that sort is less than 20 percent. Obviously A.J. is not happy with a happy medium.

A.J. is unusual among CWP constructors. He did not succumb to the crossword fever until he was newly married. His bride, Rose, was a fan who kept seeking his help in tackling difficult areas of a Sunday *Times* puzzle. After a while such forays as a solver served to whet his appetite for a taste of crossword creation.

He succeeded immediately back in Margaret Farrar's day. Incidentally, one of his humorous puzzles in the 1950s featured the names of eighteen of the leading puzzle constructors of that era. Some of the entries were:

Getting the better of a puzzler?	OUTFOXING (Anne Fox)
Best-built for Jeans?	REEDIEST (Jean Reed)
Puzzler's jazzy concerts?	JAM SESSIONS (Diana Sessions)
Puzzler's agility?	SPRYNESS (Jan Spry)
Puzzler on ice?	MALE SKATER (Sam Lake)
Puzzler with a Hart?	MOSS (Arnold Moss)

Sports fascinate A.J. As a Bay Stater living near Boston, he roots for the Red Sox, Celtics, Bruins and Patriots. Unlike most other constructors, he eagerly follows the progress of his CWP colleagues and solves several puzzles each week.

The Santoras have five children and two grandchildren, thus far. What does A.J. do for a living? Again he is sui generis. With one of his brothers, he owns a construction company. It is reasonable to assume that the edifices he erects are as carefully put together as the puzzles he constructs.

ELAINE D. SCHORR

In the 1970s many talented newcomers rose to prominence in puzzlemaking—largely under the guidance of Will Weng. Not the least of them was Elaine D. Schorr, a retired schoolteacher from Great Neck, New York.

Recently Elaine migrated to sunny San Diego, where she has engaged in horticultural pursuits and needlework and is taking courses for senior citizens at the state university in her new home town.

Elaine has been solving puzzles for most of her adult life. Her first efforts at construction were strictly for her students. She enriched her language-arts program by providing her own crosswords for the youngsters to solve. Finally, she summoned up the nerve to create a puzzle for the *Times*. It was returned with a number of suggestions for improvement, but her second attempt met with success.

To an extent, the Schorr style resembles that of Frances Hansen. Themes are unusual, titles are right on the mark and a tongue-in-cheek quality pervades the puzzle. For example, in "Whodunit?" (*Times,* May 20, 1979) two of the clues were "Diller's surgeon did it" and "Chanticleer did it." The answers, respectively, were SAVED FACE and FLEW THE COOP.

In "Impish Inferences" (*Times,* September 13, 1981) people in various occupations were transmogrified. Waiters became SERVICEMEN, conductors were called SCORE-KEEPERS, etc.

Elaine has published about 500 puzzles. Her personal favorite is "Playmates" (*Times,* May 21, 1978), which required lots of research and ingenuity. Each main entry was a Broadway play and was matched by another play in the clue. For example, KISS THE BOYS GOODBYE was defined "A Farewell to Arms."

Elaine strives for offbeat definitions and often comes up with original sparklers such as the following:

Nape drape	SCARF
Turkey tot	POULT
Hang-up of a sort	TAPESTRY
Slow flow	OOZE
Alabama abodes	MOBILE HOMES

One of Elaine's biggest thrills came a few years ago when she was asked by the University of California to conduct a session for would-be constructors. After her presentation, she Xeroxed a 15 x 15 simple pattern, entered the long words and asked the members of the group to try to fill in the crossing words. What fascinated her most was the fact that some caught on immediately while others floundered around in a tangle of non-words. At any rate, we are certain that her demonstration added more devotees to the Schorr Patrol.

RICHARD SILVESTRI

Rich is his nickname, and at least two of the synonyms for the related adjective apply — "fruitful" and "abounding in humor." The Silvestri name is probably less known to solvers than the other big names simply because he is the newest of the newcomers. His first puzzle appeared in the *Times* on January 12, 1978.

But it's a good bet that this bachelor's star will grow brighter and brighter for years to come despite the fact that his credentials don't seem to signify ability as a puzzle-maker. English was his worst subject in school, albeit he was an excellent speller.

After graduating from Colgate, Rich earned a Ph.D. at Adelphi and taught there for a while. Today he is a professor of mathematics (of all subjects!) at Nassau Community College in Garden City, New York.

Rich admits that CWP's helped him to get his first teaching job. As luck would have it, the chairman of the math department was an avid solver, and on the Sunday that he was leafing through a huge stack of applications, a Silvestri puzzle appeared in the *Times*. The chairman liked the opus, pulled out Rich's résumé, called him for an interview and hired him.

Rich adds that in his most recent interview at Nassau the committee asked more questions on the puzzlemaking craft than on the art of teaching calculus.

In his undergraduate years at Colgate, Rich joined a group who sat in the dorm lounge each Sunday and tackled the *Times* puzzle while waiting for the dinner bell. Then in graduate school at Adelphi he discovered Cryptics, loved them and soon took a stab at creating them.

Such an unusual start as a constructor probably accounts for Rich's facility in wordplay—an important feature of Cryptics. A good example is his "Polyglot" (*Times,* July 27, 1980), in which his clues seemed to be simple English words, but were actually foreign. Thus the definition "pane" became BREAD IN ITALY and "court" translated into FRENCH FOR SHORT.

Extensive research was obviously required for the "Polyglot" puzzle. It also gave the fans' intellects a workout. One forty-year devotee from Massachusetts wrote, "It was the most puzzling, exasperating, infuriating, exciting, exhilarating and rewarding puzzle I have ever done!"

The same painstaking preparation was needed for "Ess-capades" (*Times,* February 6, 1982), wherein Rich played on famous surnames beginning with S. Some clues and entries were:

Novelist's style?	IRVING'S TONE
Violinist's bird?	ISAAC'S TERN
Actress's sense of humor?	LORETTA'S WIT

What pleases this editor about a typical Silvestri creation is that it contains a minimum of esoterica and crosswordese. Probably that is why Rich's puzzles elicit lots of plaudits from solvers and no complaints.

□

A recent poll of the topnotch constructors revealed the following similarities.

1. In this age of thematic crosswords, each master craftsman begins by dreaming up an idea for a puzzle. Then cogitation and research result in a list of words and phrases, which are listed by size on scrap paper. At this point some constructors copy a published diagram, but most create their own pattern in keeping with the list. Thus, if they have collected a large number of 13- and 14-letter words, they will plot a diagram that suits those lengths. They then fill in the thematic entries, while simultaneously making sure that they haven't given themselves tough problems in the little crossing words—such as a *five*-letter word ending in J. As they proceed from there, they alter or

augment the black squares whenever necessary. In doing so, they remind themselves that a change made at the top of the puzzle entails another at the bottom, because the diagram must always be symmetrical. Finally, it should be noted that some constructors work on the bottom right corner first because it involves crossing the endings of words. It is always harder to think of a *six*-letter word ending in PO than one beginning with PO.

2. All the constructors were avid readers in childhood and still are.

3. With one exception, all were excellent spellers in school. Several were champions in spelling bees.

4. In many cases, their interest in puzzles was stimulated by a parent or an older sibling.

5. The vast majority still solve puzzles, but at least half express more interest in Cryptics than in traditional American puzzles.

6. Most are college graduates, but at least three of the very best did not go beyond high school.

7. Math was the most difficult subject for most, but there were four or five who excelled in that area.

☐

This chapter would not be complete without some mention of several other prominent crossword puzzle editors of modern times. Probably unique among them is *Eugene Sheffer,* a Columbia University professor who constructed and edited his own puzzles for the King Features Syndicate from 1928 until his recent demise. Sheffer's 13 x 13 puzzles were spurned by dyed-in-the-wool fans because they were too easy, lacked themes and contained two-letter words. But they had a great influence on millions of inexperienced solvers who broke in on his crosswords in hundreds of newspapers throughout America.

The defunct *New York Herald Tribune* also contributed to crossword puzzle fever, led by such editors as *Dorothy Kiggins, Ruth Biemiller* and *Maynard Nicholson.*

Most ubiquitous among the scores of editors of the crossword puzzle magazines that clutter drugstores, supermarkets and other places are *Charles Preston* and *Norman Hill.* The latter has even written a book called *How to Solve Crossword Puzzles.* More recently young *Douglas Heller* has surfaced as editor of umpteen *Penny Press* magazines.

True to its role as a pioneer in crossword puzzle publishing, Simon and Schuster has added a number of puzzle editors to its staff. Among them are *Miriam Raphael,* a CWP contest winner, and *Louis Sabin,* a constructor and erstwhile editor of *Boys' Life.*

But none of the above names can surpass the magnificent duo associated with Dell crossword puzzles. Four decades ago, *Kathleen Rafferty* was appointed to the editorship of a little puzzle magazine sponsored by the top officials of the Delacorte Company in the hope that they could compete with dozens of other publications of that sort.

Mrs. Rafferty had previously edited pulp magazines featuring novellas. She brought to her new post a keen knowledge of the mass market and a set of high standards from which she never deviated. Little by little, fans began to realize that the Dell puzzles were superior to the others on the stands. By 1954 the number of Dell bimonthly puzzle magazines had burgeoned to almost a score each year.

For two decades Mrs. Rafferty worked assiduously on the *Dell Crossword Dictionary*. With the approval of her immediate boss, Helen Meyer, she finally published the book. Somehow, the two were able to slip it through without the approval of owner George Delacorte. His wrath turned to joy and praise when Mrs. Rafferty's labor of love turned out to be a best seller. Over 12 million copies of this revised and updated reference book are in print now.

When Mrs. Rafferty died in 1981, the criteria for excellence that she had established were maintained by her successor, *Rosalind Moore*. An N.Y.U. graduate and a former partner in a literary agency, Mrs. Moore became assistant editor at Dell in 1954. Five years later she was moved up to the post of associate editor. Gradually she assumed more and more responsibility for the puzzle magazines while Mrs. Rafferty continued her work on the dictionary. In 1983, after the demise of her predecessor, Mrs. Moore presided over a staff of sixteen full-time employees and several free-lancers. During that year her department published a total of ninety-two magazines, paperbacks, Purse Books and other assorted puzzle pieces.

Mrs. Moore has been widowed twice, but her verve has not been quenched by tragedy. When she is not socializing with friends or family in New York or globe-trotting, she takes a busman's holiday—solving crossword puzzles.

7

Challenging Crosswords

On the assumption that most readers of this book are crossword puzzle devotees and mavens who have lost all interest in easy puzzles, this chapter will present some of the most difficult and daring creations ever concocted by constructors. Wide-open patterns and spectacular themes that resulted in a mixture of plaudits and protests from fans will be featured. Also, an attempt will be made to give readers a taste of a variety of themes that have emerged in recent years.

All the puzzles that follow are reprints of crosswords originally published in the *Times* or in Simon and Schuster books.

Let's begin with three unusual 15 x 15s. The first is by George Sphicas, a talented newcomer from New York City. The second was constructed by Vaughn P. M. Keith, a young Marylander who has recently migrated to Virginia, where he teaches Latin and doubles as a gym leader in a private school. Both puzzles are marked by an astonishingly low word count and skill in interlocking the entries without resorting to archaisms, forced expressions or other flaws.

Ernest T. Theimer, a Ph.D. from New Jersey, produced the third puzzle. It was originally published on April 1, 1982. Traditionally since Margaret Farrar's era, the April Fool's Day crossword has been a tricky creation. In one case, all the words were written backwards. A recent one by Frances Hansen repeated her famous "blank" theme. For example, "Reached an impasse" was the clue for RAN INTO A   WALL and was crossed by "party pooper": WET   ET. Solvers were required to leave a *blank* in the box where those five letters appeared in the diagram.

The Theimer puzzle contains an altogether different gimmick. You'll have to solve it to find out the trick.

The answers to the three puzzles appear on page 182.

□

Puzzle #1

ACROSS

1 Be clement
6 Scrape roughly
10 Defeat
14 Beer
15 Slave of old
16 New
17 Fragrance
18 Hebrew lyre
19 Ancient Greek contest
20 Microorganism
21 Art of weaving
22 Obfuscate
23 "No man ___ island"
24 Maxim
26 St.-Tropez season
27 Edam and Romano
29 Nahuatlan people of Mexico
31 British period beginning in
    1660, with "the"
34 Bomb-squad feats
36 Disentanglement
37 Lustrous fabric
38 Part of the throat
42 Drink that sounds helpful
43 ___ Zee, Hudson River
    bridge
46 Aberdeen native
47 Arm bone
49 Medieval coin of Italy
50 Call
51 Flat, circular plate
52 Worshiped image
53 Scope
54 Involved with
55 French department
56 A college at Oxford
57 Jejune
58 Privation
59 Condemn openly

9 Rearrangement
10 Spill the beans
11 V.P. nominee who withdrew
    in July 1972
12 Becomes portly
13 Madagascan mammal
24 Railroad conductor's inquiry
25 Subject of kinetics
28 Covert
30 Most or all
32 Macrogametes, e.g.

33 ___ serpent (fer-de-lance)
34 Reporter's concern
35 Limb muscle
37 Certain Arabs
39 Like a Giotto fresco
40 More protracted
41 Very hard
44 Army chaplain
45 In a position for push-ups
48 Skin problem
50 Cattlemen's gear

DOWN

1 East European language
2 Celtics' all-star center
3 Greek marketplaces
4 Pay for
5 Diocletian and Julian
6 Down-to-earth
7 Part of N.B.A.
8 Proboscis

Puzzle #2

ACROSS

1 Proceeds
4 Author of "The Immigrants"
8 Start of a nursery rhyme
14 Fighting temper
15 Construction item
16 Fictional sleuth ___ Lupin
17 River in China
18 Irresolute
20 Put out
22 Hindu ascetic
23 Difficult age
24 Capone, Jolson et al.
25 Italian wine
29 Antiknocks, e.g.
31 Map addendum
32 Flower receptacles
33 Consecrate
34 Current measures
37 Miami's hiemal boast
38 Babe Ruth's first name
39 Native of Shiraz
40 Ingredient of ouzo
41 Containers for colorful
   mixtures
45 Varnish ingredient
46 Police-call letters
47 Author Alex
48 ___ Haute
50 Fruity desserts, for short
51 Islands north of New Guinea
55 Op or Pop
56 "___ emptor"
57 Hindustani
58 Compass dir.
59 Isolate
60 Flay
61 Prefix with pathetic

10 High, as inflationary prices
11 "___ Mir Bist . . ."
12 ___ Arbor
13 Arm of the Medit.
19 Young maiden
21 Meccas for scholars
24 Rosary beads
26 Europe's neighbor
27 Release, as anger
28 Suffix with major or cigar
30 Phrase of understanding
33 Bates or Arkin
34 Laboratory medium
35 Part of the writing on the
   wall

36 Petits ___
37 Bassinet
39 Satellite of Saturn
41 Eng. legislative assembly
42 St. ___ , city NNW of
   London
43 At hand
44 Solar follower
49 Estimate
50 Middle: Prefix
51 King's superior
52 Cupid
53 DIII doubled
54 Annoy

DOWN

1 Khrushchev
2 Expunged
3 Tightened
4 Pentagon V.I.P.
5 Aldrich's "Story of ___
   Boy"
6 Algonquian
7 Toys
8 Pitching error
9 Lorraine Hansberry hit:
   1959

Puzzle #3

ACROSS

1 Pant
5 Charity
9 Plentiful
14 Samoan seaport
15 Appropriated
16 Salt-encrusted depression
17 Wield an ax on an ash
18 French pantomimist
19 Framework
20 How this runs
23 Choir voice
24 "___ Oncle" (vehicle for 18 Across)
25 Finally
28 Neckpiece
30 Enzymes
34 Hammer and tongs
35 Persian rug
37 Part of TNT
38 How this runs
41 Suppositions
42 Former alliance acronym
43 Playing card for a fortuneteller
44 Body pouch
46 Limb
47 Straightedges
48 Spotlight
50 Midwest airport
52 How this runs
59 Slayer of Achilles
60 Type of hairdo
61 About 2.2 lbs.
62 Violin maker
63 Mast
64 Spread
65 Circumscribe
66 Cards wool
67 Part of a three-piece suit

8 Feature in "Sugar Babies"
9 Houston athlete
10 Yacht basin
11 Stopper
12 Whip
13 Formerly, formerly
21 Reatas
22 Man of Muscat
25 Garret
26 Chewy candy
27 Loam deposit
29 Progress
31 Mart
32 Mistake
33 Winnows

35 Altair or Rigel
36 Maestro Toscanini
39 Instruct
40 Predecessor of Khrushchev
45 Gauguin milieu
47 Shavers
49 Mastic
51 King of Tyre
52 Silvery fish
53 Title
54 Mine wagon
55 Brewer's kiln
56 Finish a bathroom
57 Pub orders
58 Spoils

DOWN

1 Fishhook
2 Mimic
3 Farm structure
4 Type of pitch
5 Certify
6 Idles
7 How this runs

Diagrams with lateral symmetry have been mentioned and exemplified in a previous chapter. One of the last *Times* 23 x 23 puzzles with that pattern of black squares, "People and Places," is presented herewith in Puzzle #4. Published on May 26, 1946, it also reveals the staid, no-nonsense approach to crosswords which prevailed in that period. Incidentally, the constructor cleverly hid his full name at 86- and 88-Across. Margaret Farrar never noticed the ruse when she edited the puzzle, but was pleasantly surprised when the "perpetrator" let her know a few weeks later.

The answer to the puzzle can be found on page 183.

□

Constructors of puzzles have long memories. Apparently they also like crosswords that are real challenges with educational overtones. Or maybe they marvel at the ability of a colleague to include approximately seventeen thematic entries in a 23 x 23. All of the above reasons probably caused the choice of Herbert Ettenson's "Figures of Speech" (Puzzle #5) in a recent questionnaire asking top puzzlemakers to mention some crosswords that impressed them most. The Ettenson puzzle, which originally was published in the 1960s by Margaret Farrar, is reprinted on pages 120–21.

Note that in several instances the clue reads "man's name" or "man's nickname." This vague direction to solvers is now frowned upon.

The answer appears on page 183.

□

And now we come to more modern puzzles. The first two (Puzzles #6 and #7), by John Samson and Anne Fox, illustrate a new trend in which the clues and answers are transposed. In other words, the phrases and sentences that ordinarily are definitions now become items to be solved, and vice versa.

For example, let us say that the theme is "First Names." The solver might find the following.

Clue	Answer
Rose	AMERICAN BEAUTY
Cliff	STEEP FACE OF A ROCK
James	RIVER IN VIRGINIA
Florence	CITY IN ITALY

The Samson puzzle adds a new dimension to this idea. In his "Turnabout," time-worn clues and crosswordese are built into the puzzle itself. The answer can be found on page 183.

Anne Fox's 21 x 21 features flowers but combines the answer-becomes-clue innovation with her fondness for quotations, and also exhibits her skill in interweaving very long phrases.

The answer appears on page 184.

□

Puzzle #4: OF PEOPLE AND PLACES

ACROSS

1 Atom-smashing machines
11 Excessive nationalism
21 Self-righteously hypocritical
22 Representative of Greek culture
24 Storehouse of military supplies: Rare
25 Empire-minded person
26 Tropical twining plant
27 Tapuyan Indians
28 Girl's name
29 Compact
30 President pro tem of the Philippines
32 Burn
35 Volcano, 10,758 ft. high
37 Open inner courtyards
38 Siouan Indian
39 East Indian sheep, the nahoor
41 Chemical suffix
42 Title of respect: India
43 Low relief sculpture
44 Frenchman's "yes"
45 Russian dog-salmon
47 "Art may ___, but Nature cannot miss" — Dryden
49 City on the Arkansas
51 Close friend
52 Personality-laden atmosphere
53 Deficiency of oxygen in the blood
55 Bulge at rear of skull
56 Critical explanation of a text
58 Hebrew name for God in Book of Job
59 Conclusion
60 Republic in Soviet Russia, capital Kazan
61 Dutch navigator of the Half Moon
64 Abnormal muscular relaxation
65 Ethnic groups
69 Daughter of Cadmus
70 Objective of U. S. military planning, early in World War II
74 Censured physically
78 Of a bovine quadruped
79 Equine pace

81 Bay in Luzon
82 Spanish length measures
83 Soft globular mass
84 Girl's name
86 Any of several kings of France
88 Member of British peerage
89 River in U.S.S.R., 500 miles to the Dnieper
90 Capital of Vosges department, France
92 Pledged
94 Enjoyer of balneological pleasures
95 Decay
96 What nylons are for
99 Gateway of Shinto temple
100 Young salmon before migration seaward
102 Bengal silkworm, forms orange-red cocoons
103 Political adherent
104 States in SE Asia
105 Tradition-bound part of Mohammedan law: Var.
106 "Hot seat" of oil disputes
107 Cistern
108 Web-like membrane
110 Old corn measure, about 150 lbs.
111 Henpeck
112 Soft underpart of paw
113 Quote
114 Toothless
116 Entertained regally
118 Fabricates again
120 Defensive skin color
121 They're served with sauerkraut
125 Catnip
126 One of Cook islands
128 Man-otter victim of Loki: Norse myth
129 Palm of the hand
131 Seize uncouthly
134 Biased news
137 Organize for war
139 Converted to public ownership
140 Unrepresentative of our democracy
141 Short-lived things
142 Reactive indignation

DOWN

1 Baptize
2 Jap naval chief, shot down over the Marshalls
3 Wading bird
4 Salt marsh areas at Dnieper delta
5 Chemical sugar
6 Strong taste
7 Religious ceremonies
8 Sean ___, Irish playwright
9 Old name of Nera River, Italy
10 Foxy
11 Gypsy woman
12 Stammer
13 Italian mountain troops
14 Group of Moslem theologians
15 ___ Cruz
16 King of West Saxons: Var.
17 Dwarf cattle of South America
18 Small water-surrounded body
19 Consisting of icicles: Obs.
20 Birthplace of Mr. Truman
21 Tough fellow, in GI terms
23 Greek historian
31 Windflowers
33 Opposers of dictators
34 Join again
35 Excuses for nonappearance in court
36 Much disputed European area
37 Paint holders
40 High spot in opera
43 Sandal of ancient Roman comic actor
46 Tree choppers
48 College yell
50 Silk gossamer stuff
51 Sulk
52 Air: Prefix
54 Odic force of electricity
57 Dept. of France, Nimes, the capital
61 Nazi
62 Without ease
63 Leader of first squadron to bomb Tokyo
66 Anti-capitalist revolutionary of 1918 Russia

67 Vindicate
68 Voluptuaries
71 Plenitude: Suffix
72 Tribe of Niger
73 Siamese length measure
75 Swiss river
76 In favor of
77 Patron god of shepherds
80 White metal
83 An opinion backed by cash
85 Aromatic terebinths of the Moluccas
87 Obliging devotee to Sinatra
88 Herald
89 Mend socks
91 Ex-chief of UNRRA
93 Bedecked

94 Asst. Secy. of State for American Republic Affairs
97 "Ballad of Reading ——" Oscar Wilde
98 Sternward curve of ship's plank
100 Hero of "Great Expectations"
101 Sandarac tree
109 Former capital of Syria
113 Whimsy
115 What Robert Burns would have called a dolt
116 Burden: Dial.
117 Celestially blessed
119 Migraine

121 Ascending step
122 City in Middle Volga region
123 Gaucho weapons
124 Slippery mud
126 Semicircular basilica edifice
127 Too much: Fr.
128 Eye amorously
130 Sun-disk
132 Mohammedans' hour of prayer
133 Tendency
135 Wine measure
136 Sales notices
137 River in Austria and Yugoslavia
138 Aptitude

Puzzle #5: FIGURES OF SPEECH by Herbert Ettenson

ACROSS

1 Disport
6 Chantilly
10 Ratify
14 Housewives
19 "What's in ___ ?"
20 "An apothecary should never be out of spirits"
23 Arrange
24 Runway
25 "O frabjous day!"
26 Violet
27 Plant shoots
28 Sell
29 Went down
30 Cancel
31 Top
32 Pretense
33 Law degree
35 ___ Gwyn
37 Finials
38 Most extended
40 Man from Man
41 Hiemal hazard
43 Varangians
44 ___ windmills
45 The circus
47 Lively dance
49 Latin verb
50 Fidgety
53 Filmy piece
56 Stems
58 Angry man
60 Hemidemisemiquaver
61 Bespangle
63 Aromatic seed
64 "And faith unfaithful kept him falsely true"
66 Texas college
68 Convex moldings
69 Pine exudate
70 Brain passages
71 "Birds of a feather flock together"
74 Author's copies
75 Fold
76 Home of Lazarus
78 Schools
81 The middle: Abbr.
83 "Why, the world's mine oyster"
85 Contrite
86 Maine town
89 Newspaper section, for short
90 Yugoslav city

92 "The very identical thing itself"
96 Ground works
97 Uninspired
99 Veridical
101 Tetra-, ___ , hexa-
102 Flowers
104 Unicum
105 Curriculum
107 Child's game
108 Merman role
109 Cambridge students
111 Ear-minded
113 Concerto: Abbr.
114 ___ diem
118 Apportion
119 Lull
121 Wheel parts
123 Honey: Comb. form
124 Chemical suffix
125 Dream: Fr.
126 Example of 25 Across
128 Ancient people S of Rome
130 Craves
132 Very foolish
134 Nautical term
135 Hebrew month
136 "O come all ye faithful . . . "
138 Sample
139 In operation
140 "To take arms against a sea of troubles"
141 Willow
142 Growing out
143 Vega's constellation
144 Nieuport's river
145 Every which way

DOWN

1 Foe of Caesar
2 "For God, for country, and for Yale"
3 "I am no orator as Brutus is, but . . . a plain blunt man"
4 Outstanding
5 Members of the House
6 Most remiss
7 ___ Triomphe

8 Unfeeling
9 Substitution, as of tenses in Scripture
10 Wee: Dial
11 Picnic provender
12 Indians
13 Man's name
14 Spice
15 Venerate
16 "Illiterate him . . . from your memory," et al.
17 "She had a heart ___ how shall I say? ___ too soon made glad . . . "
18 Emphasize
20 Gourds
21 Fooyoung
22 Talus
32 Man's nickname
34 Winded
36 Props
39 Throttle
40 Yields
42 Turkic tribesman
44 Arum plant
45 Moment: Colloq.
46 Slide valve
48 Railroad
51 Gales: Slang
52 Weights
54 Conte
55 Equal: Comb. form
57 Six-year men: Abbr.
59 Man's name
61 "To the tintinnabulation that so musically wells . . . "
62 Rolls of minced meat
65 480 sheets
67 College course
72 Mata ___
73 Boundary
75 "Domini Canes" as nickname for Dominicans
76 Wand
77 Lyric poems
79 Appears
80 English river
81 Baseball great
82 "She was a phantom of delight"
84 In ___
85 Railroad branch
87 Element

88 Of certain compounds
91 Hoard
93 "To err is human, to forgive divine"
94 Draws
95 Thaumaturge
98 Soot
100 Muscovite: Abbr.
103 Ridge

105 Like a chain
106 Readiness
110 Acme
112 Igneous rock
113 Fawn
115 Ancient violin
116 Of a network
117 Fourscore
119 French painter

120 Equalizes
122 Viewpoint
125 Uplift
127 Corundum
129 Contemporary dramatist
131 Aspire
133 Canonized females: Abbr.
134 Microcosm
137 Sarnoff's outfit

Puzzle #6: TURNABOUT by John Samson

ACROSS

1 Adriatic seaport
5 Resounded
9 Riles
14 Ascend
19 Guinness
20 Russian range
21 Harden
22 Artichoke, e.g.
23 Hemp
25 Rerun
27 Lighthouses
28 Fleur-de-___
30 Housewife, in Mexico City
31 Court
32 Senator Glenn's state
34 Wait upon
38 Vous
42 Cry of amused surprise
43 "Preacher" of pitching fame
44 Car buyer's concern: Abbr.
47 Complimentary closing
48 Mars, to Menelaus
50 Signaling device
52 George's X-word brother
53 More: Comb. form
54 1051
56 Andrea ___ Robbia
59 Knight's weapon
61 Predigestion aide
62 ". . . and we all do fade as ___.": Isaiah
63 Moved hesitantly
64 Cold, wind, rain, etc.
67 Private rooms
69 ___ "Kookie" Byrnes of TV
71 Zealous
73 Saturate with H_2O
77 Topsoils
81 Brown photograph
82 Melodic
83 Big Bertha's birthplace
84 Assemble
85 Hee
89 March X-word day
91 X-word word with out
92 "Able was ___ saw Elba"
93 "The ___": Benchley book
94 Sister-in-law's daughter

96 Latvian ___
97 FDR's "Blue Eagle"
98 Some MD's
100 Venice
104 Proceed cautiously
106 X-word organic compound
107 N. A. X-word tribe
109 Overdue debt
113 Acrosses' opps.
114 Haywood of hoop fame
117 Oto
121 Alan
123 African X-word language
124 Harangue
125 ___ En-lai
126 Follow
127 Wild party
128 Name: Lat.
129 Quod ___ demonstrandum
130 To ___ (precisely)

DOWN

1 Cutting remark
2 X-word plant
3 Make requital
4 Antarctic covering
5 Storm harbinger
6 Priestly robes
7 No, to Jackie Stewart
8 Ida
9 The ___ (hubby's mate)
10 "Murder, ___"
11 Pelts
12 Independent
13 Visible
14 "When I was a lad . . . "
15 Xavier from Barcelona
16 Arab coat
17 X-word garland
18 X-word bird
24 Raid
26 One of the Beerys
29 Her, in Hamburg
33 Racetrack
35 Periods

36 Nick's X-word wife
37 Roebuck
39 Veil material
40 X-word nymph
41 Use a lever on
42 "___ Mio"
44 He had a golden touch
45 Some Harvard prep courses
46 Chief ore of lead
49 X-word inclusive abbr.
51 Hero worshipper
54 Busybody
55 Mountain peak
57 Enzyme that works on "milk sugar"
58 Let
60 Dee's predecessor
65 Plains Indians' abodes
66 Small cuts
68 Song for Sutherland
70 Author ___ Passos
72 Spud
74 "The ___ Prayer"
75 Elbe feeder
76 Tierney and Tunney
78 Aussi
79 Mil. corpsman
80 Flout (with "at")
85 Clue
86 Air: Comb. form
87 Envelop
88 X-word sword
90 Bail
95 X-word organic compound
99 Tonsorial wave
101 Minstrel jokesters
102 Charged particle
103 "Pathétique" is one
105 Sensitive touches
108 Brilliance
110 Black
111 X-word hairstyle
112 Gad about
114 X-word portico
115 X-word Adams
116 Chest sound
117 Fall away
118 X-word mulberry
119 Ribonucleic acid, for short
120 Map abbr.
122 R.C. or Prot.

Puzzle #7: OPUS ON A 20-DOWN THEME by Anne Fox

ACROSS

1 Game division
5 Hyde Park sight
9 French cup
14 Muslim scholar
18 Mixture
19 Tall timber tree of
New Zealand
20 Former
21 Mexican sandwich
22 Narcissus
26 Genus of wood sorrels
27 Masculine title
28 ___ tree
29 Florentine iris
30 Even if: Lat.
33 Possessive
35 Zest
37 "___ Alone," 1926 song
38 "Edelweiss"
44 Bunyan
45 Faith: Fr.
46 French flower
47 Ill. city
48 Violet
57 Fabric
58 Poet laureate: 1715–18
59 Greek letter
60 Boat common in the
Levant
61 Baton Rouge campus
62 Likewise: Fr.
63 Contrived
64 Chinese-American architect
65 Rose
73 Centigrade number
74 Beast of burden
75 Brother of Cain
76 Bill of a sort
77 La-di-da
79 Containing a certain gas:
Comb. form
80 Eccentric painter
81 Volume measure
85 "Morning Glory"
90 Coursed
91 Suffix with corpus
92 Buddhist people
93 Shoshoni
94 Iris
101 "The ___," B'way play,
1975

102 Item, sometimes big
103 Even if, for short
104 Wheel part
105 Attic assembly
107 Prepared with, in cookery
109 Cup or roll
111 Land on the Baltic Sea
116 Daisy
121 Type of sch.
122 Charlotte, for short
123 Peau de ___
124 Son, in English names
125 Hamlet
126 Shaped like an S-molding
127 Kept
128 Arctic sight

DOWN

1 Tramp
2 Woollcott, to friends
3 Former film star Lee
4 Clown
5 Magician's word
6 Free of
7 Relative of aimer
8 Hand holder
9 First word in many titles
10 Japanese race
11 Covered passages of a
cathedral
12 Mogadiscio native
13 Ruler: Abbr.
14 Caesar's way
15 Mark over a vowel
16 Full of nostalgia
17 Large ruminant
20 Words by George Chapman,
1607
23 Contends
24 Red, white and blue
25 Where Fuji is
31 Muslim mystic
32 With it
34 Beam
36 Capital of Ghana
38 Weaverbird of South Africa
39 Wound
40 Hebrew hymn
41 Deviate

42 Service org.
43 Some paintings
44 Letter additive
49 Kind follower, e.g.
50 King of Denmark: 1018–35
51 Lombardy lake
52 Get to
53 Sgt. Snorkel's dog, in
"Beetle Bailey"
54 Pacific island cloth
55 Nothing, in Nîmes
56 Cutting, as a remark
62 Skilled workman
63 Leafstalk
65 So long, in Italia
66 ___ de combat
67 Campus group
68 Long skirt, for short
69 Kind of service
70 French resort
71 Finish, as laundry
72 Uproar
78 Type of stick
79 Possessed
80 Netherlands city
82 Word with graph or mat
83 Waxed
84 USNA grad.
86 Tire type
87 Sgt.
88 ___ avis
89 Deception
94 Escort of a sort
95 Drive-in theater: Slang
96 Pirate
97 Sign of respect
98 Scottish poet: 1770–1835
99 Undernourished
100 Beer or miss
101 Sloshed
106 Turnpike feature
108 Entr' ___
110 Silent movie name
112 Spat
113 Bridal ___
114 Math word
115 Cutting tool
117 Postal limbo, for short
118 Leather
119 Doe's relative
120 Sma'

Puzzle #8, by Alfio Micci, exemplifies the rebus theme, in which a solver is asked to draw an object or symbol in a single box. The item to be depicted takes the place of a whole word. Here are some instances:

+ FOURS (loose knickerbockers); NE + ULTRA (acme); COMM & (order); & OVER (prep school); ✔ ERS (board game); RAIN ✔ (type of ticket); $ FISH (marine creature); TEN $ BILL (Hamilton note).

Sometimes fans are required to sketch flags, punctuation marks, horns, stars, balls, crowns and a variety of other items. In this respect, the ultimate was Vincent Osborne's feline puzzle featuring entries like *cat*ASTROPHE, WILLA *cat*HER and CON*cat*ENATION. Whenever the three-letter word appeared, solvers had to do their best to draw Tabby's face—replete with whiskers, of course. Lewis Carroll's devotees finished off their artwork with an upturned mouth, true to Cheshire tradition.

As a violinist, Mr. Micci naturally turned to musical signs when constructing a rebus puzzle. Readers are warned to be *sharp* when they tackle Puzzle #8 or they will fall *flat* on their faces. Those who are stumped should turn to page 184 for the answer.

☐

Puzzle #9, by A. J. Santora, illustrates a rebus of a different sort. Numbers are used in place of words. But a mind like Santora's is not satisfied with that simple gimmick. Instead, the numbers must fit their counterparts in the diagram! Thus, to give a hypothetical example, the clue for 9-Down might be "existence every cat enjoys" and the answer would be 9 LIVES. Will Weng, who first published the puzzle, appropriately called it "Squarely Figured."

By the way, Mr. Santora estimates that Puzzle #9 is the best one he has ever constructed. Whether you agree or not, you will find the answer on page 184.

☐

Before Will Weng became the editor of *Times* puzzles, he had won laurels as a masterful constructor of punny crosswords. During his tenure as editor (1970–77) he followed his philosophy; to wit, puzzles are essentially a game in which solvers should have a little fun while they are killing time. Hence, the Weng Era was marked by lots of crosswords that featured all kinds of wordplay. But the fundamental part of the fun was the pun.

In view of the above, it is altogether fitting and proper (excuse it, Mr. Lincoln) that we should reprint a Weng opus originally published in the *Times* by Margaret Farrar.

But before the reader turns to Puzzle #10, a quick look should be taken at two kinds of puns that regularly appear in crossword puzzles.

The first type changes the original spelling to suit the witticism. Here are some examples:

Clue	Answer
Comforter	SOOTHESAYER
Drink with a twist	WRY HIGHBALL
Needlepointer's milieu	CREWEL WORLD
A-1 clothes dryer	WRINGMASTER
Ailing gunman	SICK SHOOTER
Clip joint	WRESTAURANT
Authorship	WRITEFIELD

The second form of pun keeps the original spelling, but the humor is in the clue. Again, some examples:

Clue	Answer
Ankara race	TURKEY TROT
A kiss for the wrong miss	BLUNDERBUSS
Joint where people chat superficially	SHALLOW DIVE
Spanish coin	LATIN QUARTER
Elopers	RUNNING MATES
Rhett wearing a gag	SILENT BUTLER
Urbane raincoat	CITY SLICKER
Dupe on a warship	CARRIER PIGEON

Some editors believe that the two types of puns should never be mixed in single puzzles, in order to be fair to the fans. Others are less stringent; they feel that any solvers who are willing to wend their way through a crossword of that sort would not be flabbergasted by a change of pace. In Puzzle #10, for example, all the long entries except 48-Down change the original spelling.

Now get ready, get set, go—and wing it with Weng. Pay special attention to 125-Across, in which the master is at his best. One is reminded of the little girl who penned "Lead us not into Penn Station," when asked to write The Lord's Prayer.

The answer to Puzzle #10 appears on page 184.

□

Puzzle #8: MUSIC BOXES by Alfio Micci

ACROSS

1 Abruptly: Colloq.
5 Place for a clef
10 The women: Abbr.
14 Dark blue: Comb. form
18 Shrinks from
20 Holy: Prefix
21 Collection: Suffix
22 Like some cosmetics
23 Cremona VIP
24 Hokkaido city
25 Group of workers
26 Dickens girl
27 Akin
29 Comparative suffix
30 Take on
31 Taylor role
32 Rachmaninoff favorite
35 "East of ___"
36 Kind of verb: Abbr.
37 Habit
38 Lawn device: Abbr.
40 Color
44 Wild ___
46 Fish
48 Complete
52 Beethoven favorite
54 On edge
55 Incomplete form
56 Henri of the art world
57 Constellation called Bird of Paradise
59 Glut
61 Like: Suffix
62 Musical instrument
64 Strong
65 Left hand pages
69 Certain address
72 Passed a bid or double, at bridge
75 Phloxlike
77 Do a kitchen chore
79 Stibnite
80 Ostiole
82 Disquiet
83 Bearer of gifts
87 Sex appeal of yore
88 Corundum
91 Rubinstein favorite
93 Soft fabric
94 Plunge
95 Time abbr.
96 Heavenly animals
97 German direction
99 Yugoslavian coin
101 Nobel nutritional scientist
103 European capital
106 Chopin favorite
114 "It's ___!"
115 Algerian port
116 State: Abbr.
117 Alexandra, for one
118 Menu word
119 Hawaiian goose
120 ___ piece
122 Uses a stopwatch
123 Impetuosity
124 Codas
125 In a month of Sundays
126 Tournament units, for short
127 Record
128 Speak impolitely
129 British colors
130 Ago: Scot.

DOWN

1 Not flat or natural
2 Not as spry
3 Part of a Dickens title
4 Part of a posy
5 Device in which gold leaf is beaten
6 Use a shuttle
7 "Kiss me ___"
8 Slanted end of a wood beam
9 Key signature of 32 Across
10 Popular card game
11 Certain space probes
12 Month, in Madrid
13 Timber men
14 Gershwin favorite
15 Produce
16 French passageway
17 Fabric
19 In ___
28 Decrees
33 Strength, figuratively
34 Weapons
39 Gaiter
40 Vine
41 Transmission devices, for short
42 Italian pronoun
43 Adlai's initials
45 Stone
47 Money, in Guadaloupe
49 Milanese eating place
50 Old verb ending
51 Deer
52 A year in the future
53 See 86 Down
54 Warder
58 Kind of check
60 Geographical abbr.
63 Familiar nickname
64 Cause of mattress discomfort, in old tale
66 Bizet favorite
67 Indians
68 Stubborn: Dial.
70 ___ shoestring
71 Conditions
73 Soames' bride
74 Sinew: Fr.
76 Something for the birds
78 Monetary abbr.
80 Assn.
81 ___ fare-thee-well
82 Tongue membranes
84 Key signature of 106 Across
85 Presidential monogram
86 Plural ending
89 English region
90 Immorality
92 Old school
95 The look of the other side
98 Cuts of meat
100 ___ machine
102 Premium experts
103 Disclosed
104 Town near Salerno
105 Lists
107 Scene of action
108 "___ Louisa . . ."
109 Performance times: Abbr.
110 Zodiac sign
111 Use a crowbar
112 ___ a million
113 Civet
121 Napoleonic marshal

Puzzle #9: SQUARELY FIGURED by A.J. Santora

ACROSS

1 After-midnight hours
7 Last Commandment
13 Spring date
20 Green crust on metal
21 "Give the devil ___"
22 "Peekaboo, ___"
23 Chem. compounds
24 Italian city
25 "... sleep, perchance ___"
26 Dine
27 Sharp sound
29 Defeats
31 Goddess of infatuation
32 Malay dagger: Var.
34 Hank of yarn
36 Deer
37 Court judgment
39 New York street
42 Japanese coin
44 Makes an offer
46 Not at home
47 Cornbreads
49 In ___
50 Spar on a sail
52 Shouted
54 Eases off
58 What some scouts look for
59 Vaulter's concern
61 Renew old school ties
62 Ex-Senator from Nebraska
63 Male deer
64 Provided that
66 Fairly old auto
67 Gypsy
68 Contended
70 Smother
72 Sesame
73 Jewish month
75 Room in a casa
76 Phila. team
77 Whole
79 Part of a book
81 Hitter
83 Repeats
84 Sam and J. C. of golf
86 Note declining an invitation
87 Pulverize
88 Planet
90 Glistened

91 Strange
92 Caveman of comics
96 Friend in Paris
97 What a duffer does at times
101 Small pair
102 Raffleticket marking
104 Ulan ___
107 Anna's land
108 Spigot
109 The ___ be counted
111 In unison
114 Numerical prefix
115 Bulldog, for one
118 Verdi opera
120 Explosive
122 Expires
123 Mews: Fr.
124 Council of 325 A. D.
125 Impost at Aqueduct
126 Annoy
127 Smarts

DOWN

1 Kind of swimsuit
2 Italian spice
3 Ear trouble
4 ___ hand
5 Over again
6 Cattle feed
7 Show gratitude
8 Door piece
9 Spanish coin: Abbr.
10 Famous London address
11 Gum tree
12 Learned
13 Stage fright
14 Serviceclub units
15 Little Edward
16 Always, to poets
17 Life span of a locust
18 Exactly
19 Heraldic bars
28 Pale
30 Bribe
33 Gapes
35 Mine strike

37 More likely
38 Popular song about a highway
40 Catnap
41 Rat ___
43 Prefixes for recent
45 Lubricate
47 Mine sweeps on ships
48 Underlying layer
50 U. S. playwright
51 Peacock's pride
52 Student
53 Lao-tse's followers
55 Type of pump
56 Not ventilated
57 Mesta et al.
58 Destructive insects
60 W. W. II group
65 Pullman
69 Fordhamite
70 Douay Bible name
71 Repeat number
74 Pipecleaning tool
76 Brass in a musical
78 Arborvitaes
80 Phileas Fogg's travel time
82 Turkish title
85 Hit sign
89 Voiced sounds
91 River of Spain
92 Where 126 is
93 Put on cargo
94 Ida of films
95 Opposite of neg.
98 Young pet
99 Tahiti wrap
100 Fifth of the Indy 500
103 Sign of the flu
105 Aunt in Paris
106 Willow
109 Mouthy
110 Factual
112 Code letters
113 Send out
116 Initials on a crate
117 Elec. particle
119 Lawyer: Abbr.
121 Chemical prefix

Puzzle #10: THE PUN'S THE THING by Will Weng

ACROSS

1 Terre Haute's river
7 Tropical root plant
13 Beaten-around locale
17 Animal sound
21 Slow part, in music
22 City in New Hampshire
23 Within: Prefix
24 Ascend
25 Large, tiresome animals
27 Decree
28 B'way group
29 Music drama, in Berlin
30 Of an epoch
31 Subway for Bugs Bunny, perhaps
34 Hanger's item
36 Nile denizen, for short
38 Fancy
39 Waiter's concern
40 Chilled
42 End ___ line
45 Spread
46 Moved out
50 Summonses to a dessert
53 Pooh's cousin
56 Los ___
57 Starchy tubers
58 Time areas
59 Middle: Prefix
60 Napery
61 Kind of train
62 Odd money
63 Gay tunes
64 Man's name
65 Indian metropolis
66 Headliner of 1898
67 Despite: Fr.
68 Consecrated: Abbr.
69 Rodent's cussword
71 Jungle wire to Moscow
72 Immediately
74 Ever: Poet
75 ___ lot (is concerned)
76 Relative of an auto laundry
78 Where some animals play golf
81 Indefinite degree
84 Plaza Hotel girl
85 Ring feature
87 Shouts
88 Nickname like Ted
89 "___ mind if I do"
90 Pogo stick's predecessor
91 Horn sounds
92 Intone
93 Headland
94 Take care of
95 Mountain country
96 ___ longue
97 Direction
98 Large, untrustworthy animals
100 Spat
101 Beatnik quarters
102 Horse opera
103 Game trio
104 Sock pattern
107 Resort off Georgia, for short
109 One of the Kellys
111 Large sharks
116 What author Virginia got as a girl
120 Sinew: Fr.
122 Fish and chips
123 Sedan
124 Atoms
125 "Gladly the ___ " (Child's version of hymn line)
128 Restraint
129 Mint plant
130 Weapon
131 Meteoric shower star
132 Danube tributary
133 Former spouses
134 Tattled, gangwise
135 Pieces of cake

DOWN

1 Early Texans
2 Take as one's own
3 Farm machine
4 Feature of anc. Athens
5 Family member
6 Water, as a lawn
7 How doughnuts are fried
8 Casals
9 Inner: Prefix
10 Burn partly
11 Subtle atmosphere
12 Native sections, as in Algiers
13 Suit
14 Oneness
15 Office copy, for short
16 Items from the oven
17 Marlon
18 Wash lightly
19 Active
20 Abbey Theater name
26 Shaped in a curve
32 Enter with a flourish
33 War god
35 Alp-climbing gear
37 Occasional import from Canada
41 These, in France
43 Coal or gas
44 Cooking meas.
45 Bullfight cheers
46 Effective
47 Vibrant
48 Silly Ottawan, maybe
49 So be it
50 Papier ___
51 Nautical term
52 Before bellum
53 What a Liege barber cuts
54 Houston player
55 Trousers, in Berlin
57 Get the answer
59 Industrial plants
61 Dissolve by percolating
62 Beast of burden
63 Rubber source
65 Impenetrable
66 Iffy answer
67 Poetic times
69 Vaunt
70 Intimidate
71 President 90 years ago
73 Ball players
75 Curtailed
76 German poet and critic
77 Times of yore
78 What a ten-goal man wears
79 Arctic sight

80 Early Canadians
82 On edge
83 Stopping place
85 Short distance
86 Famous Croat
88 "... in them ___ hills"
90 Old World lizard
91 Small meal
92 Abyss
94 Laterally
95 Small bird

96 Fashion
98 30 minutes of football
99 Self-propelled coach
100 Raise doubt
101 Air-race markers
103 Where the filter goes
104 Mindful (of)
105 French city
106 ___ on the ground floor
107 Slight burn
108 Sigmas

110 Result
112 Perth ___ , N. J.
113 City in N. H.
114 Walking ___ (happy)
115 Irrational numbers
117 Mislead
118 Silkworm
119 Ilk
121 Subsided
126 NCO
127 Goddess: Lat.

Puzzle #11, by Maura B. Jacobson, is called "Upsa-Doozy" — and it's really a doozy! Originally published in *New York* magazine on April 5, 1982, it typifies the kind of shenanigans that go on around April Fool's Day. Note how the numbers are reversed. What is usually 1-Down becomes 1-Up and is found at the bottom of the puzzle! To give you a start, the answer to that item is NIB, written backwards.

Constructor Louis Baron states that this crossword is one of the most interesting he has ever solved. Certainly it is eminently fair to fans who are flexible enough to turn topsy-turvy.

The answer to Puzzle #11 appears on page 185.

□

With regard to Puzzles #12 and #13, explanations as to their genesis are in order, and so is the first person singular.

As a published poet and recipient of an M.A. degree in English literature, I had always been consumed by a burning desire to combine two of my great passions — crossword puzzles and famous quotations. Encouraged by Margaret Farrar, I published a few puzzles wherein the Across entries featured a quote. An example for a 21 x 21 puzzle is the following:

> THERE IS NO FRIGATE LIKE A
> BOOK TO TAKE US LANDS AWAY.

Those lines from a poem by Emily Dickinson were perfectly suited to my needs. The quotation broke into two parts, each having 21 letters. Individual words would not be split from line to line, and the entire statement lent itself to a 21 x 21 puzzle.

But sometimes a quotation would break up evenly into more than two parts. Here's an example from "The Song of Songs":

> MANY WATERS CANNOT   (16)
> QUENCH LOVE: (10)
> NEITHER CAN   (10)
> THE FLOODS DROWN IT.   (16)

But there were times when a good quote would contain a two-letter word in the middle. These verses from Longfellow's "Hiawatha" will serve as an example:

> AS UNTO THE BOW THE CORD   (19)
> IS,   (2)
> SO UNTO THE MAN IS WOMAN.   (19)

Since two-letter words are verboten in the best puzzles, necessity generated the creation of the U-Quote, which involved a devilish little trick: Solvers had to read Part III of the quotation *Upwards*. This is how the quotation looked in the middle of the diagram.

```
A       N
S       A
U       M
N       O
T       W
O       S
T       I
H       N
E       A
B       M
O       E
W       H
T       T
H       O
E       T
C       N
O       U
R       O
D  I  S  S
```

Of course, some of the letters in those two long vertical word ladders were connected by Across entries and others were separated by black squares.

A natural offshoot of the U-Quote was the Boxquote, which added another dimension. Part III of the saying read *backwards* and Part IV read *upwards*. Incidentally, good Boxquotes are hard to find, because the first letter of the quotation must be the same as the last letter in order to mesh perfectly. Here's an example from Tennyson's "In Memoriam."

```
T  I  M  E  A  M  A
S              N
U              I
D              A
G              C
N              S
I  R  E  T  T  A  C
```

The above illustrates a problem that occurs in quotation puzzles. Solvers must figure out where one word ends and another begins. Also, they must estimate where punctuation marks are needed. In case the word square makes no sense to you the quote reads, TIME, A MANIAC SCATTERING DUST.

In the 1940s the *New York Herald Tribune* published some of my Diagonograms. A brief statement above the diagram would inform solvers that after they had completed the puzzle they should read diagonally from the top left letter to the one at the bottom right. A hidden 15-letter word or phrase, such as CROSSWORD PUZZLE, would emerge as a sort of bonus.

Why not use the idea for small quotations? For example, "Brevity is the soul of wit" (from *Hamlet*) has 21 letters — just right for a diagonal message in a 21 x 21 puzzle. The Diagonogram becomes a Slide-Quote. By the way, that type of puzzle presents the most difficult challenge a constructor can face.

Since some excellent quotations did not lend themselves to any of the above ideas, once again necessity mothered invention. To overcome the problem, Circles in the Square was created. Puzzle #12 is an example of that type of crossword. The answer can be found on page 185.

All of the foregoing puzzles are regular features of *Simon and Schuster's Crossword Book of Quotations*. The U-Quote, Boxquote, Slide-Quote and Circles in the Square first appeared in that series, which began in 1966 under the aegis of editor Helen Barrow.

But previously in 1964 Margaret Farrar had published the first Stepquote in the *Times* Sunday *Magazine*. The puzzle caused a sensation that it didn't really deserve. In my opinion, the Stepquote is just one of many devices created by constructors looking for a new way to excite the interest of puzzle mavens.

Probably the catalyst for the hubbub was the fact that Mrs. Farrar chose not to baby the fans by indicating that the quotation would drop down like a staircase from top left to bottom right. Nor did she ask the artist to draw heavy lines around the Stepquote. Her feeling was that the title and the sequential definitions would be enough to tip off the solvers that something unusual was afoot.

What happened when the fans encountered the puzzle amazed us both. Letters of praise and protest poured in from almost every state in the Union. Those who had caught on to the idea were ecstatic. Some compared it with Acrostics, because the unkeyed letters at the crossings of the angles required them to use brainpower to fill in the missing letters. That group remains avid today; every month inquiries arrive at the *Times*: When will you publish another Stepquote?

On the other hand, thousands of fans were frustrated. One woman complained that she had looked up Stepquote in her unabridged dictionary and couldn't find it. Hundreds called their librarians, who were no help at all. A doctor in New York phoned Mrs. Farrar on the following Wednesday and begged her for the answer, because his two nurses had been so baffled by the puzzle that they had neglected their work for two solid days.

Probably the most significant result was that the reactions pro and con occupied the entire "Letters to the Editor" of the *Times* Sunday *Magazine*—a rarity indeed!

People ask, "How did you think of such an idea as the Stepquote?" The answer is that it evolved from the Diagonogram. The original plan was to make the first part of the quotation extend across to the middle of the diagram. Part II would then proceed vertically to the bottom and Part III would move horizontally to the bottom right corner. But ten minutes of experimentation revealed that the concept was impractical. Those Across letters added up to 11 apiece for a 21 x 21 puzzle. Each would have to be accompanied by at least two other 11-letter entries—not impossible but difficult to repeat time after time.

Well then, what compromise could be made? The thought struck me that a series of shorter steps would do the trick. A tentative diagram was sketched and scrutinized. Yes, the idea was viable! But how many letters would be needed for those steps? A quick count disclosed that 41 would be perfect for a 21 x 21 puzzle and 45 for a 23 x 23.

Next came the research in books of quotations. Finally, a sardonic O'Neill statement popped up: "Contentment is a warm sty for eaters and sleepers." Not a very happy thought. In retrospect, it's surprising that Mrs. Farrar did not turn it down as an "ugh-ly" observation. But it contained exactly 41 letters—just the right number for a 21 x 21 puzzle. The result was as follows:

Note that there are eight "blind spots" where the angles intersect. This was the reason that so many solvers were completely confounded by the puzzle. Further experimentation has shown that those unkeyed areas can almost be cut in half. Puzzle #13 is an example. There are only five parts in the Stepquote, as contrasted with nine in the original one.

A good Stepquote, like all other quotation puzzles, should include the source and the author's name. In Puzzle #13, the source is omitted, but there is a good reason: The last five words in the Stepquote also form the title of the poem from which the quotation was taken. However, solvers will discover a bonus, as seven other references to the poet and his works have been included in the puzzle—a giant step ahead of the first Stepquote.

The answer to Puzzle #13 appears on page 186.

□

Nobody can say that Margaret Farrar was a conservative editor of *Times* puzzles. Not only was she daring enough to publish the first Stepquote, but she permitted other by-products of regular quotation puzzles to appear. For example, Frances Hansen was allowed to quote herself.

But, really, no editor could resist those lighthearted, original Hansen limericks. For example:

> An aesthetic old man of Duluth
> Went to live in a telephone booth;
> One day, feeling hot,
> He abandoned the spot:
> "To perspire," he remarked, "is uncouth."

The fans were delighted, although a few grumbled about the splitting of words like Duluth from line to line. Mrs. Hansen's colleagues were pleased, too. A few (notably Tap Osborn and Alfio Micci) exhibited the sincerest form of flattery by submitting their own limericks.

Not one to rest on her laurels, Mrs. Hansen turned to other forms of original verse. Puzzle #14, entitled "Poetic License," displays the same kind of offbeat wit that sparkles in her limericks. Note that there are no runovers; each line of the verse has exactly 23 letters—a feat in itself! The answer is on page 186.

□

The Hansen innovation was only one of the many breakthroughs promoted by Margaret Farrar, and later by Will Weng. For example, several decades ago Father Edward J. O'Brien electrified the crossword puzzle world by embodying "Tom Swifties" in a Sunday opus. In response to fans' requests, he repeated the idea several times. Below are some of his adverbial quips taken from a puzzle edited by Will Weng.

Clue	Answer
" 'Cards?' asked Tom ____"	WISTFULLY
" 'Neap,' said Tom ____"	TIDILY
" 'It adds up,' Tom said ____"	SUMMARILY

The mention of Father O'Brien reminds me of his *A Compendium of Cruciverbalists* — a directory of constructors which he compiled after a 1974 luncheon in honor of Margaret Farrar's fiftieth anniversary as a puzzle editor. That get-together at a New York City hotel was a memorable occasion indeed. For the first time in the history of Puzzledom constructors from all over the United States were able to meet each other.

As sponsors of the event, Mrs. Maleska and I were thrilled by the response. About sixty constructors and their spouses attended the affair, and not one of them had spilled the beans to Mrs. Farrar. She had expected a quiet tête-à-tête — just three of us. The look of surprise that lit up her face when she entered the room will always be remembered by every constructor.

Most interesting were the reactions of lesser-known constructors upon seeing the "celebrities": "Ooh, there's Jack Luzzatto!" "So that's what Herb Ettenson looks like!" "William Lutwiniak is a tall one, isn't he?"

But the most appreciated constructor of all was A. B. Canning, our Texas tycoon. He picked up the tab for the drinks.

One of Father O'Brien's other fascinations is Spoonerisms. Always superambitious, he once attempted a diagram in which the reversal was placed directly under the original phrase. Here's an example:

MOLLY CODDLE
COLLIE MODEL

Not so enterprising, but nonetheless rewarding to the solver, is Puzzle #15. Enjoy! Enjoy! The answer appears on page 186.

□

Puzzle #11: UPSA-DOOZY by Maura B. Jacobson

ACROSS

1 Indira's dad
6 Pre-coll. school
10 San. Dept. pickup
15 Character in "What's Happening"
18 Become frosted
19 Artifice
20 Biblical prophet
21 Shade of green
22 Puncture
23 Not taken in by
24 Bridge seats
25 Slithery slayers
26 Fragmentize
28 Dill, old style
29 Family insignia
30 Blockade
31 Polygraph findings
33 Fanatic
35 False fronts
37 Uhlan's weapon
39 Part of a serial
42 "A Bell for ___ "
43 "Message" shirt
45 "___ Rosenkavalier"
46 Powerful explosive
47 Off one's feed
48 Hair tendril
50 Viet ___
51 Massage
52 Loki's daughter
53 Wears the crown
55 Courtroom words
57 Having knobs
59 Term for a worm
60 Borgnine
61 Melville adventure
63 Alt.
64 C.I.A.'s predecessor
65 Catch on
66 Reason for this confusion
69 And others: Abbr.
71 Dye receptacle
73 Altar locale
75 Verne captain
76 Comparison-shops
79 ___ du lieber
80 Getting one's goat
82 Quick to learn
84 Secluded path
85 Jackie's sister
86 Airport-tower workers: Abbr.
87 Of the dawn
89 Moslem priest
91 RR stop
92 Moral philosophies
94 Flop
95 ___ -fi
96 Basketry twig
98 Pedicure site
100 Tall-clown's prop
102 Comatose states
104 Parading properly
106 ___ about
107 Flax product
108 Seaweeds
110 One of the Ladds
112 Cardinal's cap
114 Siamese coin
115 Full-grown
116 Samoan capital
117 Rubber city
121 Ceremonial act
122 Fistfight
123 Work at the bar
124 "With this ring ___ wed"
125 Personal tags, for short
126 Busybody
127 Cooperstown's Roush, et al.
128 Not any person

UP

1 Beak
2 Medieval shield
3 L.B.J. beagle
4 Kind of dressing
5 Sandy Dennis film, 1967
6 Makes objection to
7 Littlest of a litter
8 Actress Parsons
9 City in Illinois
10 Bronowski P.B.S. series
11 Equine color
12 Enough: Fr.
13 Sofa of a sort
14 Isn't out of
15 Meet the challenge
16 Elec. units
17 Say in fun
21 Vocalist Julius
27 Have another birthday
29 "Sound of Music" song
30 Attempting Everest
32 Within: Prefix
34 "Comes ___ in the day's occupations"
35 Savoir- ___
36 Freud's colleague
38 Therefore
40 Activists
41 Immigrants' island
44 Finial
49 Ending with novel or violin
50 Winning
51 Partner of rock
54 Order to Dobbin
56 "Le Coq ___ "
58 Antique auto
62 Barcelona bravo
66 Poses questions
67 Noted architect
68 Alley of the comics
70 Sesame
71 Gentleman's gentleman
72 Vinegar: Comb. form
74 Berliner's toast
76 Kegler's gp.
77 Log in
78 Name on the world's tallest building
81 Buntline and Calmer
83 Twitch
88 Server's edge, informally
90 Deceives
93 Congenital
95 Like a tiger
97 Reprove
99 Hard to lift
101 Lung-shaped
103 ___ for tat
105 Outermost planet
108 Hillside dugout
109 ___ back (unflappable)
111 Type of saxophone
113 Marmalade ingredient
115 Onager
118 Greek letter
119 Vintner's prefix
120 Born

Puzzle #12: ENCIRCLED WISDOM by Eugene T. Maleska

ACROSS

1 Boy
7 Tidbit
13 One of Macbeth's titles
18 "Walden" writer
19 Idle
20 Actor Leslie
22 Famous ferry
23 Very ornate
24 Farrell's "A World ___ Made"
25 High note
26 Bowling button
28 Over
30 G.P.'s group
31 Utah ski resort
33 Old Scratch
35 Shadow-box
36 Anchor position
38 Purse items
40 Scottish uncle
41 Adjective suffix
43 Johnson of TV
44 Veronese duo
49 Straw boss
51 Kazan
52 Romeo and Juliet, e.g.
54 Mine entrance
55 Adjusts anew
59 Initials for a 1933 act
60 Portia's maid
64 Lodge member
65 Costume
67 Chalcedony
69 Stage direction
70 Yalies
72 One of Macbeth's victims
76 Safari quarry
77 French upper house
79 Cheerless
80 Homeric work
82 Italian's "Yes!"
83 Muffin variety
86 Jewish eve
88 Ten-o'clock scholar's problem
90 Feedback of a sort
91 Composer Erik
93 "___ shanter"
94 Activating
98 Nobleman in "Henry VIII"
103 Mrs., in Poland
104 Alpaca's habitat

106 "We'll ___ a cup . . ." (Burns)
107 Suffix with Indo and Poly
108 Tagging along
110 Mailed
112 Old-womanish
115 "King ___," quotation source
116 Wine: Prefix
117 Greek courtesan
120 "Lend ___"
122 Disencumber
123 Tarry
125 "You ___ !"
127 Basis of argument
129 Fishing gear
130 Will subject
131 Duchess in "Henry VI, Part II"
132 Awaken
133 Judged
134 Blush

DOWN

1 Lacking depth
2 Hamlet's friend
3 Dadaism founder
4 Shift
5 Dog ___ (shabby)
6 Charlotte ___
7 Puppet Snerd
8 Siouan
9 Costa ___
10 Smudges
11 Fire or narrow
12 Governor in "Much Ado"
13 Hammett's man
14 Lariat part
15 Disciple's emotion
16 Scene of "Love's Labour's Lost"
17 Holy hermit
18 Caught in ___
21 Dry-goods merchant
27 Knievel
29 Armenian capital
32 Play backer

34 Dud
37 Sampling
39 Blissful: Ger.
42 Relinquish
45 Actor Bruce
46 City in Egypt
47 Actress Bergner
48 French town
50 Laugh: Fr.
53 Famed N. Y. restaurateur
55 Singer Della
56 Miss Terry
57 "Every inch ___"
58 Nile growth
61 The world, to Jacques
62 Trucking rigs
63 Realms
66 Combustible heaps
68 Uninteresting
71 Messenger in "Merchant"
73 Danton's colleague
74 Ukases
75 Deadly
78 Check mark
81 Word for rum
84 Vessel
85 Like John
87 Flora and fauna
89 Unusual
92 Sprang from
94 Barkers' come-ons
95 Basket
96 Shylock's adversary
97 Lubricated
99 Related
100 Alkaloid
101 Relationship
102 Pantry
105 Misgiving
109 Merry cries
111 Overdone
113 Shunned one
114 Inventor Pliny ___
118 Irish Gaelic
119 Mr. Bede
121 Donna or Rex
124 Zoo animal
126 Native: Suff.
128 Like Ophelia, in Act IV

The circled letters from left to right, starting at the top, contain a fool's wise advice.

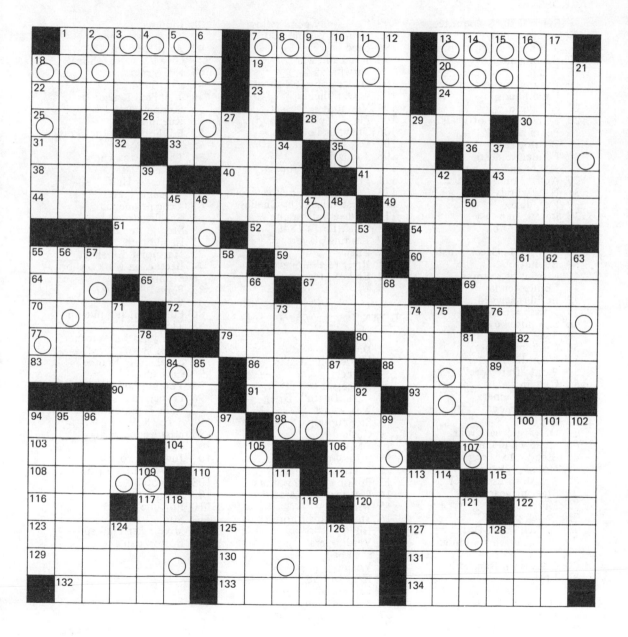

Puzzle #13: STEPQUOTE by Eugene T. Maleska

ACROSS

1 Start of the Stepquote, (along heavy line from top left to bottom right)
9 Señor's Saturday
15 Jazzman Fountain
19 Ethiopian emperor
20 Field hands
22 Effluvium
23 Belmont gate officials
24 Poem of 1847
25 Chariot race
26 Feudal domestic
27 Madre and Leone
29 Actor James
31 N. Z. woody vine
32 Fish dish
33 Below, in poesy
34 Vacuum tube
36 Revolution
38 Tempo, in Greek music
39 Big butte
40 Citizen of Kerman
41 Condescends
43 Edible seaweed
45 Jewish month
46 S.A. monkeys
48 Sweet alcohol
50 Guidonian note
52 "You Know ___"
54 Word after "woe"
57 Certain songs
59 "I ___ Camera"
61 Soft, in Siena
62 Recency
64 Of a fraternal order
66 Medieval helmet
67 Stepquote
69 Noted pollster
70 British forest officer
73 Steering-gear units
75 Matchless
76 Capek play
77 French saint: Dec. 1
79 "Once upon a midnight ___"
80 Cries from Hamlet
81 Erode
83 Poetic form
85 Ant
87 Descartes

89 "___ jolly good fellow"
92 Emulates Brünnhilde
96 Seed
98 Road and wart
99 Nitwits
101 Office copy, for short
102 K.O. punches
104 Vermont ski resort
105 Pig ___ poke
106 They, in Tours
107 Gypsy's reading matter
108 Tapeworms
110 Topic in the tropics
111 Pro ___
113 Container for pekoe
115 Verse tragedy by Shelley
117 Made a hole in one
118 "___ Lee": 1849
119 Leading players
120 Zilch
121 River to the Aegean
122 End of Stepquote

DOWN

1 Maintains
2 Divulges
3 Mexican herdsman
4 Darnel
5 Successor to F.D.R.
6 "___ Death": Grieg
7 Wearisome
8 Stepquote part
9 Gushed
10 Deity of Islam
11 Ethnologist Franz
12 Leather-puncher
13 Prolonged tennis units
14 Port west of Karachi
15 Wire grass
16 Stepquote author
17 Hired
18 Verdi opera
21 Coal bed
28 Vogue
30 Hang or hob
34 Persian fairy
35 Kind of blue
37 Cash-register recordings

38 Inquire
39 Took no chances
42 Artist's board
44 Give a ___ to (shun)
45 Fitzgerald
47 ___ Saud
49 ___ Paul Kruger
51 Somme capital
52 Rue in a story
53 Boyhood love of 16 down
55 Ridicule
56 Those in the know
58 Poem of 1831
60 Port near Haifa
61 Volcanic crater
63 Attic promenade
65 Egglike stones
68 Stepquote part
71 In addition
72 Marsupial, for short
74 Beethoven work: Abbr.
78 Stool pigeon
82 Period
84 Wooden pegs
86 Pub. company pile-up
88 Tide
90 Henry Aaron's mother
91 Swiss town
93 Stephen, in France
94 Cure-all
95 Totalitarian policy
96 Persian rug
97 "The Haunted ___ ," poem of 1839
98 Miss Reddy et al.
100 Pheasant
103 Judo workout
104 Hawthorne's birthplace
108 Verboten
109 Wheys
110 Fortune's child
112 Stir
114 Mixologist's milieu
116 Boston fish

Puzzle #14: POETIC LICENSE by Frances Hansen

ACROSS

1 Attacked
6 Dated
11 Old Venetian medal
16 Driver of a kind
21 Superior to
22 "____ thee every hour . . . "
23 A. Doyle's middle name
24 Name meaning "of noble rank"
25 Biblical inventor of flutes and lutes
26 Word with head or hand
27 Girl
28 Egyptian notable
29 Start of a verse
33 Small-minded
34 Dowry
35 Fiddler or hermit
36 House hardware
37 Nigerian tribe
39 Surrender, as one's heart
41 Writer or rasher
44 What "item" is of "time"
48 Shipment, for short
49 El or Jose
51 Fine Japanese china
56 Oliver's audacious request
57 Manufacturers' org.
59 Fit for the job
61 Dwelling
63 Church corner
64 More of verse
70 Occasion
71 He had a whale of a time
72 Linden tree
73 Province of E. Cuba
74 Deepest down
76 Monogram of Prufrock's creator
77 Elegance
78 Wayne's name in "True Grit"
79 Abraham's father
81 Mowgli's early home
82 Croc's cousin
84 Tartuffe's creator
88 Drag strip for Ben Hur
90 Afflict
91 Only vertebrate to possess true hair
96 Dance
97 Neck area
98 Festive
100 New Zealand native

101 More of the verse
105 Molt, to a Yorkshireman
106 Collection
107 "____ take arms against a sea . . . "
108 Aunt, in Acapulco
109 Source: Abbr.
110 Astronaut Gagarin's namesakes
112 Irish patriot Robert: 1778–1803
114 On the double!
117 Synthetic rubber base
119 Confused
121 Name meaning "hairy"
122 Govt. pension plan
123 Canaanite commander: Judges 4:2
127 Doctor Dolittle's Sophie, for one
130 King, in Portugal
132 VMI and MIT
136 End of the verse
142 Full of pith
143 Skip over a vowel
144 Do an editor's job
145 "He maketh me ____ down . . . "
146 Ruined city of Edom, noted for carvings
147 Like most baskets
148 "____ thee late a rosy wreath . . . ": Jonson
149 A Fitzgerald
150 Dutch painter Jan
151 Exhausted
152 Zodiac sign
153 Krupp works locale

DOWN

1 Title of Mecca pilgrim
2 "Like ____ on a log"
3 Gillis, of TV reruns
4 Belay's partner
5 Communications satellite
6 Tommyrot!
7 Chipped in
8 Jack London's Larsen

9 Bumpers or Bayh
10 Whirlpool
11 Happen
12 Name in music lore
13 Site of a rescue mission, July 3, 1976
14 Placed
15 Writer Claude
16 Oleg, in his fashion
17 Not give ____
18 Hound, as one's footsteps
19 "The Tiger" poet
20 Editor/novelist Edmund Hodgson
30 Ruler of a sort
31 Household need
32 Cry of discovery
38 Triple Crown winner, 1935
40 Corset strip
42 Tart
43 Twist
44 Friends, to Titus
45 "____ is an island . . . "
46 Suffix for planet or sanit
47 Plaster of Paris
49 Attach, in a way
50 Plastics ingredient
52 ____-nest
53 Make ____ (get rich)
54 Income, on the Left Bank
55 Toucher-up of imperfect dyes
58 Conductor Zubin
60 Most severe
62 ". . . ____ in the inn"
65 Sonnet units
66 Chore that boys abhor
67 White House nickname
68 Like some orations
69 Three-dimensional scene
75 Saint of Avila: 1515–82
80 Languishes
81 Take off; split
83 Apportion
84 "I saw ____ kissing Santa . . . "
85 "It All Depends ____ "
86 Ring-tailed or ruffed primate
87 "Lord, ____ ?": Matthew 26:22
89 Western resort
90 Ripen

92 Barbara or Hoople
93 Poet Marianne
94 Actor Alan
95 Belgian city on the Meuse
99 Faulty
102 Reputation
103 Hits on the head
104 Dines at home
111 "The Time of Your Life"
     author
113 Bulky
115 Father of Xerxes

116 Jason or Quixote, e.g.
118 Where sampans go to
     and fro
120 Marble
121 City lines
123 Knuckleheads
124 "Experiment to me/Is
     everyone ___ ":
     Emily Dickinson
125 Emulate Dorothy Hamill
126 ___ nous
128 Saxony city

129 Common contraction
131 "Of Thee ___ "
133 Blackthorns
134 Cultivates
135 Mean: Slang
137 "Man Bites Dog," e.g.
138 Swaying loosely
139 XXXVIII years after the
     Battle of Hastings
140 Digging a new subject
141 Shakespearean actor
     Edmund

Puzzle #15: SPOONERIZING by Sam Lake

ACROSS

1 Level
5 Sailors' patron saint
9 Shh!
13 Don Juan's delight
17 Hindu caste
18 Family member
20 She wrote "Them"
22 Cloy; glut
23 Aftershave powder
24 Artist's complaint re a
    drama
26 Shipshape
27 Hebrew song
29 Cancels
30 ___ Park, N.Y.C.
32 Tennyson's "___ Arden"
34 Limiting conditions
36 Entangling
37 Husky bred in the U.S.S.R.
40 Command in a Western
42 Comprehensive
45 Library treasures
46 Script direction
48 Monroe's "___ Good
    Feeling"
50 Autry birthplace, in Texas
51 Paul's friend
53 Paganini's hometown
55 Aligns
57 Tackle
58 ___ Yisrael (Palestine)
60 "Like Niobe, all ___"
62 ___ City, Calif.
64 Marshall Plan initials
65 Shadrach's friend
67 Newsy digest
69 Stratas of the Met
71 Medicinal plant
72 "Peace ___ time":
    Chamberlain
73 Mottled
74 Yalie's rival
76 Strategic Pacific island
77 Late Greek tycoon
81 Hamlet's cry
82 Author of "State Fair"
84 ___ Tuva, U.S.S.R. region
86 Seven, in Sicily
87 Ditto
89 Pea and bean
91 Trotsky and Jaworski
93 Café au ___
94 Wild; savage

96 German child's hero
98 Changed the décor
100 Mauna ___
101 Whirled; purled
103 Slander
105 Counterirritant
107 Within: Prefix
109 Goya's "Maja" et al.
111 Bobby-soxer's "Of course!"
112 Continual
115 Freshen
117 Puget Sound port
120 Broadway group
121 He can't spell chickadee
124 Burden
125 City in Utah
126 Tropical climber
127 Garb for Calpurnia
128 Abominable Snowman
129 Sense; think
130 "___ for All Seasons"
131 What Simon does
132 Concordes

DOWN

1 Small one: Suffix
2 Patty ingredient
3 Girl makes pies, not
    yummy to the tummy
4 ___ Creed: A.D. 325
5 Attractive
6 Roman 52
7 Recuperate
8 Nonet minus one
9 Playwright's cayuse
    emporium
10 Assembly-line group: Abbr.
11 For men only
12 Legatees
13 Starfish or minor planet
14 Do actors do this?
15 Of the ear
16 "Aspostle of the Franks"
19 Angler for congers
21 Gang's language
25 Cattail of India
28 Knowledge
31 Brewer's purchase

33 Read Walton without
    interest
35 Alarming trimmer in a
    wagon
37 Western capital
38 Toughen
39 Hawaiian bird
41 One of 24
43 Plaza
44 Northlander
47 Leo's April ailment
49 Soles beatin' out a
    jazzman's rhythm
52 Allen or Frome
54 Fight site
56 Coil of yarn
59 Epsom ___
61 Carson was one
63 Precincts
66 Blazers
68 Synonym for 15 Down
70 Car that "bombed"
74 Like cryptograms
75 ___ band (cattle on
    parade, proverbially)
78 Old whetstones twisted by
    icy pellets
79 Compound suffix
80 Attack
81 "___ with Lather,"
    musical soap opera
83 Void's partner
85 Carol or Coward
88 What a sane male turns at
    sea
90 Station wagon
92 Frank, Nancy et al.
95 Native of Riga
97 Cicero's "I sit"
99 Philippine tree
102 Talk like a Georgian
104 Periods of fasting
106 Hatfields' foes
108 Idiocy
110 Religious groups
112 Dogie
113 Small shoe size
114 Colliery vehicle
116 Command to Dobbin
118 Jeff's partner
119 Without any changes
122 Key to heredity
123 Culbertson

And now we come to a quartet of unusual *Times* Sunday crosswords that have generated floods of mail from the fans. In each case, the letters could be divided into three types:

    a. "Awful! I couldn't even get started!"
    b. "I solved it, but I really don't understand it."
    c. "Marvelous! The best ever! Let's have more!"

As stated in a previous chapter, no crossword puzzle editor can please all of the fans all of the time. Some solvers are more experienced or more adaptable to innovations than others. Also, many tyros step into waters that are over their heads; they fail to realize that they should continue to hone their skills on easy puzzles in the front sections of crossword puzzle magazines. Editors who are worth their salt cannot continually kowtow to Group A or even Group B. Chances that often lead to advances must be taken.

Will Weng took a courageous chance when he published Puzzle #16 by William Lutwiniak. This startler contains seven unclued numbers and another item in which neither the number nor the clue is indicated! The title, "Do-It-Yourself," gave a sly hint, but some neophytes were still baffled. A few gave up immediately and chided the *Times* for sloppy typography. But others worked on the crossing words until the light dawned. Suddenly they realized that there was a method in the Lutwiniak-Weng madness. Let us hope that sophisticated readers of this book will do the same. Stumped solvers can find the answer on page 187.

□

Puzzle #17, by Bert H. Kruse, presents a different problem. Solvers are asked to play a game of word association. Once again, the title, "Some Two-Steps," is a subtle signal to fans that they should not fill in the first word that occurs to them; instead they should go to the second step. Below are some samples, none of which can be found in the puzzle. They merely serve to indicate how the game is played:

Clue	Step 1	Step 2, Answer
Jungle beasts	LIONS	DETROIT ELEVEN
Moby Dick, e.g.	NOVEL	NEW AND UNUSUAL
N.Y.C. borough	QUEENS	ANNE AND MARY

If still confused, the solver should turn to page 187 for the answer.

□

Jim Page, a CBS executive, created Puzzle #18 and soon discovered that some fans were not on his wavelength. Others, however, tuned in cleverly and hailed his opus as the most interesting they had ever solved in the Sunday *Times*. His puzzle bears some resemblance to the previous one by Mr. Kruse, because solvers should not take the definitions literally. The title asks fans to "Unglue the Clues"—in other words, to take the sections of the definitions apart and think of words to fit each section.

The samples below are not to be found in the puzzle; they simply provide a hint as to what lies in store for anyone tackling this blockbuster.

Clue	*Answer*
Red herring	SKELTON / PRONOUN / CIRCLE
peregrinate	A DUMAS / SMILE / CONSUMED

Solvers who still are baffled will find the answer on page 187.

□

Puzzle #19 has an interesting history. The constructor, Ronald Friedman, came out of the blue and submitted "Strip Tees" to this editor. A glance at the puzzle revealed that he had eliminated all the T's from the main entries but had not dropped them from the smaller words. A letter was immediately dispatched to him. He was commended for his ingenious idea and his apt title, but it was pointed out to him that fans would expect all the T's to be expunged. The letter concluded with a challenge to meet that immense task. Since he had never published a puzzle before, it was assumed that Mr. Friedman would shrug his shoulders, curse the editor and quit.

Quite the contrary! A month later, the revised puzzle arrived. Mirabile dictu, every T had been taken out! Furthermore, the puzzle lived up to all the rules and contained a minimum of esoterica.

On August 19, 1979, the puzzle appeared in the *Times*. The reaction was sensational. In this case, very few solvers found the puzzle impossible to complete. The title had specifically informed them what the gimmick was, and the rather easy clues and familiar words had carried them along to success. In essence, Group C far outnumbered Groups A and B. Among the commendations were letters from fans who had been solving Sunday *Times* puzzles since their inception in 1942. Some of them called it "the greatest" accomplishment in crosswords that they had ever come across. Yours truly is inclined to agree.

What happened to Mr. Friedman? Subsequently he submitted "Noels" as a reprise. The L's were missing, but the rest of the puzzle fell far short of his magnum opus. Since then, he has never been heard from again.

The answer to Puzzle #19 appears on page 188.

Puzzle #16: DO-IT-YOURSELF by William Lutwiniak

ACROSS

1 Communicates in a way
7 Clever
12 Circus member
16 Celtic searobber
21 Grain bristle
22 Of hair
23 Come into view
24 Invierno month
25
*
29 Card game
30 Produces
32 A.L. player
33 Dairy animals
37 Famous last words
38 Footloose one
39 Sesame
40 ____ dictum
42 Diminutive ending
43 Reservoir outlet
48 Passover ceremony
49
55 Inhabitant: Suffix
56 Elms and oaks
57 Word for a weak infield
58 Make happy
59 Black: Lat.
60 Solitary
61 Is footloose
62 Miss Bow
63 Greek letters
64 Café-table leavings
65 ____ nuit
66 Word with full
67 Reconnoiter
68 Chemical ending
69
71 Large vessels
72 Cacophony
74 Holbrook
75 Port of Morocco
76 Windsor or Vernon
78
83 Cartographic item
86 Wine pitchers
87 Badgers
88 Mecca people
89 Tijuana money
90 Catface
91 Crabby
92 Tête-____

93 Life and gravy
94 S.A. toucan
95 Reporter's query
96 Interference
97 Whether ____
98 Night before
99
101 Rustic crossover
102 Abandons hope
104 Gardner
105 Part of the hand
106 Hill-dweller
107 Chair panel
109 Wild goat
112 N.C.O.'s
113 Coiffure
116 Luster
117 Resident of Apia
119
121
127 Dye
128 Tropical tree
129 Plane, in France
130 Eden
131 Wails
132 Recuperate
133 Made tracks
134 Alphabetized

DOWN

1 Untrained
2 "Exodus" man
3 Morse symbol
4 Somewhat: Suffix
5 Indian of West
6 Dinnerware item
7 Estranged
8 Mirabile ____
9 French pronoun
10 French winter resort
11 Organ effects
12 Outlandish bit of luck
13 Recluse
14 Ages and ages
15 ____ Darya

16 Running a temperature
17 U.S. dramatist
18 Warm-sea fish
19 U.S.S.R. city
20 Took a cab
26 Do handwork
28 Reason
31 Swear
33 Having ribs
34 First coed college in U.S.
35
36 Dutch masterpieces
38 Red, to Caesar
41 Gaelic
43 Desolate
44 Plant fiber
45
46 Roman hall
47 Fermenting agents
49 Ascended
50 Times of day
51 Native of Qishm
52 Caesar's was Julius
53 Casaba, e.g.
54 "Ah, me!"
59 Port of Ghana
62 Carne's partner
65 Alpine wind
66 Social units
67 Is mournful
69 Wire measures
70 Mountain passes
71 Swiss card game
73 Alamogordo's county
75 Old stringed instrument
76 Figured expenses
77 Niche
78 N.Z. native
79 Iron, in Bonn
80 Port of Brazil
81 Garbo
82 South American
84 Arthurian locale
85 Circus harbingers
87 Beer and ale
89 Doors, in Lyon
91 Soho domestic
92 Up, in baseball
93 Piffle
95 ____ prohibition
96 City of Georgia

 99 Fits of temper
100 Noisy outburst
103 "___ my glove"
105 Ear part
107 Queen of ___
108 Bicycle part
109 Western resort

110 Have ___ of one's own
111 Sweetie
113 Bumpkin
114 Lily plant
115 Winnie ___ Pu
116 Snick and ___
117 To-do

118 Atlantic pact
120 German pronoun
122 Egg cells
123 Rocky height
124 Liable
125 Whopper
126 Shaver

Puzzle #17: SOME TWO-STEPS by Bert H. Kruse

ACROSS

1 Mess
6 Ark landfall
12 Appoint
16 Golf club
21 Different
22 Singer Vic
23 Arabian head cord
24 Mexican Indian
25 New York City
27 North African kingdom
29 Kind of plate
30 Begins
31 Fyodor and Alexis
33 Toscanini
34 Broke a Commandment
35 House plant
36 Sioux
37 ___ Mahal
40 Plural ending
41 Struck
43 Part of 70 Across
46 Deduced
49 U. S. Nobelist in Literature: 1938
52 D.C. tax collectors
54 Lofty
55 Vacation
57 Breaks a Commandment
58 Fitzgerald forte
59 Kind of jaw
60 Bassanio's beloved
62 Miss Kett
63 Rossetti's "___ Beatrix"
64 The old sod
65 Demi follower
66 Actor Jack
68 Safari figure
69 Soviet rep.
70 Shakespearean tragedy
72 An Argonaut
73 Headliner: Aug. 6, 1926
75 Faith: Fr.
76 Emerson, ___ Concord
77 Genetic offshoots
78 Ravel masterpiece
82 Surpass
85 Out-of-date
86 " . . . ___ passion to tatters"
87 Noted Swiss poet: 1821–81
88 Resort east of Altdorf
89 Island group off Ireland
90 Beat pounders
91 Caught

93 ___ code
94 Hogarth subject
95 Mount sacred to the Muses
97 Thug
98 Originate
99 Hot time in Paree
100 Hit song of 1912, with "My"
102 F. L. Wright's home in Wis.
105 "The Praise of Folly" author
108 Occupied
110 Spareable item
111 French possessive
112 Those born July 23–August 22
113 Hair style
115 Canyon mouths
117 Drenched
120 Playwright Tad
121 Erstwhile source of plumes
122 Anent
126 U. S. anthropologist: 1901–78
128 Vodka drink
131 Cold period in Spain
132 Light a fire under
133 University board member
134 Sam or Toby
135 Island in Taiwan Strait
136 Imperative, e.g.
137 Talks back
138 Paravane

DOWN

1 Anderson's "___ Your Houses"
2 Roman emperor
3 Oates book
4 Give up
5 Charlemagne's dom.
6 Fatty
7 Blacksnake
8 Chemical compounds
9 Wallabies, for short
10 Tropical herb
11 Having left a will
12 Brazilian port
13 Money in Israel
14 Atlas material

15 Building part
16 Rose of ___
17 Doughboy's leg covering
18 Koolau Range site
19 Done
20 Notorious uxoricide
26 Scowl
28 The Sprats, e.g.
32 Luges
34 Paddock papas
35 Italian philosopher: 1822–1905
36 Florida city
37 Dyes
38 Chameleons
39 Bumppo's creator
42 Zero
43 Ticket
44 "Essay on Man" author
45 More incensed
47 Besides
48 Matelot's wheel-rope
50 County in Colo.
51 Cessation
53 Excel
56 Previously, previously
58 NATO's late cousin
60 Containers for liquids
61 Tilden in 1876
63 Plague
65 Trio
67 Keep ___ (persevere)
68 Bialy's relative
70 Goes one's way
71 ___ effort
72 Encrusted
74 Lorna of fiction
76 Knowing
77 Pharmacist's waxy preparation
78 Seven: Comb. form
79 "Dondi" cartoonist
80 Shirt ruffles
81 Large pulpitdesk
83 Antipodean
84 Grooms
85 Bell the cat
86 Frogs' kin
88 Essence
90 Bag man
92 "___ Dei"
93 "Mikado" trio
95 Thackeray's "Henry ___"
96 "___ Romance," 1936

101 Piscators
103 Halts
104 Unwilling
106 Kin of birches
107 So long
109 Holes-in-one, often
113 W. African antelope

114 Inquired
116 Pickle
117 Noah's firstborn
118 Chaplin's widow
119 Plankton collector
120 Spanish Superrealist
121 Roe

122 Pittypat in "G.W.T.W."
123 Conventicle group
124 Prefix for prompter
125 Humdinger
127 Kind of runner
129 Teachers' org.
130 Quid pro ___

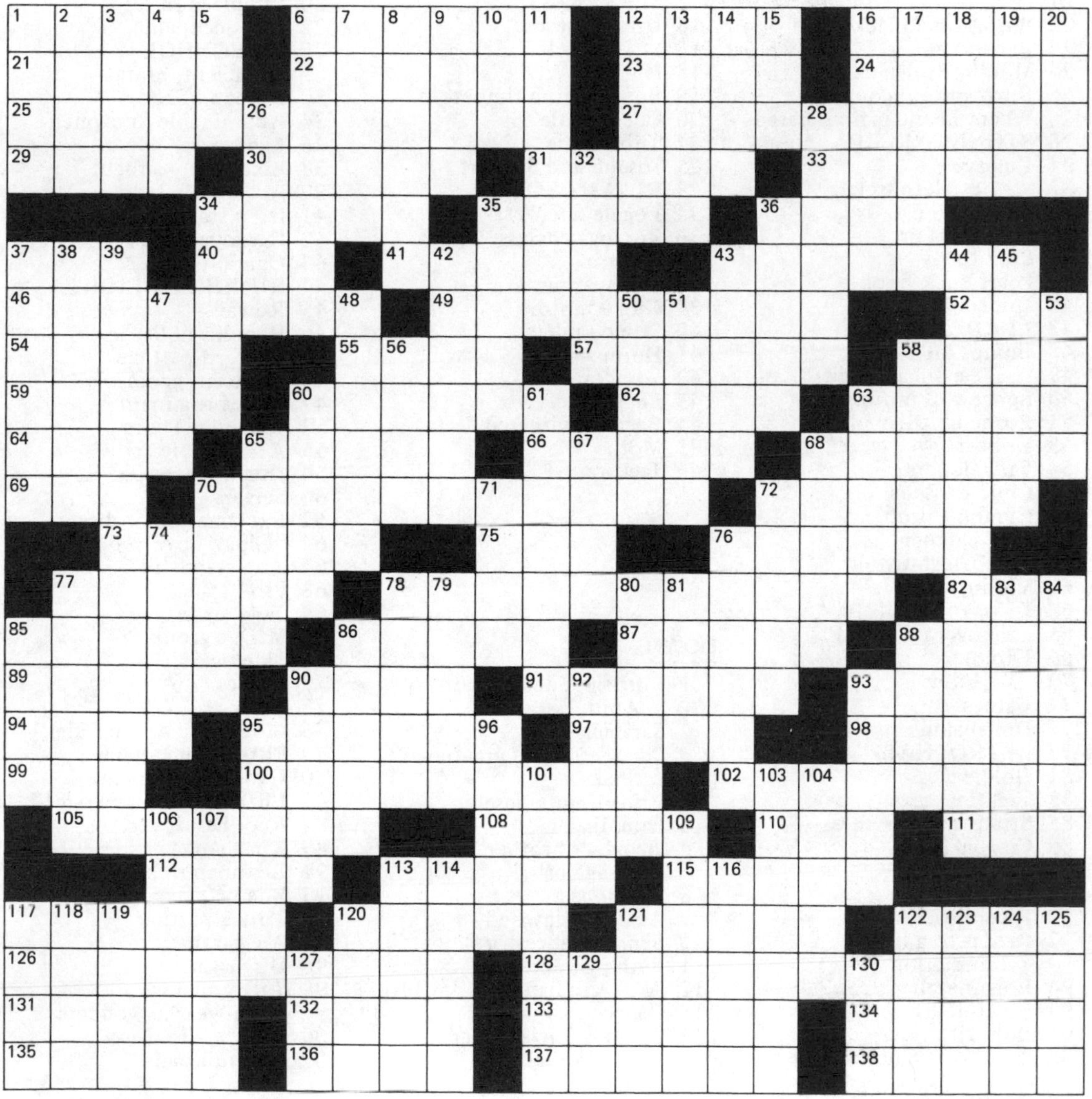

[Crossword grid with numbered cells: 1–138]

Puzzle #18: UNGLUE THE CLUES by Jim Page

ACROSS

1 Nobelist in Physics: 1944
5 World's busiest airport
10 Position: Comb. form
15 Comic
18 Argentine press
21 Ora pro ___
22 Writes on a blackboard
23 Bar order
24 Moulin Rouge dance
25 Burst or burgeon
26 Where Leander floundered
28 STONEWALLED
31 Lineage
32 ___ as Methuselah
33 Part of A.E.C.
35 Stage curtain
37 Clay today
38 Pearl Buck book
40 Joint
42 LEADENNESS
48 Bumps into
49 ___ ear (hearkened)
50 Spore sacs in fungi
51 Borne by the wind
53 Upbeat
54 Parishioners
55 Child of Zeus
57 Cyrano's problem
58 Cow catcher
59 Baseball statistics
61 Violin string
63 Dross of metal
65 ___ over (ponder)
66 Lariat
70 ___ Flow
74 Witnesses
77 Dimension
78 BETROTHAL
81 Goldie
83 Treatise
85 Stradivari's teacher
86 City in Tenn.
87 Concert halls
88 Swear at
90 River near Gerona
92 Parties to a legal
     transaction
94 Fortuneteller's card
97 Fleur-de-lis
101 Boil with rage
105 "___ of a Salesman"

106 "___ the West Wind"
107 Fundamental
109 Queenly nickname
110 Romans' small shields
111 Clans
112 SPARERIBS
115 Urban eyesore
116 St., ave., etc.
118 Marker
119 Boat-bottom timber
120 Click beetle
122 Tubers' kin
125 Joseph and Stewart
129 RIGAMAROLE
134 Locale out West
136 Zoological class: Comb.
     form
137 Chopper parts
139 Gun a motor
140 Stone tablets
141 Dorm sound
142 Wonder
143 Beatitudes verb
144 Became withered
145 Moth
146 Jackstay

DOWN

1 Correspondence courtesy:
     Abbr.
2 Saracens
3 "___ afraid of greatness":
     Shak.
4 Bring upon oneself
5 Humdinger
6 Hengist's brother
7 Is up against
8 Hilarious
9 Actress Winwood
10 Semites' ancestor
11 Bath powder
12 "___ are liars": Psalm 116
13 Daggers
14 "Who is Silvia? what ___
     . . .": Shak.

15 Lack of justice
16 Writer Rand
17 Obtain
19 Time of youthful
     inexperience
20 Fireplace fixture
22 Lab occupant
27 PIGEONHOLES
29 Sufficient, of old
30 Roman official
34 Abominable Snowmen
36 Land map
38 Like Lindy's flight
39 Actor Skinner
41 It, in Italy
42 Use a yardstick
43 Quarantines
44 HUNDREDWEIGHT
45 Rowan
46 Hamill's milieu
47 Charged particle
48 SE Asian peninsula
49 Andes ruminant
52 These, in Tours
55 A ___ Able
56 Down-Under people
60 Salvers
62 Exclamation of disgust
64 "Gipsy Love" composer
67 ___ standstill
68 Pro ___
69 Nets' ex-league
71 M.D.'s group
72 Sidekick
73 Curve
75 Glow
76 "Ida! ___ Apple Cider"
79 Pittsburgh catcher
80 Handle a problem
82 Elizabethan playwright
84 Reo, Essex, etc.
89 Kinsman
91 Boatman's chore
93 Edenic place
94 Turn's partner
95 An Astaire
96 Disgusting
98 Talk gibberish
99 Horn-wearing goddess
100 Thus, to Tacitus
102 City railroads

103 Asian festival
104 Golfer's problem
108 City on Tokyo Bay
110 Ecdysiasts
113 "Heads I win; tails ____"
114 Duck or color
116 Speak a piece

117 Market figure
121 Part of a switch
123 Hound
124 Cubic meter
126 Horse opera
127 Utah resort
128 Gaza or Sunset

130 Stake
131 "If ____ My Way"
132 Peen of a hammer
133 Row
134 Bikini part
135 Poetic preposition
138 Episcopacy

Puzzle #19: STRIP TEES by Ronald Friedman

ACROSS

1 Type of post
7 Former Yankee pitcher
11 African lake or republic
15 Convenes
18 Yield to gluttony
19 Hawaii and Alaska in 1958: Abbr.
20 Addiction
21 Poetry of a people
23 David Frost's "TW3" of TV
26 Main artery
27 Kefauver
28 Rouses
29 Wild and excited
31 Fifty forming one
34 Stumble
36 Doctrines
37 Advances slowly
38 Turner's agcy.
39 Eye-opener
42 Serve food for a banquet
43 Landon
44 Pleaded
45 Moon's age on Jan. 1
47 She-bear, in Granada
50 Basketball targets
52 Ragged
56 Debases
58 Turtles
61 Playground item
63 ___ Benedict
64 Pule or mewl
65 Maris or Williams
66 City on the Merrimack
68 Inoculation or jigger
70 Quote
71 Pigs' kin
72 Suffix for gang or team
73 Pronoun
74 Pagan
76 Reese
77 Fool's gold
79 High schooler's problem
80 Heckled
82 Musical passages
85 Enjoyed oneself
87 Flow
89 Greet
90 Meat dish
91 Writing pad
92 Small amount

95 Floor piece
96 Honolulu is here
98 Poe tale, with "The"
103 Throw stones at
104 Stop for gas
106 New Rochelle college
107 Separate carefully
108 Cash or charm
109 Obsolete
111 Slide
112 Deep cut
114 Houston athlete
115 Bikini adjectives
122 Decayed
123 Margarine
124 Land west of Wales
125 One who samples oolong
126 Boy
127 Floating or swimming
128 Rent payer
129 Provides funds for

DOWN

1 Something to pledge
2 Gardner
3 Morning moisture
4 Most wrathful
5 Nutcrackers' suites
6 One who collects
7 Actor Ayres
8 Pulled apart
9 Gift
10 Soliciting
11 Dance step
12 Melt
13 To the stern
14 Perry's adversaries
15 Spiritualists' meeting
16 Tim's tune
17 Sally
22 Black Hawk's tribe
24 Trying
25 Number of Bears or Pigs
30 Makes into law
31 Criticize severely

32 He tries to suit the customer
33 Popular refrain
35 Michelangelo works
39 Omen
40 Keats work
41 Announce formally
46 Prefix for fix
48 Musician's transition
49 Analyze ore
51 Track
53 Shoots dice anew
54 Nondrinker
55 Lower in rank
57 Dead heats
59 Ringing of bells
60 Born: Fr.
62 Remainder
67 Policeman, at times
68 Former Iranian rulers
69 Six-armed Greek goddess
71 Board's partner
72 Detect
75 Degree of warmth
76 Cross out
78 Actress Louise
81 Swiss hero
82 Metalworkers
83 Electrical needs
84 Addison's colleague
86 Used the tub
88 Biblical weed
93 Pretend
94 Continental army volunteer
97 Basically, in Nice
99 Site of the Teatro São Carlos
100 Norse god of mischief
101 Sweet liqueur
102 ___-waiting
104 Crowd sound
105 Antiseptic
108 Leading
110 American inventor
113 Cygnet
116 Affirmative vote
117 Part of Q.E.D.
118 Harold of comics
119 This, in Valencia
120 Salamander
121 Time periods: Abbr.

8

Diagramless Puzzles

Back in 1925, Margaret Farrar and her two colleagues — Prosper Buranelli and F. Gregory Hartswick — were accustomed to meeting for lunch at a restaurant. They would carry with them a pile of puzzles to be edited. On one occasion they discovered that the diagram for one of the puzzles was missing. No problem for Hartswick! Using the clues, he drew up the proper diagram on the back of a menu. Thus, the diagramless puzzle was fortuitously born.

Mrs. Farrar introduced the diagramless in the *Times* in the 1940s. Since then her policy of publishing that type of puzzle every fourth Sunday has been followed.

Has the diagramless puzzle caught on? Well, yes and no. A rather small but rabid group of fans prefers this challenge above such other offshoots as Puns and Anagrams or Cryptics. On the other hand, when Simon and Schuster published a book of diagramless puzzles edited by Mrs. Farrar, the investment did not pay off.

One of the chief reasons that diagramless puzzles have not achieved widespread popularity is the mind-boggling effort they require to solve. Also, the average fan must set aside several hours to complete one. But the greatest deterrent is that 1-Across in most diagramless puzzles does not occupy the top left box in a rectangle. It may appear as far back as the twentieth box in a 23 x 23 puzzle or anywhere in between. To help neophytes, some puzzle magazines tell the solver where to find the "starting box," but dyed-in-the-wool fans resent this crutch. They would rather limp along and discover the secret themselves.

An additional obstacle to the popularity of the genre is that well-meaning explanations for solving become so complicated that the learner gives up. But let's see if we can overcome that problem with a few simple statements.

In reality, every crossword puzzle can be solved without a diagram. The key to the evolution of the pattern is the numbers for the clues. If you have never solved a diagramless puzzle before, start by solving a regular printed puzzle using a blank piece of graph paper instead of the printed diagram. When you finish the puzzle you will have produced the proper diagram.

The above is easy because you know you are working with a perfectly square pattern. The challenge of solving a true diagramless puzzle lies in the fact that the pattern, although symmetrical, is also of irregular shape, with many indentations. Thus, solvers will need to work on sections of the puzzle separately until they discover how the sections come together—much in the fashion of completing a jigsaw puzzle.

Example:

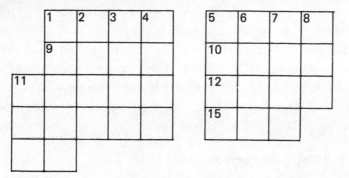

At this point, the solver realizes that numbers 13 and 14 do not appear in the Across column. An examination of the clues indicates these numbers go Down *only*; therefore, they must be placed in the word at 12-Across. See what happens now:

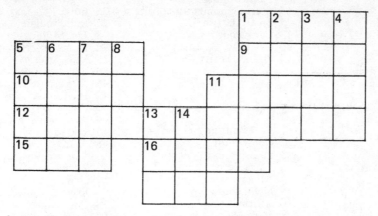

The clue at 12-Across, "open-handedness," indicates a noun suffix is required. Such an ending appears under 11-Across.

Enough of explanations. As John Dewey said, "We learn by doing." On the pages that immediately follow you will find the clues for two diagramless puzzles. Now get yourself several sheets of graph paper and discover what fun you've been missing all your life. Incidentally, you'll be pleased to learn that the definitions are simple and the entries are almost devoid of esoterica. Those are two criteria for most diagramless puzzles—the theory being that the challenge is stiff enough without trickery or abstrusity.

Finally, you will see that the two diagramless puzzles presented herewith are the traditional type. The end results are jagged but symmetrical patterns that are not intended to form some object, but each does have a theme.

In that connection, some constructors like to build diagramless puzzles that give the solver an extra surprise after the puzzle has been completed. Norton Rhoades, for example, recently used the Alamo as a theme, and the diagram formed the shape of that memorable shrine. One of Stephen Shalom's creations emerged as a telephone; another, with a monetary theme, produced a dollar sign.

In Will Weng's day the ultimate in shaping diagramless puzzles was reached by Stanley A. Kurzban. The outlines of New York State appeared and inside the puzzle chief cities like Utica, Rochester and New York were located exactly where they are on a map. The only flaw in that opus was the irregular, asymmetrical pattern which drove some of the less experienced fans up the wall.

Diagramless #1: 15 × 22 by Dick Dempsey

ACROSS

1 Lincoln
4 Actress Myrna
7 Colophon
9 Republic name: 1937–49
10 Adjective for this diversion
13 Exclamation of discovery
15 Arena cry
16 Adherent
19 Buttons or Skelton
20 Masefield heroine
21 Menagerie
22 Daily diversion
29 Small case
30 Of an age
31 Indian group
32 Rim
33 Reference for solvers
37 Craggy hill
38 Energy unit
39 U.S. 66, e.g.
40 Suffix with Euclid
41 Middleton products
47 Swamp
48 ___ bene
50 Prefix meaning "both"
51 Torment
52 Taub product
59 Fort ___, Calif.
60 Pub order
61 Knock

62 Pumpkin or pecan ___
63 Gullet
64 Pasha's cousin
65 Starting points for solvers
72 Small flatfish
73 Card game
74 Yoko
75 Ordinal suffix

DOWN

1 Foreman finisher in '74
2 Constrictor
3 ___ and dart, decorative molding
4 Abner's size
5 Metal source
6 Affirmative
8 U. of Maine site
9 Correct
10 Grooves made by cabinet-makers
11 Winged
12 Hot sound
13 Circle segment
14 Pronoun
17 Hurok
18 Lou (The ___) Groza

23 Hemo or thermo follower
24 ___ as (for example)
25 Sage
26 Equal
27 Indic tongue
28 Jagged lines
34 Home entertainer
35 Main arteries
36 Pressing
41 Mendicant's request
42 Island near Jamaica
43 Check
44 Actress Swenson
45 D.C. group
46 Asterisk
47 Smoothed wood
49 Prizes
52 Dad
53 Psychic Geller
54 Condemns
55 Jai ___
56 Salamanders
57 West
58 Agent
66 Tokyo's old name
67 Strike out
68 Nigerian people
69 D-day commander
70 Cereal grass
71 Extreme degree

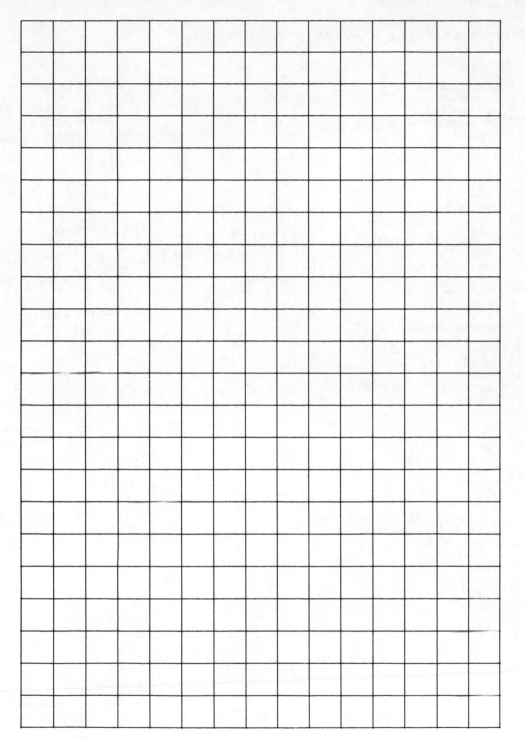

Diagramless #2: 20 × 21 by Kathryn K. Righter

ACROSS

1 Waldorf and Caesar
7 Elementary text
8 Mab and Titania
9 Reverence
11 Augment
12 Computer input
14 Two-legged dragon
16 Egyptian goddess
20 Polish
22 Repair
25 Julep herb
26 Torrid
27 Caviar
28 Creature in Persian folklore
29 Partner of every
31 Compositions for two
33 Affirm
34 Greek letter
35 Cuckoo
36 Pippin
39 Well-known Pilgrim
41 Expansive
43 Brogans
44 Billiard shot
45 This: Fr.
46 ___ favor (please, in Ponce)
47 Blurt out
49 Shut
51 Bristle
53 Slime
54 Golf score
55 Ship-shaped clock
56 Press
57 River in Italy
59 Dirndl
61 Imparted
62 Monster famed for riddles
64 Commercial transaction
65 Meaning: Abbr.
68 Tugboat service
69 Winged horse
72 Vestments
73 Snuggle

DOWN

1 Health resort
2 Onassis
3 Money in Verona
4 Ringed in by
5 Act
6 Potential grads
8 Gala celebration
9 Tennis term
10 Surge
13 Limb
14 Hecate and Duessa
15 Thetis and Galatea
16 Place on a skewer
17 Strainers
18 Concerning
19 Agitate
20 Haggard novel
21 Stores up selfishly
23 Negative word
24 Of the: Fr.
30 Sharpen
31 Crow's cousin

32 Fabled beasts
36 Vipers
37 Bird of fable
38 Redcap
39 Hippolyta
40 Potential
42 Summer in Nice
47 Seethe
48 Learning
49 I.R.S. employee
50 Small ape
52 To the rear
58 Goddess of plenty
59 Farm building
60 Was cognizant
63 Fedoras
65 Greek commune
66 Protection
67 Truth; reality
69 Greek god
70 Salt, in Sedan
71 Custom

The answers to Diagramless Puzzles #1 and #2 appear on page 189.

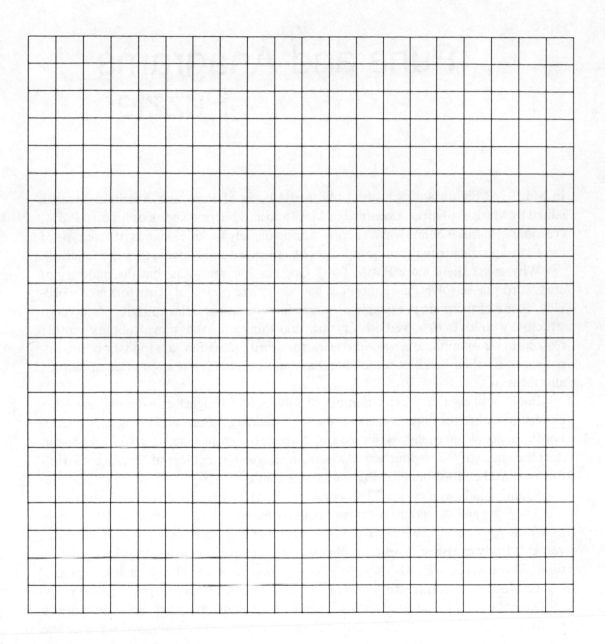

9

Puns and Anagrams
Puzzles

In May 1963 Simon and Schuster published a book of Puns and Anagrams puzzles edited by Margaret Farrar. Constructor Mel Taub also put out a book of his own P.&A. creations. Neither volume was a success. Unfortunately the aficionados of that type of crossword puzzle are in the minority. But, like the diagramless fans, they are fanatical.

Why aren't there more P.&A. fans? One possible reason is that the majority of crossword puzzle solvers are sobersides who don't like puns and other forms of word-play. Some of them are the people who "graduate" to diagramless puzzles. A top constructor, who loves to solve both Cryptics and Puns and Anagrams, submits another reason. In his opinion, average American crossword puzzle fans are too lazy or too impatient to try their hands at something that requires extra cerebration or an additional allotment of time.

But it is likely that a great number of solvers of "straight" crosswords just don't understand what they are required to do when tackling a Puns and Anagrams puzzle. For those people an explanation is due, and who is better qualified to give such a lesson than the queen of Puzzledom herself? Here, then, is an abridgment of Margaret Farrar's foreword to her 1963 book of Puns and Anagrams.

"Candy made with cream." The word you need has seven letters. What's the word?

The Puns and Anagrams crossword is an evolution that started back in 1924, when, as Will Rogers put it, the general public learned the difference between horizontal and vertical. Early crosswords were simplicities, made of short words and primary definitions. Those were the EMU-MOA-ROC days, when a tree was always "a woody plant."

Gradually, as constructors became more venturesome, and solvers more accustomed to the gambit, the puzzles took on a more ambitious character. Rules were drawn up by an interested group called the National Puzzlers' Association, and the style was set for America's crosswords: allover interlock; open, symmetrical pattern using one-sixth or less black squares; no unkeyed letters (i.e., letters appearing in one word only);

due restraint in the use of obsolete, obscure words; only a one-word answer per definition.

But as early as 1928, the humorous puzzle made its appearance in books, and in magazines such as *Judge*. Ted Shayne proceeded to take off on many a flight of fancy in his "Cockeyed Crosswords," which achieved fame in the pages of the once-popular *Liberty* magazine. And later Albert Morehead, aided and abetted by Jack Luzzatto, published the book *Double-Talk Puzzles*.

When the Sunday *New York Times Magazine* inaugurated a puzzle page in 1942, Puns and Anagrams became a permanent resident of the lower half of the page. The topical puzzle, mainstay of crossword popularity, kept to its straight defining style, but the Puns and Anagrams were, to quote from *Judge's* earlier statement of the case, "not edited in conformity with any rules whatever. Our only requisites are that the spaces shall be square; some must be black and others vacant; some of the spaces shall contain neat little cardinal numbers; and above all, the definitions shall be ambidextrous and witty."

Over the years, Puns and Anagrams came to acquire special characteristics. No un-keyed letters were allowed, so that the solver would always have two clues to each letter. The puzzles had to be first-class constructions with a low word total, thereby avoiding most of those unconcealable repeater words. And they were made with the specific aim of lending themselves to the Puns and Anagrams treatment, containing words capable of being twisted into amusing anagrams or amenable to entertaining camouflage of other sorts.

How does one go about solving a Puns and Anagrams puzzle? Well, not in an orthodox manner, that's certain. Let's go back to the definition at the beginning of this exposition — a seven-letter word defined as "candy made with cream." We suppose the word will be the name of a candy. But in this sort of puzzle, "made with cream" is likely to mean that the final *word* has the word *cream* in it. If we juggle the letters in *cream* (remembering that there are two more letters to be added), does anything suggest itself? Why, of course, *caramel* — a "candy made with cream"!

There are, of course, many helpful hints. An important one, as we have just seen, is Do exactly as you are told. Many clues contain concealed *instructions* in words such as *add, back, use, turn,* etc., that tell the solver how to proceed. "Backbite" may be *pin*, reversed from *nip*.

The clue to a four-letter word may read "appropriate part of Vermont." "Appropri-ate" telegraphs two meanings — "specially suitable or proper" and, as a verb, "take or confiscate." What can one take from "Vermont" that will be specially suitable? The answer, *vert* which means "green," is certainly suitable to the Green Mountain State.

Spotting an anagram is a primary step of great value in getting ahead. If the clue

Puns and Anagrams by Mel Taub

ACROSS

1 They're getting up in the world
8 Pollutes the seabeds
15 Line for G.I. to man
16 W.W. II queue?
17 Site of Bay Area A.M.A. deal
18 Term for all you med. students
19 Did rite?
20 She's for railroads, that is
22 It's the same as in. or yd.
23 Give it a ___ (triple it)
24 End of a cat or nap, but not a catnap
25 In South Carolina, #1 sch. subj.
26 Herr Reiner's middle name
28 Simon says he's a king
30 Ted and I are even
31 Tailor's activity with ribbed fabrics
33 One way to remove a beard
35 A ragtag U.N. biggie
37 Ans.: Expert
40 He turned on ladies and Persians
44 He raises cane with Veronica
45 Sink that's most wonderful
47 Xt
48 Diminutive gal from Ill.
49 Kind of line in business
50 Group causing guns to go off
51 A Morse code symbol
53 Opposite of outlost
55 Short Long Island Army cop
56 Finding someone a gin mate
58 Hopefully, like smog in L.A. in 2001
60 Angered swordsman's position
61 Home of camel tamer, i.e.
62 He has a voice that will not rest
63 He broke rear leg while carousing

DOWN

1 Make men star, fashionably
2 Concern of Dr. Atkins or Alice
3 Like jewelry of Anita, e.g.
4 Rick's predecessor
5 A way for G. to get ration
6 Rowed, in effect
7 Establishing link to stag
8 Dot's in mood to play this
9 Handy item when on the fence
10 Start of Ger. game
11 Companion of an Abner
12 Stanislas is here, as is Eli
13 Cleaned and adjusted boot
14 Shore disease
21 Musical event for Lions' gang
27 Guest who made the grade
28 Note: radical is bogged down
29 Participated in NATO's council
30 Peculiarity of most artists
32 Dearth of resin?
34 A U.N. follower?
36 Stranger makes men cower
37 Expands details
38 The TV I need must be clear
39 In golf, i.e., a hazard
41 A medical point
42 Blackbird spouse; a live one, too
43 It binds like plaster
46 Stand-in for playwright in RR terminals
52 Mr. Lipton?
53 It comes before in re
54 It's on the watch
55 L'Gershwin
57 Half the trains in N.Y.C.
59 Dress bare stone at night's onset

writer has been clever enough, the anagram will be well concealed: "Just the same, it's Henri" has *Matisse* hidden in "same it's." "Praises an Egyptian god" is easy for *Serapis*.

Partial anagrams are also fair play when a complete one cannot be employed.

And the astute solver watches out for connective words, innocently dropped in, that will provide big hints — *with, from, to, about, in, off,* and so on. For example, "Washington with cap off" will come out *ital* — that is, *capital* with "cap off."

The sharp-eyed solver will realize that Roman numerals in a clue are useful as letters — or that ordinary numbers, as in "the 5 and 10," may become V and X in a word.

"One" or "1" often indicates I, but "eye" may get into the act too. "Are" or "our" can suggest R, and "see" or "sea" will be fairly obvious for C. A question mark usually telegraphs a really bad pun coming up.

These tips reveal only a few of the tricks used, but enough to get you started — with the fair warning that there are ad-lib proceedings ahead. At first reading, a clue may make no sense at all. But let your mind wander a little . . . the light will dawn. Or leave one mystifying clue and go on to the next. The second time around, the sense often appears like magic.

Even a neophyte has an excellent chance of solving Puns and Anagrams. Remember that these puzzles are built of proper words, and that by tradition the solver is often provided with two clues for every letter. If the Across entries baffle you, a look at the Down list may give the extra hint that will crack a whole corner. Enjoy being baffled for a bit, knowing that the moment of truth will come, attended by a wonderful exhilaration when you've written the right word into the right place.

□

As every experienced Puns and Anagrams fan knows, for several decades Mel Taub has been recognized as the best constructor of that type of puzzle. Incidentally, he is also one of the top creators of American Cryptics. It takes him five times longer to put together a P.&A. puzzle than to construct a Cryptic. The former contains 68 to 74 words, all of which must be interlocked; the latter consists of 26 to 32 words, and the constructor's task is eased by the use of unkeyed letters.

Mel has added his own touch to Puns and Anagrams. He has loosened the rules in order to provide more leeway to the constructor and simultaneously make the clues more sensible. For example his definition for ONIONS in a recent puzzle was "They're added soon in recipes." The anagram is "soon in." The extra phrase "in recipes" helps to tip off the solver that some kind of food is called for. In the pre-Taub era that phrase was not permitted. Although the clues were more clean-cut, the puzzles were often more difficult to solve.

Here are some other Taubisms:

Clue	Answer	Explanation
Score at the middle of the eleventh	EVEN	EL(EVEN)TH
He took article from garbage	BAGGER	GARBAGE minus A
Kind o' classed?	ICON	ICON-O-CLAST
Time before Dick ate?	ERA	ERA-DIC-ATE
Ringer I took on as lawyer	BELL I	BELL + I
Mag's follower	GOT	MAG-GOT
431 or 471 awesome miles	SEA	

That last one is one of the many Taubian innovations. The solver is required to figure out that S is the fourth letter of "awesome," E is the third or seventh letter, and A is the first letter. Get it?

Mel plays all kinds of other tricks with letters. For instance, a recent clue for FLICK was "flambaste," and VEER was once defined as "___ off to see the vizard." Worse yet, ERECTOR was signaled by "correge man of poritics?" (Sometimes this wordmaster is inscrutable.) Casey, standing for K-C, is one of Mel's favorite names. Thus, CREAKED is clued as "Walked on old joints like Casey Reade."

Puns are Mel's meat. A FINN is "a European with five bucks" and TENNER is defined as "Bill gets the drift?" His anagrams are sharp, too. As examples consider just two: SENATOR ("one star in the Capitol"); SMEARED ("branded me as Red").

By this time, you should be ready to match wits with M.T. If you don't let yourself get discouraged, you won't come up empty (pun intended).

If you must peek, the answer appears on page 189.

American Cryptics

Every year, more and more experienced crossword puzzle solvers in the United States are turning to Cryptics created by American constructors and are discovering a new form of fun and excitement. In a letter to this writer, one fan recently wrote, "Thanks for publishing the Cryptics! After solving regular crosswords for three decades, I was beginning to get bored—probably because the challenge decreased as familiarity increased. Now I feel reborn, in a way. It's like starting all over again; once more I have to shift my brain into high gear, and each time I unravel a word in the puzzle I feel like a conqueror!"

There seem to be three groups of solvers who don't go in for American Cryptics:

1. those who have no interest whatsoever in puns, anagrams and other types of wordplay
2. those who like Puns and Anagrams puzzles but are unwilling or unable to proceed to the next step
3. those who have tried British Cryptics and have been frustrated.

Let Group One rest in peace; Group Two requires a bit of prodding to climb the next step of the ladder to new thrills. Group Three should be advised to try again—this time with an authentic American Cryptic that contains no references to rugby, cricket, small English towns and obscure quotations. Nor will the American puzzle resort to strange letter codes with which the British solvers have become familiar.

For the reader whose appetite for solving American Cryptics has been whetted, two typical ones will be presented a bit later along with instructions and tips to neophytes. But prior to that treat, a few words should be said on behalf of the British. After all, they made the London *Times* editors eat humble pie in 1930 when those arbiters finally succumbed to the CWP craze and published a puzzle. Back in 1924 the newspaper had scoffed at the crosswords fad in an article entitled "An Enslaved America."

But the British eventually went beyond mere imitation of Americans. Led by

Edward Powys Mather, a translator and literary critic who preferred witty definitions to the stodgy American ones of that day, they gradually evolved their own brand of crossword puzzle. Mather loved to pit his ingenious mind against the brains of the highbrows. Specializing in fiendishly tricky clues, he chose an appropriate pseudonym — Torquemada (after the notorious Spanish grand inquisitor). To Mather, humor and wordplay were the supreme goals, and all obstructions were discarded. Hence, he threw aside the idea that every letter in an Across word must also fit into a Down word. His unkeyed creations were emulated by such other British greats as Afrit and Ximenes (noms de plume, of course).

Addiction to Cryptics soon spread throughout Great Britain, and almost every newspaper in the United Kingdom was forced to publish a puzzle. Today any traveler who takes a train or bus in England will see many fellow passengers poring over such definitions as "The bunippedd" (6,2,3,3), "She upset dean, I gathered" (5) and "A pram for a stroller?" (8,5).

The answers to that trio, by the way, are NIPPED IN THE BUD; DIANE; and CARRIAGE TRADE.

Recently this editor was asked by the head of a British crossword club to send him a typical 15 x 15 American puzzle for the edification and enjoyment of his clientele. The puzzle was printed in his little magazine and the club members were invited to submit their reactions. As might have been expected, the great majority disliked the puzzle because it required them to match knowledge — rather than wits — with the constructor. Also the American idiom baffled them. Such entries as YENTA and BEAN BALL were beyond their ken.

Are the British cleverer and less knowledgeable than Americans? Probably not. The moral seems to be that CWP fans are more comfortable with the type of puzzle that is familiar to them and tend to shy away from what is new and different.

At any rate, the purpose of the following paragraphs is to help American solvers break through the Cryptics barrier and eventually come to enjoy an exciting challenge.

HOW TO SOLVE CRYPTIC PUZZLES

First of all, Cryptics are eminently fair! Somewhere in every definition you will find the true meaning of the word — usually stated directly and sometimes implied. Along with the "straight" clue, you'll find other words and phrases which involve some kind of verbal high jinks — and that's where the fun begins.

Let's discuss *anagrams*, for example. Suppose that the definition reads "Story that got Ryan mad" (4). The answer is YARN. Of course, "story" is the synonym. The anagram is "Ryan." But you might ask why "mad" is included. The reason is that "Ryan" is a crazy spelling for YARN.

To make solving a bit easier, constructors often signal the presence of an anagram by placing an adjective before it. Watch for words like *addled, confused, clumsy, inept* and *eccentric*. Sometimes an adverb like *perhaps* or *possibly* tips you off to an anagram. For instance, a definition might read "This kind of hen could possibly make son rich" (7). CORNISH is the answer and "son rich" is the possible other arrangement of the letters.

Occasionally a verb gives the anagram away. For example, the clue might be "Roast cracked up the ballplayer" (5). If you "crack up" "roast," you'll find ASTRO (any Houston baseball player). Incidentally, rules relating to punctuation and syntax are often violated in Cryptics. In the above example, one might expect a colon or dash after "cracked up," but such separators are deliberately omitted—the better to mystify you.

Another example is "Disturb the bear in sleep" (8). The verb tells you to "disturb" (break up) what follows. The anagram is "the bear in" and those letters become HIBER-NATE when "disturbed."

The following anagram recalls a feat of Moses: "Where water was *erased* radically" (3,3). The answer is RED SEA. By the way, note how the numbers after the clue tell you that two three-letter words are called for.

Sometimes Cryptics constructors resort to partial anagrams. In the puzzle that follows this exposition a clue reads "Hide most of the schedule." The answer is SECLUDE. Note how "hide" provides the real meaning while "schedule" contains most of the letters in SECLUDE.

Reversals are special forms of anagrams. Here's a simple example: "Deserters go back on a star" (4). The answer is RATS. The word "back" denotes that "star" should be reversed. Some other indicators are *backward, receding* and *returning*.

Variations of the reverse method occur in Down words. Since the opposite direction is *upward,* some form of that word might be used. For instance, let us say that the clue for 2-Down is "Star goes up the river" (4). The answer is AVON. The ascending star, of course, is NOVA. Incidentally, the clue slyly tries to deceive you into imagining a leading Hollywood actor being sent to jail. This type of elfish deceit is part of the game. If you're gullible, you're more likely to be fallible!

Sometimes a reversal in a Down word is signaled by "north" or "northward." Examine the following, for instance: "Tram travels northward to get to the market" (4). The answer is MART (for "market"). Notice how the tram is going upward—or "northward," since north is always at the top in maps and other charts.

Similarly, in Across words, you may find "east" or "west" in the clue. The former often indicates a direction to the right and the latter suggests a leftward direction. Here's an example of a reversal combined with a geographic reference: "Zoo animal; it returns from W. Germany" (5). The answer is TIGER. Note how *it* "returns" (reads backward). "W. Germany" indicates that the left portion of Germany (Ger) is called for.

Another Cryptics technique is the use of *two meanings.* Such clues are comparatively easy. Some examples are "dull walker" (PEDESTRIAN) and "Do a striptease while jets leave" (TAKE OFF).

Word splitting, commonly called *charades,* is still another device. Consider the following:

Signatory	Sign a tory
Redisplayed	Red is played
Buckskin	Buck's kin
Hippocrates	Hippo crates

You can imagine the delight of constructors when they use such words and manage to create sensible clues for the charades. You can also picture the satisfaction a solver gains when the light dawns!

Contained or *hidden words and phrases* are another source of puzzlement and pleasure in Cryptics. Here again, the parts of words are split, but they are concealed somewhere in the clue. Examine the following:

"Garb worn by some in re*d hot I*ndia" (5)
"Reverberated through part of the Luthe*ran g*athering" (4)

In the first example the five-letter "contained" word is *dhoti;* in the second clue, *rang* is hidden. Incidentally, note how both definitions make good sense — a prime requisite, especially for "containers." Also, watch out for signals like *part, partly, some* and *to some extent.*

Homophones, which are closely related to puns, crop up occasionally. They are usually indicated by such phrases as "I hear," "by the sound of it," "you say," and others referring to listening or speaking. Here are two examples.

"I hear spot in fence to peek through isn't complete" (8)
"A pleasant evening, 'tis said, doesn't last long" (6)

In the first instance the "straight" answer is KNOTHOLE and the homophone is *not whole.* In the second example, FINITE comes from *fine night.*

Puns and other forms of *wordplay* are the highlights of Cryptics. Top constructors feature these devices far more than anagrams, double meanings and other techniques. When you see a long entry, it's advisable to look first for some type of play on words. Here's an excellent example: "It's used for exercise in the Sioux fraternity" (6,4). The answer is INDIAN CLUB, which is certainly "used for exercise." The rest of the definition is a pun. Puns, by the way, are sometimes signaled by a question mark after the clue.

A more intricate technique, which I call *enclosures,* is practiced by several constructors. Consider the following clue, for instance: "Soundly winning out in Ali's milieu" (7).

The answer is ROUTING ("soundly winning"). The clue should be read "Soundly winning—out in Ali's milieu." Note how "out" is enclosed by "ring." Thus, ROUTING becomes R(OUT)ING.

The technique of enclosing one word denoted within another is often tipped off by prepositions such as *about, around, embraces, encircles* or similar verbs.

Here's an example using "about" as a signal: "To get Broadway role, how would Miss Le Gallienne go about it?" (5). Miss Le Gallienne is EVA, of course. Now place the letters of EVA about (meaning *around*) IT and you get EV(IT)A.

In the following example an enclosure is combined with an anagram and a letter gimmick: "Strode awkwardly around the ring; then settled down" (7).

"Awkwardly" tells you that "strode" is involved in some kind of anagram, and "around" indicates a possible enclosure. The straight clue is "settled down" or RO(O)STED. Note how ROSTED (an anagram for "strode") encloses the O. In this case, O stands for "ring" because of its shape.

The above leads to a brief outline of *letter gimmicks*. Here are some of the tricks used in Cryptics.

A article, high mark	N measure (en) or north
B bee, Bea, be	O ring, nothing, cipher
C 100	R are
D 500	S south
E east	T tee, tea
G gee or grand (for 1,000)	U you
I eye or 1	V five
J Jay	W west
K Kay	X ex
L 50	Y why
M 1,000 or measure (em)	

Combinations involving Latin numerals (IV, LI, etc.) also abound, as well as college degrees and titles (A.B., M.A., C.E., d.a., att., r.n., etc.).

Abbreviations are often signaled by adjectives like *little, short,* etc. Thus "the diminutive lieutenant" indicates the presence of LT somewhere in the answer, and "the tiny street" tells you that ST must appear in the word you are looking for.

Be alert for the phrase "that is," because it often stands for IE. Also words beginning with "un" are likely to be converted into some reference to the U.N. in the clue. And, oh yes, watch out for the word *hesitation*. It translates into ER or UR (alluding to speakers).

Still another trick with abbreviations or single letters is the use of "head," "leader" or similar words. Consider the following: "Senate leader sets the wheels in motion for swindles" (4). This clue breaks down into s + CAMS.

Foreign articles such as *la, el, le, les* are often cleverly inserted in a clue. Take the following, for example: "The Spanish got tired of it all, but worked hard anyway" (7).

> The Spanish = LA (note lack of punctuation; ordinarily a colon would follow "The")
> tired of it all = BORED
> LABORED = answer

Incidentally, note how a good Cryptic clue makes some sort of sense.

Needless to say, there is much more to the Cryptics game. If you keep your wits about you and constantly stay on guard against the constructors' artful dodges, you'll learn more and more as you go along. And finally, like millions of others, you'll be hooked. But the side effects are benignant. Aside from the sheer pleasure of successfully meeting a challenge, you'll feel the ecstasy that comes from knowing that you haven't let your brains grow rusty.

Also, if you are a solver of regular crossword puzzles, you'll be glad to leave the realms of the emus, gnus, anoas, moas, esnes, leks, Otoes, Arus and evoes. Constructors of Cryptics avoid crosswordese like the plague. In fact, a good Cryptic contains only common words and phrases.

Now you should be ready to try your hand at a relatively easy Cryptic. The one that follows was prepared by *Mel Rosen,* a versatile editor-constructor whose regular occupation is in the computer-analysis field. This puzzle was specially chosen for tyros because it contains lots of complete anagrams and a few partial ones. Keep in mind that the anagrams are usually signaled by adverbs like "clumsily" and adverbial phrases such as "strangely enough." Sometimes a verb like "disturbed" will tip you off to the fact that certain letters in the clue have scrambled the letters in the answer.

The puzzle also contains several good puns and one reversal at 11-Across. The clue at 20-Across is typical of many Cryptics.

Good luck! But if you are stumped, the answer to the puzzle plus an explanation of the clues can be found on page 190.

If you have solved the warm-up Cryptic, you are now ready for one that is a bit more difficult. This puzzle was constructed by *Fred R. Homburger,* a Cryptics expert from Pennsylvania. Amazingly enough, English is Mr. Homburger's second language.

Cryptic #1

ACROSS

1 Travelers in space; they're excellent photographers! (8,5)
10 Meet anger in an inept way and yet reach harmony (9)
11 Book written on reverse half of vellum (5)
12 Magnificent, tall, A-1 father is disturbed (8)
13 So Celt is possibly concealed here! (6)
14 Gave the orders as autographed (8)
16 Clumsily set two times to fly (6)
18 Who stupidly shared stage with dancer? (6)
20 Ditch around resort is constructed with speed (8)
22 The "ace" of witchcraft strangely enough (6)
23 He'll patch things up concerning the matchmaker (8)
26 Unrefined, like some educators (5)
27 See Zoe cringe uncomfortably (9)
28 Musician when confused, seems retiring (13)

DOWN

2 Charges crazily in almost ruthless fashion (7)
3 Open type of urn (5)
4 Tried tea, tried tea (8)
5 Robbin' hood's weapons (4)
6 Pat lunges awkwardly and gets twisted (7,2)
7 While discombobulated, make six tries to call again (7)
8 Two brothers badly chop China road, the marks are evident! (5,3,5)
9 Provides blankets in the stable? Dapper Dans would fit the role! (7,6)
15 Quality displayed by sergeants in turmoil (9)
17 Squelches all unusual licenses (8)
19 Hide most of the schedule (7)
21 Tiny woodchopper demolishes one small mountain tree (7)
24 Gas that may cause a horrible groan (5)
25 Lake: Part of a series (4)

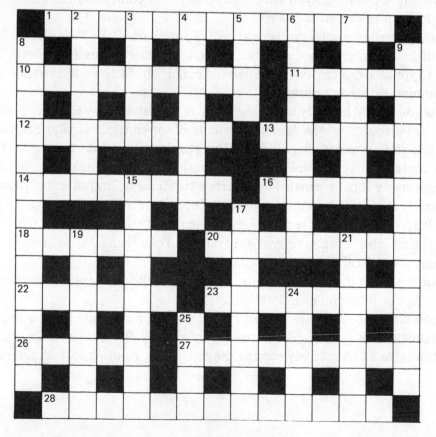

The answer to Mr. Homburger's Cryptic, along with explanations of the clues, can be found on page 191.

If you have caught the fever and wish to solve additional puzzles of this type, Simon and Schuster has published Series #1 and Series #2 of a *Book of Cryptic Crossword Puzzles*. Each volume contains fifty puzzles constructed by American experts. Among them are Edward Buckler, the late Hume Craft, Alice Kaufman, Derrick Niederman, Will Shortz, Stephanie Spadaccini, Jim Strossman, Walter Webb, Barbara Wells and Bob Yarashus.

Some top constructors of Sunday puzzles have also developed skill in creating Cryptics. They include Henry Hook, Jack Luzzatto, Tap Osborn, Arthur Schulman and the inimitable Mel Taub.

Moreover, it should be noted that songwriter Stephen Sondheim has published his own brand of challenging Cryptics. Intricate, mind-boggling offshoots of the genre have also been originated by at least two eminent teams: Emily Cox–Henry Rathvon and E. R. Galli–Richard Maltby. Mr. Maltby, by the way, wrote and directed the Broadway musical *Ain't Misbehavin'*. He received a Tony Award for Best Direction, and the musical itself won a Tony for 1977–78.

□

Finally, a word must be said about crossword puzzles in languages other than English. Italian publications call the game *enigma a parole incrociate* (sometimes shortened to *parole incrociate*). The East Germans and Russians use crosswords as a propaganda device. Definitions are loaded with attacks on capitalism. The French have evolved their own form: One-word clues are embodied in the black squares, and arrows emanating from those squares point to the proper boxes to be filled in by the solver.

English, however, seems to be most conducive to Arthur Wynne's creation. The Romance languages, especially Italian, have too many vowels. Many German words are as long as a crocodile's tail and wouldn't fit into a 15 x 15 diagram. English, on the other hand, has a nice mixture of consonants and vowels. Above all, thanks to the Anglo-Saxon and the American penchant for abridging words, English contains a host of monosyllables that come in handy when filling in the cracks between the longer entries. The reader is invited to test this statement. Turn to any page in a foreign language dictionary and count the words containing fewer than six letters. Then try the same method with an English lexicon. The contrast will astonish you.

Cryptic #2

ACROSS

1 Construction of this highway system buries London gallery (10)
6 Mark the end of a film award (4)
10 Try to surpass Australian bird when tardy (7)
11 Laments because a splint broke (7)
12 Least, tiny, little flower? (7)
13 Movie-maker arrived with endless cheer (6)
16 Kindled some prayers (6)
17 Calamity described as direst (8)
18 Follower of band or barm (3)
19 Disturbed over such warranties (8)
21 Isolate a dark red color (6)
24 In case of shortage, try air mixture (6)
25 These angels minced phrases (7)
28 First lady can relax on this mountain (7)
29 One who listens to an accountant (7)
30 Don't eat quickly! (4)
31 Even a monarch has a chance to put his car here (7,3)

DOWN

1 Article from Time (4)
2 Traveler's small change may be insufficient to pay for these (7,8)
3 Arrange once more in regal costume (7)
4 Fastens cravat to eat a meal (4,2)
5 Sort of writer? (4)
7 Event on Hilton Co. property (10,5)
8 Place to eat rarest tuna, well marinated (10)
9 Prohibit collection of fruit (6)
14 At this intersection, an accident was caused by local fever (10)
15 Offer made twice to 500 (3)
17 A god in Brindisi (3)
18 Pictures from the party (3)
20 This madman may run amok and tease a poor hare (6)
22 What some birds have, but also give up (7)
23 Comment repeatedly made on return from viewing "Kramer vs. Kramer" (6)
26 Porch partly constructed from best oak (4)
27 Second-grade deserter is a naughty child (4)

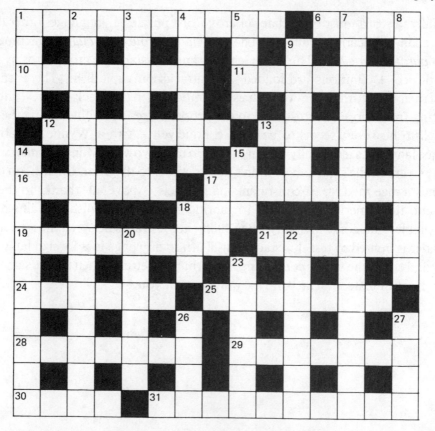

APPENDIX:
Solutions to Puzzles

Puzzles 1, 2, 3, 4, 10, 12, 15, 16, 17, 18 and 19 in chapter 7, as well as the two diagramless puzzles and the Puns and Anagrams puzzle have been copyrighted by The New York Times Company and are reprinted by permission.

ANSWERS TO TRUE-FALSE TEST ON PAGE 32

1. True (It's also a city and a river in Russia).
2. False ("The love of money is the root of all evil").
3. True (See *W-3*).
4. True (See *Book of Who*).
5. False (See Bartlett).
6. True (See the musical).
7. True (See encyclopedias).
8. False (Vergil led Dante).
9. False (The locomotive was a she).
10. False (He wrote *Messiah*).
11. True (See *W-3* or *W-2*).
12. False (Either is correct; see *New World Dictionary*).
13. True (See encyclopedias).
14. False (See a rabbi).
15. False (The original dish was made of corn and cranberry beans).
16. False (It's now the pula; see new almanacs).
17. False (Cio-Cio-San; see the libretto).
18. True (See *Webster's Biographical Dictionary*).
19. True (This Erato was the wife of Arcas).
20. True (See World Almanac: Lew Lehr).
21. False (See any new lexicon).
22. False (See *N.W.D.*).
23. False (See *W-3*).
24. True (See *W-2*; this was Pythias's original name).
25. False (It's a lagomorph).

RATINGS

100%	Take over as CWP editor.
88 – 98%	You've made the grade as chief aide.
72 – 84%	Apply for a proofer's job.
52 – 68%	Maybe you can be backup proofer.
Below 52%	Solving is your salve and salvation.

ANSWER TO "LATERAL SYMMETRY" PUZZLE [PAGE 55]

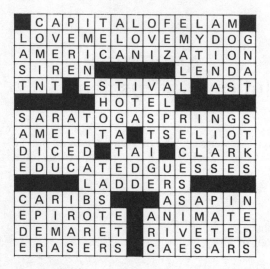

```
 CAPITALOFELAM
LOVEMELOVEMYDOG
AMERICANIZATION
SIREN     LENDA
TNT ESTIVAL AST
    HOTEL
SARATOGASPRINGS
AMELITA TSELIOT
DICED TAI CLARK
EDUCATEDGUESSES
   LADDERS
CARIBS   ASAPIN
EPIROTE ANIMATE
DEMARET RIVETED
ERASERS CAESARS
```

PUZZLE #1

```
SPARE RASP BEST
LAGER ESNE LATE
AROMA ASOR AGON
VIRUS LOOM BLUR
ISAN DICTUM ETE
CHEESES TOLTEC
 RESTORATION
DEACTIVATIONS
 EXTRICATION
SATEEN TONSILS
ADE TAPPAN SCOT
ULNA TARI PHONE
DISC IDOL RANGE
INON ORNE ORIEL
SERE NEED DECRY
```

PUZZLE #2

```
NET FAST BAABAA
IRE IBAR ARSENE
KAN VACILLATING
ISSUED FAKIR
TEENS ALS SOAVE
ADDITIVES INSET
  VASES ANOINT
AMPERES CLIMATE
GEORGE IRANI
ANISE PAINTCANS
RESIN APB HALEY
 TERRE MELBAS
ADMIRALTIES ART
CAVEAT URDU NBE
ENISLE SKIN SYM
```

PUZZLE #3

```
GASP ALMS AMPLE
APIA TOOK SALAR
FELL TATI TRUSS
FROMLEFTTORIGHT
  BASSO MON
ATLAST BOA ASES
TOOLS SENNA TRI
TFELOTTHGIRMORF
IFS SEATO TAROT
CYST ARM RULERS
  ARC OHARE
ONTHEHORIZONTAL
PARIS AFRO KILO
AMATI SPAR OLEO
HEMIN TUMS VEST
```

PUZZLE #4

```
CYCLOTRONS  CHAUVINISM
PHARISAICAL HELLENISTIC
ARMAMENTARY IMPERIALIST
LIANA GES    IMA TERSE
OSMENA SEAR ETNA PATIOS
OTO SNA YNE SRI BAS OUI
KETA ERR TULSA PAL AURA
ANOXEMIA INION EXEGESIS
   ELOAH FINIS TATAR
HUDSON ATONY   TRIBES
INO DEFENSE SLAPPED OXY
TROT SUBIC VARAS   BLOB
LELIA LOUIS BARON DESNA
EPINAL SWORN   BATHER
ROT LEGS TORII PARR ERI
IST SHAN SONNA IRAN VAT
TELA MOY NAG PAD CITE
EDENTAL FETED REMAKES
   TAN SPARERIBS NEP
ATIU OTER VOLA GRAB
PROPAGANDA MILITARIZE
SOCIALIZED UNAMERICAN
EPHEMERALS RESENTMENT
```

PUZZLE #5

```
CAPER LACE SEAL   MAMAS
ANAME PARONOMASIA ADAPT
STRIP EXCLAMATION COLOR
CIONS PEDDLE SANK ERASE
ACME POSE LLB NELL EPIS
LONGEST GAEL SLEET ROS
TILTAT BIGTOP   GALOP
AMO RESTIVE WISP STIPES
RAGER NOTE ENSTAR ANISE
OXYMORON SMU TORI RESIN
ITERS APHORISM   MSS
PLEAT BETHANY SECTS
CTR METAPHOR SORRY
ORONO ROTO NIS PLEONASM
BASES STODGY TRUE PENTA
BLOOMS ONER COURSES TAG
ANNIE SIZARS AUDILE
CTO CARPE METE RESPITE
RIMS MELI ENE REVE AHME
ITALI BEGS INSANE ABEAM
NISAN EXHORTATION TASTE
GOING CATACHRESIS OSIER
ENATE LYRA YSER MESSY
```

PUZZLE #6

```
BARI RANG MIFFS SCALE
ALEC ALAI INURE TUBER
ROPEFIBER SCREENAGAIN
BEACONS LIS SENORA
YARD OHIO ATTEND
PARTOFRSVP OHO ROE
MPG YOURS ARES FLARE
IRA PLEO MLITOCAESAR
DELLA LANCE SALIVA
ALEAF EDGED ELEMENTS
SANCTA EDD ARDENT
WATERLOG LOAMS SEPIA
ARIOSE ESSEN ERECT
HAWSPARTNER IDES EKE
IEREI DEEP NIECE SSR
NRA GPS SEEIACROSS
TIPTOE ENOL OTOE
ARREAR DNS SPENCER
EARCOMBFORM ACTORALDA
BANTU ORATE CHOU TAIL
BLAST NOMEN ERAT ATEE
```

PUZZLE #7

```
HALF│PRAM│■│TASSE│■│IMAM
OLIO│RIMU│■│WHILOM│■│TACO
BELOVEDOFTHENYMPHECHO
OXALIS│■│FRA│UPA│■│ORRIS
■│ETSI│■│ITS│■│ELAN│■│ONE
■│THESOUNDOFMUSICSONG│■
PAUL│■│FOI│■│LIS│■│■│CHI
SHRINKINGCOLORORULTRA
SATEEN│■│ROWE│■│ETA│SAIC
■│LSU│■│MEME│■│PAT│■│PEI
CHRISTMASORSECONDHAND
IOO│■│■│ASS│■│SETH│■│IOU
ARTY│OXO│■│DALI│■│CUBAGE
OSCARWINNERFORHEPBURN
■│RAN│■│CLE│■│LAO│■│UTES
■│GODDESSOFTHERAINBOW│■
WIZ│■│IDEA│■│THO│■│AXLE
AGORA│■│ALA│■│EGG│LATVIA
DONALDDUCKSGIRLFRIEND
ELEM│LOTTIE│■│SOIE│FITZ
DORP│■│OGEED│■│HELD│FLOE
```

PUZZLE #8

```
SLAP│■│STAFF│■│MMES│CYAN
HATES│HAGIO│■│IANA│OILY
AMATI│OTARU│■│CREW│NELL
RELATED│IER│■│HIRE│CLEO
PRELUDEINC#MINOR│EDEN
■│IRR│■│USAGE│■│SPR│■
LILAC│OAT│■│CARP│UTTER
MINUETING│■│TENSE│TORSO
MATISSE│APUS│■│SATIATE
INE│■│SITAR│■│POTENT│■
VERSOS│KEYNOTE│LEFTIN
CYMOSE│■│KNEAD│■│ORE
STOMATE│FEAR│■│OFFERER
OOMPH│EMERY│MELODYINF
CASHA│DIVE│GST│URSAE
■│OST│■│DINAR│■│ORR│■
BERN│BALLADEINAbMAJOR
ABOY│ORAN│DEL│■│TSARINA
ROTI│NENE│INONE│■│TIMES
ELAN│ENDS│NEVER│SEMIS
DISC│SASS│■│GREYS│SYNE
```

PUZZLE #9

```
ITO4AM│■│THE10TH│JUNE17TH
PATINA│■│HISDUE│■│ISEEYOU
IMINES│■│ANCONA│TODREAM
EAT│WHANG│WORSTS│■│ATE
CRIS│■│SKEIN│■│DOE│ARRET
EAST40TH│■│RIN│PROPOSES
■│AWAY│■│PONES│■│SITU│■
SPRIT│SANGOUT│■│LETSUP
TALENT│CROSSBAR│REUNE
HRUSKA│HART│SOAS│66CAR
ROM│STROVE│STIFLE│TIL
IYAR│SALA│76ERS│ENTIRE
PAGE80│MANATBAT│ECHOES
SNEADS│REGRETS│POUND
■│MARS│SHONE│EERY
ALLEYOOP│AMI│BREAKS100
FOURS│NO103│BATOR│SIAM
TAP│LASTTO│ASONE│TRI
EDITION│ERNANI│AMATOL
RUNSOUT│MUETTE│NICENE
125POUNDS│PESTER│STINGS
```

PUZZLE #10

PUZZLE #11

PUZZLE #12

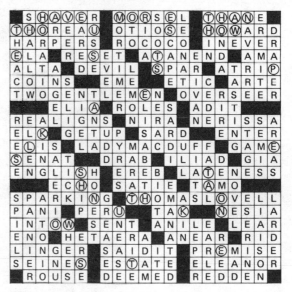

"Have more than thou showest,
Speak less than thou knowest..."
—SHAKESPEARE, from *King Lear* I, IV, 132

PUZZLE #13

PUZZLE #14

"All that we see or seem
Is but a dream within a dream."
—Poe, from "A Dream Within a Dream"

PUZZLE #15

PUZZLE #16

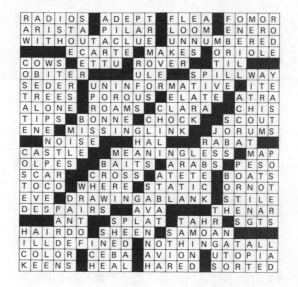

PUZZLE #17

PUZZLE #18

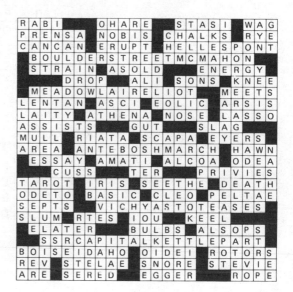

PUZZLE #19

EXAMPLES [PAGE 161]

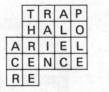

DIAGRAMLESS #1

DIAGRAMLESS #2

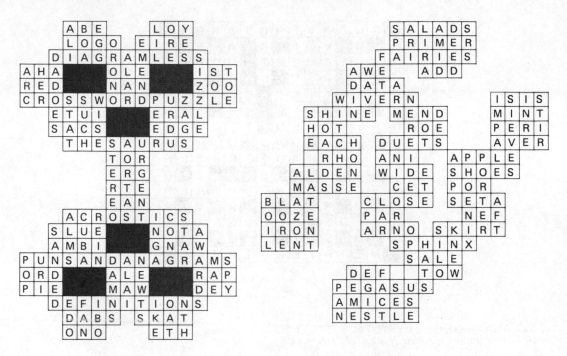

PUNS AND ANAGRAMS

CRYPTIC #1

EXPLANATIONS OF CRYPTIC #1
(*All items containing an asterisk are anagrams.*)

ACROSS

1   Two meanings (comets and marksmen)
10 Meet anger*
11 On (reversed) + vel
12 Tall, A-1 pa (father)
13 So Celt*
14 As + signed
16 Set + set (two times)
18 Shared (reference to Dancer and Dasher in Christmas poem)
20 Di-spa-tch (resort = spa)
22 The ace*
23 Re-pairer
26 "Crude" is part of "educators"
27 Zoe cringe*
28 Seems retiring*

DOWN

2   Ruthless (minus s)*
3   Overt-urn
4   Tried tea* (anagram repeated to fit meaning of "iterated")
5   Pun on Robin Hood's
6   Pat lunges*
7   VI (six) tries*
8   Chop China road; also, pun on Marx
9   Two meanings (the first is a pun)
15 Sergeants*
17 Licenses*
19 Sc (h) edule
21 1 mt + tree (1=i)
24 Groan: Anag. of argon
25 Part of a sERIEs

CRYPTIC #2

EXPLANATIONS OF CRYPTIC #2
(*All items containing an asterisk are anagrams*)

ACROSS

1 Inters (buries) Tate (London Gallery)
6 (O)scar
10 Emu + late
11 A splint*
12 Mini + mum
13 Came + ra(h)
16 Lit + any
17 As direst*
18 Band (aid) barm (aid)
19 Over such*
21 Two meanings
24 Try air*
25 Phrases*
28 Eve + rest
29 Two meanings
30 Two meanings
31 Par (even) king (monarch) lot (chance)

DOWN

1 Time*
2 Pun on "quarters"
3 In regal*
4 Tie (cravat) sup (to eat a meal)
5 Type (writer)
7 Event on Hilton Co.*
8 Rarest tuna*
9 Ban (prohibit) ana (collection)
14 Local fever*
15 Bi (twice) D (500)
17 Brin DISi
18 The pARTy
19 Ha(tt)er: tt = tease and haer = poor hare
22 A band on
23 Reversal = Kramer-remark
26 From be ST OA k
27 B (second-grade)`rat (deserter)